# Indianapolis Motor Speedway.
## Greatest Race Course in the World.

WITHDRAWN

WITHDRAWN

D1592423

# INDY:
# Racing Before The 500

*By D. Bruce Scott*

IUPUI
UNIVERSITY LIBRARY
755 WEST MICHIGAN STREET
INDIANAPOLIS, IN 46202-5195

# INDY:
# Racing Before The 500

Copyright © 2005 by D. Bruce Scott

All rights reserved. No part of this book may be reproduced or transmitted in any form or by any means, electronic, mechanical, including photocopying, recording, or by any informational storage and retrieval system, without permission in writing from the publisher, except for the inclusion of brief quotations in a review.

Library of Congress Control Number: 2005921738
ISBN 0-9766149-0-1

Printed in the United States of America

First Edition

Published by
*INDIANA REFLECTIONS LLC*
Batesville, Indiana
www.indianareflections.com

Foreword by Donald Davidson

Edited by Hetty Gray

Produced by
*PPC BOOKS*
Redington Shores, Florida

# Dedication

This book is dedicated to the memory of the founders, drivers, team members, spectators and other participants who played a part in the early history of the Indianapolis Motor Speedway. Their persistence to continue despite adversity and their passion for competition gave future generations the world's finest racing facility to be enjoyed by all.

# Foreword

If it were possible to conduct a quiz among the many millions of people who have ever attended an Indianapolis 500, watched it on television, listened to it on the radio, or read about it in some form, chances are that a surprising number of them would know that the race was held for the first time in 1911. Not only would a goodly percentage be able to add that it was won by Ray Harroun in a Marmon "Wasp," but the general public around the world might be surprised to learn just how many central Indiana *grade school* students would have been able to reel off these facts over the years.

What is *not* so well known; however, is that the track was actually in its third season in 1911 and that there had been an abundance of motor racing at the Indianapolis Motor Speedway before anyone even *dreamed* of conducting a 500-mile race. Still, more might be surprised to learn that there was a very strong aviation presence in the early days, that a championship gas-filled balloon race and a program of motorcycle events had already been held before the first automobile ever fired up for competition, and that the world record for altitude was broken not once but twice at the Speedway, months before the concept of a 500-mile race had entered anyone's mind.

As far as automobile races were concerned, there were four (arguably five) meets, a typical program spread over three days. Each day comprised a series of short races for a variety of different classes of stripped-down passenger cars, a couple of "run what you brung" free-for-alls and a longer race to end the day's proceedings, normally concluding around sundown.

Because there were so many short events in a day's time—some lining up with only three cars—others who have written about those days have generally concentrated only on the major 100, 200, 250, and 300-mile events. Anyone who wished to learn more was obliged either to spend seemingly endless hours at a library, reading the amazingly detailed reports in the *Indianapolis Star*, *News*, and *Sun* (later the *Times*) on an eye-taxing microfilm viewer, or else travel to Chicago or Detroit in search of bound volumes of the excellent trade magazines of the day.

"Somebody ought to write a book," people would say. Easier said than done.

When a rather soft-spoken Bruce Scott first contacted me in the fall of 2003 and told me of his intentions, I was—and I hope he will agree—neither particularly encouraging or discouraging, especially when he told me he had never before tried to write anything of this magnitude. Many a well-meaning effort in the past has ground to a halt when the author came to the sobering realization that it is a heck of a lot easier to read a book than to write one.

Bruce came to see me a few days later, mainly for the purpose of showing me some "box scores" he had developed on a computer and to see whether or not I could provide some missing first names for lesser-known drivers (a common problem for researchers of all early-day sports) and perhaps identify hometowns for some of the drivers and car manufacturers.

I was truly amazed at what he had done. Others have attempted to chronicle the early events at the

Indianapolis Motor Speedway over the years, but nothing I had ever seen came anywhere close to comparing with the charts he had compiled. They were beautifully laid out and color-coded, and were, for a stats freak like me, delightfully easy to read and digest.

But these were still early days and he was still faced with the ordeal of actually *writing* a book. I also believed that in spite of the Speedway photo archives having a reasonably healthy selection of images from those days, the illustrating of his book might present a challenge.

The end result is really quite astounding. Through a variety of sources he himself acknowledges elsewhere in this book, he was able to gather an extraordinary collection of images of aviation and balloons at the track, local hotels and buildings, an appropriate selection to cover the much lamented absence of motorcycle shots at the Speedway, and, most impressively, more stereoscopic images from the August 1909 meet than just about any of us realized existed. Pictorially, it is a real eye-opener, especially the 1909 stereoscopic shots when viewed through special three-D enhancing glasses. Most current participants have absolutely no clue as to the conditions endured by their counterparts a century ago.

As with most projects, there was even more work involved with this one than is immediately apparent. His original version told the story, with great imagination, through the eyes of a fictitious Marmon employee. When I pointed out that others had certainly used this technique but that historian types were not generally in favor of it (as with a much criticized Ronald Reagan biography of a few years ago) he said that friends had already convinced him that he should go with the more traditional approach.

He returned a few weeks later, having eliminated hundreds of hours of creative writing and retold the story in "third person." And he hadn't settled for just the automobile races, but had delved into the motorcycle events, the aviation meet, and the balloon races with painstaking detail. In fact, even balloonists and aviators with no interest in either the Indianapolis Motor Speedway or motor racing for that matter, would find this work of interest.

In the meantime, the book has been through a couple more transformations in order to arrive at the final version. His intention was for it to stand the test of time as a cherished reference work.

We believe that he has succeeded.


Donald Davidson
Historian
Indianapolis Motor Speedway

# Acknowledgements

When I first came up with the idea to write about the events at the Indianapolis Motor Speedway prior to the first Indianapolis 500 it was hard for me to believe that someone had not previously completed such a project. However, upon my first visit to the Marion County Public Library, I began to understand why no one had tackled the subject. The daunting task that lay ahead of me immediately came to light as I sat peering through the viewer of a microfilm machine at the fine print of a 1908 *Indianapolis Star*. There were so many events and stories from this two-year period relating to the Speedway that the necessary research effort alone seemed insurmountable! This didn't even include all of the writing, editing, and gathering of photographs that would be required. I quickly realized that if I had any hope at all of pulling everything together I was going to need help from others.

The key to the successful completion of this book was undoubtedly the patience and understanding of my wife. From day one she never questioned that I would follow this project through or complained that I was spending too much time on it. She even jumped in to help throughout the process. She willingly filled the following roles: both a source and sounding board for ideas, a manuscript editor, babysitter for our son, cheerleader, photo editor, proofreader, cover designer, and researcher. I watched in amazement and amusement one day in St. Louis as this woman blazed a trail through the research files of the Missouri Historical Society. Never have I seen anyone accomplish so much in so little time as she did that afternoon! Despite her limited interest in racing, she developed a genuine fascination for the story as it began to take shape. This book is truly as much hers as it is mine.

The historical accuracy of the facts presented in this book was not only of primary importance to me but also became an obsession! I was fortunate enough to have strong support in verifying the accuracy of my research. Indianapolis Motor Speedway Historian Donald Davidson provided tremendous assistance to me in this regard. Besides graciously agreeing to write the foreword for the book, he took the time on more than one occasion to review my research for accuracy and edit the manuscript. His additional insight provided guidance to further research, allowing me to present a more complete perspective of the story. He also made some excellent photographs available for my use, which added a great deal to the presentation of these historical events. Dave Goss, Vice President of the National Indy 500 Collectors Club, impressed me by providing copies of almost every program from the events during 1909 – 1910. This proved to be invaluable to me in verifying the validity of my research. Finally, Tom Rollings and John Blazier granted me permission to include their thorough research on the brick paving of the Speedway.

A story with as much historical significance as this one would not be complete without good photographs. Therefore, a lot of time and effort was purposely spent on searching and obtaining them for this book. Numerous photos have been included, giving the reader a better feel for the time period. I consider my contact with racing historian Joe Freeman as the first big break in completing the book. Mr. Freeman patiently listened as I explained my project and asked permission to use his 26 rare stereoscopic photographs taken at the Speedway during the August 1909 automobile races. He never hesitated to offer his photos or his help and I am deeply appreciative of his kindness. I know he never realized it at the time, but his generosity early in the task supplied the fuel to see it through to the end. Incredibly, as rare as these photographs are, fate led me to Grant Meitzler as the project was winding down. Grant just happened to have several of these photographs as well, including 11 that Mr. Freeman did not possess. This allowed me to include 37 of the original set of 40 stereoscopic photographs in the book. These are astounding pictures and really help bring to life the events of the time. John Darlington, President of the National Indy 500 Collectors Club, provided me with an outstanding picture of the Speedway during the brick paving in the fall of 1909 and pictures of a rare pamphlet advertising the first auto races held at the Indianapolis Motor Speedway. Several photos were obtained from the Indianapolis Motor Speedway Photo Shop. The staff was very patient and helpful each time I worked with them. Wright State University in Dayton, Ohio, proved to be a valuable source of photographs and information for the aviation meet and balloon races. Archivist Toni Jeske, who assisted me during my research, provided terrific customer service. She went out of her way to help me locate old magazines and look through them for specific information. Wright State is lucky to have an employee like her! Rob Medina of Rights and Reproductions at the Chicago Historical Society provided some wonderful photographs with prompt and efficient service while Anthony Miles of the Hoosier Auto Show and Swap Meet supplied the great photo of the 1910 Marmon racing team that is on the front cover. Stephen Wright was kind enough to take time from his busy schedule to provide several photos for use in the chapter on the motorcycle races. Photographs for this chapter were hard to procure so I am grateful to him for his assistance. Additional photographs were provided by; the Indiana Historical Society, Brooklands Museum Photo Archive, Alfred P. Sloan Museum in Flint, Michigan, the National Automotive History Collection at the Detroit Public Library, Missouri Historical Society, the Smithsonian National Air and Space Museum, and the Library of Congress.

Finally, the support that I received from my family and friends that were aware of this project was remarkable. They gave up their time to read drafts of the manuscript, offered feedback, and provided encouragement along the way. A special thank you goes to the following for all of their help: my mother and father, my brothers, my aunt Rita and my uncle Dave. A heartfelt thank you also goes out to Hetty Gray who willingly offered the benefit of her publishing and editing experience to me. She was a pleasure to work with and her contribution was extremely helpful to me.

# Table of Contents

# Introduction

The Indianapolis Motor Speedway has been an American institution since its first year of existence in 1909, yet the common belief is that the Speedway was built for the inaugural Indianapolis 500 in 1911. Thousands of people visit the Speedway every year without giving much thought to how, when, and why it was built. After all, it's easy to take the Speedway for granted since it has been at the corner of 16ᵗʰ Street and Georgetown Road for as long as anyone can remember. There have been cosmetic changes to the Speedway and the cars and speeds have improved dramatically but the Indianapolis Motor Speedway itself has consistently remained as the focal point for auto racing throughout the world for almost 100 years.

Many people would be surprised to learn that the Speedway played host to an exciting and varied schedule of events in the years leading up to the inaugural Indianapolis 500, or International Sweepstakes as it was called then. During this busy two-year period from 1909–1910, there were over 80 auto races and a handful of motorcycle races held at the Speedway. The Wright brothers also paid a visit to the Speedway to participate in a week-long aviation meet. In addition to these events there were two National Balloon Championships and in December 1909 a two-day session was held to test the newly laid brick racing surface.

These two years were perhaps the most critical time in the Speedway's existence as the events of this period helped to determine the future success of the Speedway. There have been several good books documenting the history of the Indianapolis 500 but, strangely, very little has been written about the years at the Speedway before the Indianapolis 500. As time has passed these events have been forgotten, and now only the very astute fan is fully aware of the exciting events held at the Indianapolis Motor Speedway during 1909–1910.

As the 100ᵗʰ anniversary of the building of the Indianapolis Motor Speedway nears, the following pages tell the fascinating history that was made at this American institution in the years before it became famous for the annual Indianapolis 500-mile race. This is history that has remained unknown to most race fans. It has played such an important role in the tradition that we have enjoyed through the years and will enjoy for many years to come. All of the events presented here are true and have been recreated based on accounts given by the participants and the local media of the time. It is my hope that this book will transport you back to 1909 as if you are part of the activities rather than merely reading facts from a history book. Please join me on this fascinating journey of the groundbreaking events at the Indianapolis Motor Speedway from inception through the first two years of its illustrious history.

*Chapter 1*

# A Dream Becomes a Reality

Speeding over the bricks down the front stretch at a little over 40 miles per hour in his white Stoddard-Dayton passenger car, Carl Fisher took a quick glance beside him to see the front row starters of Lewis Strang, Ralph DePalma, Harry Endicott, and Johnny Aitken bearing down rapidly on the starting line. Huge clouds of smoke from their engines hid the other speed demons that made up the rest of the 40-car field behind them. With the eyes of 80,000 cheering spectators locked on the seemingly endless line of racers, Fisher swerved the pace car off to the left and into the pits at the very moment the thundering machines were ready to swallow him up. In the same instant, Fred "Pop" Wagner waved the starter's flag as the cars roared past the wire to begin the first annual 500-Mile International Sweepstakes race at the Indianapolis Motor Speedway.

Carl Fisher must have been beaming with pride on that late May morning in 1911. A dream of his just a few short years before, now was not only a reality but also the envy of all in the world of auto racing. Fisher began to seriously pursue his dream of a big race track in 1905. In July of that year he helped represent America in the James Gordon Bennett Cup races in France. It was during this trip that Fisher recognized the superiority of foreign autos after the American cars were badly outclassed by their European counterparts in the races. Upon his return, he warned others that if America didn't start producing better automobiles they would likely lose the industry to Europe. One key to accomplishing this, many believed, was to use racing as a means to test the cars before they were sold to the public. Testing would provide the opportunity to identify and eliminate any imperfections. America, Fisher pointed out, lacked the proper facilities for such testing.

Shortly after his return from France, Tom Taggert, former Indianapolis Mayor from 1895 – 1901, urged him to build a race track in French Lick, Indiana. The site had great potential, highlighted by the mammoth French Lick Springs Hotel of which Taggert was part owner. Viewed as one of the world's most elegant spas and noted for its gambling activities, it would attract the crowds and provide the required lodging for guests while the railroads serving the area would meet the transportation demand. Ultimately,

1

Fisher decided against the location after he failed to find a piece of land level enough to accommodate a large race track.

The dream continued to occupy Fisher's mind, which led to discussions with the Indiana State Fair Board about a possible site for his venture. Subsequently, this effort also proved unsuccessful when a survey revealed that nothing larger than a two-mile track could be built. Shortly thereafter, the discouraged Fisher sent the following letter to the editor of *Motor Age* magazine.

Dear Sir:

I note with considerable interest that you are taking up individual opinions regarding the advisability of racing on large tracks. As you are probably aware, a large track of 3 to 5 miles in diameter (sic), with a width of 100 to 150 feet, has been a hobby of mine for the past three years, and I have done a great deal of work toward a track of this kind. The proposed track at French Lick fell through, for the reason that enough level ground could not be secured for a track of sufficient size. After considerable time and investigation arrangements were made with our Fair Board in Indianapolis for the ground for a 3-mile track, but after a careful survey it was found impossible to put more than a 2-mile track on it.

Very few people understand what an immense difference there is between a mile track and a 3-mile track, and to do this it will be necessary to have a drawing to scale of a 1, 3, and 5-mile tracks in order to convey properly to the average driver the respective sizes. I have been an interested spectator in most of the big track meets and road races in this country and France – including the Vanderbilt and Bennett – and it is my opinion that the only successful racing course, and the one which will ultimately find favor with both drivers and the public, will be a 3 or 5-mile circular course.

There is no question in my mind that track racing on mile tracks is doomed. The average horse track is narrow, has fences that are dangerous, and is always dusty or muddy, and with high speed cars, where wide skids are necessary, racing becomes so dangerous that frequently the fastest car, from a slow start or other temporary delay, gets off in the rear without chance of ever gaining the front on account of continuous seas of dust and skidding cars ahead that would make it too dangerous to attempt to pass. This condition would not exist on a 3 or 5-mile track.

To the spectators, there is very little enjoyment in seeing a 25 or 50-mile road race, where immense crowds throng the course and where only fleeting glimpses can be had of the cars as they come and go down the road. There is no accommodation for the public in a race of this kind, and the thousands of dollars spent in advertising and for special privileges that go to private individuals could well come into the purse of the management of a 3 or 5-mile track. The American manufacturers annually spend thousands of dollars in building high speed racing cars to compete with French cars and without possible chance of winning, and I think this is largely due to the fact that American drivers do not have a chance to thoroughly test their cars continuously at high speed for weak spots in construction, or to become entirely familiar with and have their car under perfect control at very high speeds.

There is no question in my mind that it takes weeks and months of practice handling a car at 75, 80, and 90 miles an hour to be able to properly gauge distances, numerous road conditions, and the response of the car to such conditions. It has been my experience that quite a number of racing cars, when tested over the best roads we had in this country, seemed to have wonderful speed. There was no accurate way to time them for any distance, and the best anybody could do was to guess at what the cars were doing.

It seems to me a 5-mile track, properly laid out, without fences to endanger drivers, with proper grandstands, supply stores for gasoline and oil, and other accommodations would net for one meet such as the Vanderbilt Cup race a sufficient amount to pay half of the entire cost of the track. With the present record of 52 seconds on a mile track, I am confident a 3-mile track 100 feet wide will stand a speed of 100 miles an hour, and that a 5-mile track will stand a speed of 2 miles a minute.

In diagrams I have seen of a 5-mile track it is possible at any point of the curve to see in a direct line 800 feet ahead and a curve of this kind, when gradual and continuous, is not nearly as severe as some of the short, choppy curves at Ormond Beach, where a speed of 2 miles a minute was made by a couple of contestants in the meet in the south last winter.

(Signed) C. G. Fisher

The letter eloquently summed up Carl Fisher's feelings about track racing and his desire for such a facility. However, with no further prospects identified, Fisher turned his immediate attention to other interests.

Then, during a return trip to Europe in 1907, his dream was given renewed spark by a visit to the Brooklands, a two-and-three-quarter-mile race course made of concrete with banked turns. Located near the town of Weybridge in Surrey, England, the Brooklands was very similar to the track that Fisher envisioned for America. Although the dream continued to occupy Fisher's mind, he received little widespread support as auto racing was relatively new in America and certainly not the most popular spectator sport.

*A car racing on the Brooklands race course in England during the early 1900s. The Brooklands pro-vided renewed spark for Carl Fisher's dream of a race track for America. (Photo courtesy of the Brooklands Museum Photo Archive)*

Eventually, the intrigue of the automobile, coupled with Indiana's growing industrial climate, would work in his favor. Both created an environment conducive to such a venture and would play a prominent role in the birth of the world's greatest race course. Indiana had been introduced to the automobile by Kokomo's Elwood Haynes in 1894, but the industry would not establish a stronghold in the state until the early 1900s. Prior to this, railroads had been built to the point where the state had developed an extensive railway system, one of the best in the country. As a result, this created the need for workers to provide the necessary support for the railroads. The efficient railway system also attracted new industry as evidenced by the numerous carriage and buggy businesses and countless bicycle shops that sprang up throughout the state. Fortunately for Indiana, the state's industry was given an additional boost by the discovery of a natural gas field within its boundaries before the turn of the century, providing a low-cost energy source. Likewise, the transportation network had been enhanced by the establishment of an electrical interurban system. All of these developments provided several key elements necessary to support a successful auto-mobile industry. The carriage and buggy businesses, as well as bicycle shops, employed laborers who were qualified to build automobiles. Equally as important, the vast railroad system would help supply the re-quired materials and provide a means to ship the final product.

The opportunities available within the state, Indianapolis in particular, attracted many ambitious and talented individuals. Four of these men would meet through mutual interests to form the partnership for the Indianapolis Motor Speedway. They came to Indianapolis at different times, and under different circumstances, but it was their love for the automobile that drew them together.

One of these men was Arthur Newby. Born in Monrovia, Indiana, on December 29, 1865, Newby spent the majority of his childhood in Kansas. After returning to Indiana for a brief stay in Mooresville, he moved to Indianapolis in 1881 at the age of 15. One of his first jobs was at Nordyke & Marmon, first as a bookkeeper then later as the office manager. He then worked for Hay & Willits Manufacturing Company, producers of Outing Bicycles. In addition to starting the Zig-Zag Cycling Club in 1890, he also built the famed Newby Oval in 1898, a quarter-mile bicycle track that was highly regarded throughout the country. He later became partners with Charles E. Test and Edward Fletcher in the Indianapolis Chain and Stamping Company. The company produced bicycle chains, supplying a large portion of the market at the time. Shortly after 1900, Newby joined the National Motor Vehicle Company where he served as a Director prior to becoming the President. His influence helped move the company from the production of electric cars to gasoline-powered cars.

Although younger than Newby, James Allison had arrived in Indianapolis one year before him. Allison was born in Marcellus, Michigan on August 11, 1872 and moved to Indianapolis with his family in 1880. In his youth he worked as a newspaper boy and messenger. Allison eventually quit school at the age of 12 to work at his father's business, the Allison Coupon Company. When his father died James took over running the business with his two brothers at the age of 18. Soon afterwards, Allison joined the Zig-Zag Cycling Club where he met Arthur Newby, the club's founder, and Carl Fisher. The three became friends and formed a lasting bond.

Carl Fisher, undoubtedly the driving force behind the Indianapolis Motor Speedway, was born in Greensburg, Indiana, on January 12, 1874. He moved to Indianapolis as a teenager and opened a bicycle shop with his brothers in 1891. The lure of the automobile had such a firm grasp on him that he had converted his bicycle shop into an auto dealership well before the industry started to prosper. The Fisher Automobile Company, where he sold several makes of automobiles, was located on 400 North Capitol

*Carl Fisher sitting in his race car at the Harlem race track located near Roosevelt Road and Hannah Avenue in Forest Park, Illinois. (Chicago Daily News negatives collection, SDN-002710. Courtesy of the Chicago Historical Society)*

Boulevard. Naturally, the progression from bicycle racer to auto racer soon followed. During the early 1900s, he toured the Midwest, giving auto racing exhibitions with the likes of Barney Oldfield and Webb Jay, two of the most famous race drivers of the time. In 1904, Fisher even held the world's record for two miles by completing the distance in 2:02 on the Harlem dirt track in Forest Park, Illinois, near Chicago. Also in 1904, he happened to meet a man by the name of Percy Avery who held the patent for a method of using compressed gas to supply headlamps for automobiles. Fisher persuaded James Allison to join him in a business venture with Mr. Avery and the three of them formed the Concentrated Acetylene Company located at 211 East South Street. In 1906, the name was changed to Prest-O-Lite Company. The company quickly began supplying headlamps to almost every automobile manufacturer in the country. This successful venture provided Fisher's main source of income to finance the Speedway project.

The last of the four partners to arrive in the city was Frank Wheeler. He was born in Manchester, Iowa, on October 24, 1864. Prior to moving to Indianapolis in 1904, he had lived in California and worked as a traveling salesman. Through the years, Wheeler had always insisted that he made and lost two fortunes before moving to Indianapolis. Not long after his arrival, he met George Schebler, the inventor of a carburetor. Mr. Wheeler partnered with him and provided the money to start a manufacturing plant for the Wheeler-Schebler Company, making it one of the largest producers of gasoline engine carburetors in the country.

The automobile industry had seized Indiana quickly. By 1906, almost 100 car manufacturers had been or were in operation in Indiana, many of them located in Indianapolis. The city emerged as one of the leaders in the industry along with Detroit, Michigan. Companies such as National Motor Vehicle and Nordyke & Marmon had huge expansive factories, employing several hundred factory workers. Nordyke & Marmon, originally a producer of milling equipment, had relocated from Richmond, Indiana, in 1876 and ventured into the automobile industry in 1902. The company covered eight and a half acres at the corner of Kentucky Avenue and Morris Street. The facility was so vast that Daniel Marmon, Howard Marmon's father and President of the company, often remarked that he was "tired of walking to Vincennes and back"[1] when he made the 700-foot long trek to the end of the main building. National, located at 1105 East 22nd Street, was just as immense and led all other Indianapolis-based auto manufacturers in 1906 with its production of nearly 900 vehicles.

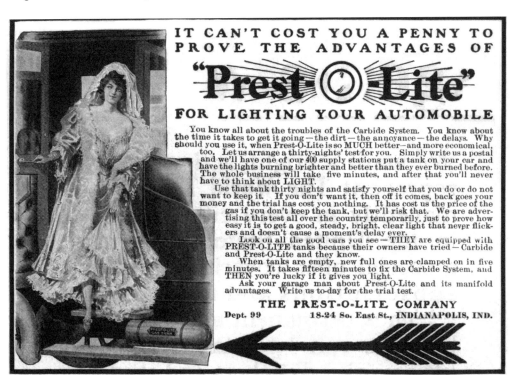

*A 1907 magazine ad for the Prest-O-Lite Company. Note the Prest-O-Lite tank mounted on the running board of the auto. (The World Today magazine)*

As the automobile industry started to flourish, so did the auto parts manufacturers. Companies like Prest-O-Lite and Wheeler-Schebler emerged as the result of new opportunities while other businesses redirected their efforts to prosper from the "horseless carriage." The Remy Company of Anderson, Indiana, was one such example. Started as a home wiring business in 1896 by Frank and Perry Remy, the company transformed into a manufacturer of magnetos, a device that provided a spark to the engine of an auto during the starting process.

Meanwhile, Carl Fisher refused to let his dream of building a race track die. He frequently shared this idea with his friends and business acquaintances. In her book *Fabulous Hoosier*, Carl's wife Jane, told how he even drew his vision of the Speedway on a table cloth at Horace "Pop" Haynes' restaurant. The establishment on Pennsylvania Street was a popular lunch spot for Fisher and his friends. It was there that hours were passed telling stories and sharing thoughts on bicycles, automobiles, aeroplanes, and anything else that interested the group. Apparently, providing illustrations on a table cloth was routine for them.

*The Nordyke & Marmon Company as it appeared in the early 1900s. (Photo courtesy of the Indiana Historical Society, Bass Photo Co. Collection, negative # 4491)*

Finally, in the fall of 1908, Fisher asked Indianapolis real estate agent and friend Lem Trotter to keep an eye out for some land within five miles or so of downtown Indianapolis that would be suitable for a race track. Trotter, who would later be instrumental in founding the town of Speedway, showed Fisher four adjacent 80-acre tracts of land five miles northwest of Monument Circle. The Ben Hur traction line and the Big Four railroad ran along the land, which was part of the old Pressley farm. The spot was perfect by Fisher's standards. It was flat and big enough for the kind of facility he envisioned, the traction line and railroad nearby would solve his transportation issues, and the distance from Indianapolis was ideal. The Chenoweth family, owners of three of the 80-acre tracts, was willing to sell for $200 per acre. However, Kevi Munter, owner of the 80-acre tract on the southwest corner, wanted $300 per acre. It's likely that Mr. Munter knew that he was sitting on the key piece of land for the project. The Ben Hur traction line ran along this corner, which is why the main entrance was placed in this location. Thus, for $72,000 Fisher could secure the land needed to build his dream.

By December 12, 1908, Lem Trotter had secured the options required to buy the land. The anxious Fisher already had a preliminary plan for the property, which included a three-mile race track. He had also been busy forming the partnership for his project. Joining Fisher were James Allison, Stoughton Fletcher, Arthur Newby, and Frank Wheeler. Fletcher, President of the Fletcher National Bank, later withdrew at the bank's urging because the investment was not consistent with their conservative reputation.

The articles of incorporation for the Indianapolis Motor Speedway Company were filed on February 8, 1909, at a capitalized value of $250,000. Both Fisher and Allison had contributed $75,000 apiece while Wheeler and Newby each contributed $50,000. The officers of the corporation were: President Carl Fisher, first Vice President Arthur Newby, second Vice President Frank Wheeler, and Secretary-Treasurer James Allison.

During late February and early March of 1909 the partners established that the surface of the track would be consistent with that used on many dirt roads of the time, crushed stone and asphaltum oil on a firm clay base. Additionally, after much debate, a proposed schedule of events for the first year was agreed upon. It was decided that the Speedway would open up with the National Championship Balloon race on June 5 under the sponsorship of the Aero Club of America followed by automobile races during the July 4 weekend. There would also be motorcycle races held in August in connection with the Federation of American Motorcyclists convention to be held in Indianapolis during that time. The season would wind up with more automobile races over the Labor Day weekend.

*A steamroller works on the Speedway's racing surface during May 1909. ( Motor Age magazine June 1909)*

By mid-March the building of the new Speedway was ready to begin. Just days before Indianapolis was to host the automobile show, the paper announced that the contract with King Brothers of Montezuma, Indiana, for the grading of the racing surface had been agreed upon and that the work was to be completed in 60 days. Further, a New York engineer, P. T. Andrews, had been hired as the Superintendent of Construction. Mr. Andrews was very influential in the final design of the Speedway. He cautioned the partners that they had no chance at all of finishing the Speedway by the July 4th auto races and that they would be very fortunate to have it done by the motorcycle races in August. In his opinion, most of the construction could be completed; however, the problem was going to be dealing with the little creek flowing across the southwest corner of the property. Mr. Andrews suggested that two bridges be built over the creek instead of relying on a culvert that could cause problems if there was a heavy rainfall. Additionally, he suggested that the design of the Speedway be changed as well. Andrews urged that a two-and-a-half-mile track would fit on the land better because it would not be as close to the property lines, leaving room to build additional grandstands in the future. Upon Mr. Andrews' recommendations, the final mileage of the outside course was agreed upon as follows: each turn would be a quarter of a mile in length, the straightaways would be five-eighths of a mile, and the two short stretches between the turns would be one-eighth of a mile for a total distance of two and one half miles. The partners' wishes for a five-mile track could still be realized by adding one-half mile on the inside road course, allowing for the original two-mile "W" shape of the inner road course to be rounded out, eliminating the sharp curves. This plan allowed the cars to pass the main grandstand three times and be visible on any part of the five-mile Speedway. (Incidentally, although the inner road course was part of the original plans it was never built.) After making these changes, the estimated final cost of the Speedway was $220,000, which was a little less than the original $250,000 estimate.

Based on Mr. Andrews' advice, the partners agreed that they had no choice but to alter their proposed schedule of events for the summer. They finally decided that they could go ahead with the balloon race on June 5, even if the race track itself was not completed. They agreed to keep the motorcycle races on the schedule for August 13 and 14; however, the July 4 auto races would have to be rescheduled. Besides, Arthur Newby thought that the auto manufacturers could use the extra time to prepare for the races. Therefore, he proposed moving the races to Labor Day weekend. Carl Fisher did not want to wait that long in order to start getting a return on their investment. He suggested moving the auto races to the weekend following the motorcycle races and have additional auto races in early October. After some discussion, the partners finally decided to move the July 4 auto races to August 19 – 21 and schedule additional auto races in early October.

Work on the Speedway began immediately after the contract for grading was signed. The work crew consisted of close to 500 men, approximately 300 mules, and several road scrapers and rollers of various tonnages. After the grading produced a smooth, firm surface, two inches of creek gravel was spread uniformly over the entire outer track and rolled with a 15-ton roller. This was followed by a two-inch layer of crushed limestone that was rolled with an eight-ton roller after which two gallons of taroid per square yard were poured on top. One to two inches of crushed stone chips were then applied followed by another coat of taroid at the rate of eight to ten gallons per square yard. Finally, a thin layer of crushed stone ranging from dust size to two inches was applied followed by a final rolling with a 3-ton roller. The April rains had kept the workers from completing the track in the area of the bridges in the southwest turn; however, the bleachers for the June balloon race were almost complete.

Publicity for the Speedway began to increase after the group hired Ernest Moross as Director of Contests. Mr. Moross, the manager of Barney Oldfield, was widely known as one of the nation's best press agents. He persuaded the group to arrange for the local press to be given a tour around the Speedway. During the month of May, a group from various press organizations was driven around the Speedway in two Overlands and a Stoddard-Dayton. This plan had worked exactly as Mr. Moross had hoped. The

*Carl Fisher drives members of the press around the Indianapolis Motor Speedway in a Stoddard-Dayton during early May 1909. (Photo courtesy of the Indianapolis Motor Speedway)*

Speedway was featured in many newspapers across the country and locally was the talk of the town. The only hitch in the plan was that Mr. Andrews had to put large timbers in the creek so that the cars could successfully complete a full circuit of the course. Not long after the tour, the local newspapers began reporting that large crowds were visiting the grounds everyday to watch the progress being made. The activity was not confined to the grading of the track. A large group of men were busy on several buildings that were necessary for a racetrack of this size. Pipes from the gas plant of the Indiana Gas Company were laid to the area at the south end of the Speedway to accommodate the hot air balloons that would ascend from there for June's balloon race. Workers were also busy painting the various buildings and the eight-foot board fence surrounding the grounds white with green trim. This color scheme had been decided upon earlier and would to be used throughout the grounds.

The racing community was anxious for the Speedway to be completed. Lewis Strang, winner of the Savannah, Briarcliff, and Lowell road races had already made a visit to the Speedway. He had stopped while en route to Florida where he participated in the Daytona Beach races. While here, he was the guest of Mr. Losey of the Buick-Losey Dealership who accompanied him to the Speedway to inspect the site and talk to the engineers. The newspaper showed a picture of Mr. Strang looking over a miniature racetrack on exhibit at the southeast corner of the site. The eight-foot long model was made of cement and was a good representation of what the outer course of the Speedway would look like when completed. The newspapers reported that Mr. Strang was the only American who had raced on the famous Brooklands racecourse in England and therefore knew a thing or two about racetracks. He told the local press that "I am of the opinion that the local track when completed will be capable of standing terrific speed and predict that the Brooklands records will be smashed here within the first year."[2] Mr. Strang said that he believed that the Buick Motor Company would enter the full team in all events that its stock and special racing cars were eligible to compete and that they would definitely be here for the first races on the new track. Strang, Louis Chevrolet, and Bob Burman made up the Buick racing team. Chevrolet drove a Fiat for years and at the time was best remembered as the man who defeated Barney Oldfield in ten out of eleven races in 1905.[3] Bob Burman had recently won the 100-mile championship race at New Orleans. Many drivers expressed that even though there were other racetracks being built, the Speedway would be the premier racetrack in this country and they were anxious to be a part of the races in August.

*Buick driver Lewis Strang looking over a model of the Speedway in early 1909 during the construction phase. This was in the vicinity of where the Speedway Motel sits today. (Photo courtesy of the Indianapolis Motor Speedway)*

Frank Wheeler had accepted designs by Tiffany for a seven-and-a-half-foot tall silver cup that he would award on behalf of the Wheeler-Schebler Company to one of the winners of the August automobile races. There were several other trophies and medals that were being offered for the races. Others included: the Prest-O-Lite trophy, the Remy Grand Brassard, and the G & J Tires trophy.

By the middle part of May, there was still much work to be done on the racetrack itself but the construction of the various structures was progressing nicely. The bleachers to be used for the balloon race were complete which assured the partners that the balloon race would go on as scheduled. Meanwhile, as the first entrants for the balloon race began to arrive in Indianapolis, Carl Fisher split his time between overseeing the construction efforts and visiting the Coliseum at the Indiana State Fairgrounds where the balloons were being given inflation tests. Fisher also needed to find the time to qualify himself for the event as he hoped to be a participant in the race as well. Since the race would be run under international rules, the pilots had to be a veteran of at least ten ascensions, including one at night. Fisher had completed six ascensions while in Europe and two in the United States, leaving him two short of the required ten. He had planned to use the remaining days in the month to complete his last two required ascensions and had announced that he would be making the first of these two ascensions from the Speedway in late May.

*One side of a flyer advertising the August 1909 automobile races at the Indianapolis Motor Speedway. This aerial view shows the inside course originally planned as part of the Speedway. (Courtesy of John Darlington)*

*One side of a flyer advertising the August 1909 automobile races at the Indianapolis Motor Speedway. Featured are the four founding partners and the Wheeler-Schebler trophy. (Courtesy of John Darlington)*

*Chapter 2*

# "Gas Bags" Sail From the Speedway

On Saturday, May 22, Carl Fisher prepared for the initial balloon ascension from the Indianapolis Motor Speedway. The *Indianapolis Star* reported that Fisher and Captain George Bumbaugh went up in C. A. Coey's 40,000-cubic-foot balloon *Kathleen*. The pair was assisted by about 50 men who stationed themselves along the 600-foot drag rope while some of the sightseers who were at the Speedway on Saturday helped with the inflation of the balloon. The pair rose to a height of about 3,000 feet and sailed southwest upon leaving the Speedway grounds before making three landings that were hampered by strong winds. After their first descent in Bridgeport (about 15 miles from Indianapolis), the second one was made about five miles south of Bridgeport in Decatur Township before finally arriving near Valley Mills. This gave Fisher his ninth qualified trip and left him with only a nighttime ascension to complete in order to qualify for the balloon race on the 5th of June.

The following Saturday Fisher and Bumbaugh made another flight from the Speedway with four other occupants in a brand new balloon called the *Hoosier*. Mr. Bumbaugh had just completed building the balloon for the Indiana Aero Club to be used by Captain Thomas Baldwin of New York in the national balloon race. Accompanying the pair were Mr. and Mrs. Coey of Chicago and two local newspaper reporters. This was the first time that the 80,000-cubic-foot balloon had been flown and Mrs. Coey was quoted in the papers as saying that she was quite nervous by the fact that the balloon had never been tested. The group arose from the Speedway at 5:00 p.m. and drifted to the northwest for about 40 minutes before coming down in a field on the farm of Charles Howard. The trip was performed at an expense of about $1 per minute. The costs consisted of inflating the balloon, transporting it out of the field, and reimbursing for damages done. A rail fence was torn down for several feet during the descent and a telephone wire was ripped from its post. While it looked like the landing was made in a desolate location, within minutes nearly a hundred people had made their way to the site.

*George Bumbaugh and C.A. Coey before a balloon race in Chicago, Illinois, on July 4, 1908. (Chicago Daily News negatives collection, SDN-054007. Courtesy of the Chicago Historical Society)*

Over the next few days, Carl Fisher completed his nighttime ascension and qualified for the balloon race. By this time, it was known that there would be two balloon races on June 5. With three of the original twelve entrants withdrawing and three failing to meet the qualifying standards, the organizers decided to go ahead with the National Balloon Championship race for the six qualified entrants and hold a handicap race for the three entrants who had failed to qualify. An additional qualification for the national race required that the gas capacity of the balloons be between 60,000 and 78,000 cubic feet.

The *Indianapolis Star* published a picture of the prizes that would be awarded to the winners of each race. For the balloon traveling the farthest in the handicap race, the Merchants' Association of Indianapolis provided a silver cup valued at $300. The Aero Club of America awarded a beautiful trophy consisting of a gold hot air balloon resting on a black marble base for the winner of the national championship. Additionally, Carl Fisher announced that he would award a commemorative silver plate worth $350 and a special cup to the contestants that remained in the air the longest in the national race and handicap race, respectively.

Indiana Governor Thomas Marshall and his wife accepted an invitation from the Aero Club of America to deliver the farewell address to the race entrants. The organizers erected a large platform in front of the bleachers which would allow the inflated balloons to be led in single file past the Governor and the rest of the spectators before they took to the sky. The pilots and their aides for the balloon races were as follows.

### National Championship Balloon Race Entrants

- Carl Fisher and Captain George Bumbaugh of Indianapolis in the *Indiana*
- Captain Thomas Baldwin of New York and Charles Walsh of Mt. Vernon, New York, in the *Hoosier*
- A.H. Morgan and J.H. Wade, Jr., of Cleveland in the *Cleveland*
- Albert Bond Lambert and H.E. Honeywell of St. Louis in the *St. Louis 3*
- John Berry and Paul McCullough of St. Louis in the *University City*
- Holland Forbes and Captain Clifford B. Harmon of New York in the *New York*

### Handicap Balloon Race Entrants

- Dr. Goethe Link and Russ Irvin of Indianapolis in the *Indianapolis*
- Dr. H.W. Thompson of Salem, Ohio, and W.E. Mast of Canton, Ohio, in the *Ohio*
- C.A. Coey and Jack Bennett of Chicago in the *Chicago*

*The silver cup awarded by Carl Fisher to the balloonist that remained in the air the longest during the handicap race. (Photo courtesy of the Indianapolis Motor Speedway)*

*The trophy awarded by the Aero Club of America to the winner of the 1909 National Championship balloon race. (Fly magazine, June 1909)*

Major H. B. Hersey, one of the United States Government Weather Bureau experts, was called in to provide the entrants with information concerning air currents and weather conditions. Alan Hawley of New York, Field Manager for the races, had complete charge of the grounds. Others assisting Mr. Hawley were timekeeper Charles Glidden of Boston, Charles Edwards of New York, and W. T. Blythe, the local weather bureau expert. Charles Glidden was well known in the automobile world as the donor of the trophy for the famous Glidden tour automobile reliability run. Upon seeing the Speedway for the first time, he reportedly said that it was a glorious sight and exceeded even the press agents' stories.

The entire city of Indianapolis had come alive for this inaugural event at the Speedway. Numerous spectators arrived by Thursday, June 3, to visit the Speedway and view the facilities for Saturday's festivities. Many of them were shocked by the magnitude of the Speedway. Likewise, the entrants were very impressed by the facilities which included gas pipes that could supply one dozen balloons simultaneously, emit 80,000 cubic feet of gas per hour and were reinforced by special joints costing $1,600 each.

The Aero Club of America had set up its headquarters in the Claypool Hotel, which was being referred to as "balloon alley". The atmosphere surrounding the hotel was magical as hundreds of visitors tried to catch a glimpse of the aeronauts and view the many large banners and other prizes on exhibit that had been won at various international events. The balloon pilots captivated the crowd with stories of their past experiences.

*The Claypool Hotel as it appeared in the early 1900s. Located at the corner of Washington and Illinois Streets, the Claypool served as the headquarters for the Aero Club of America during the balloon races hosted by the Indianapolis Motor Speedway in June 1909 and again in September 1910. (Photo courtesy of the Indiana Historical Society, Bass Photo Co. Collection, negative # 27543)*

"I remember one incident," said Captain Thomas Baldwin, "when we were making an ascension in France, a storm came up which turned from a rain into a hail storm when we were a half-a-mile above the clouds. The cold air and hail were beating against the great gasbag and caused the gas to contract, and we made a descent that was far from being of a consoling nature. We quickly unloaded ballast and when we rose, we reached another warm current of air and as the gas expanded we rose to a height that made it hard for us to breathe after being in the low altitudes. Then it became necessary to let out more gas to descend to a normal height, but, in so doing, we again hit the cold currents, which further contracted our gas so that we had to descend to the ground and the speed in which we did so imperiled our lives. Small time was there to climb into the ropes and wait for the basket to hit the earth, which it did with a thud that would likely have proved fatal to us had we neglected to properly protect ourselves by climbing into the rigging."[1]

Holland Forbes, the man who would be piloting the *New York* balloon told how he fell out of the sky in his balloon for a half-mile over Germany a few years ago. "I was in the big Berlin race with Augustus Post," Mr. Forbes said. "We were in the big balloon the *Conqueror* racing for the international cup and within five minutes of the start we were 2,900 feet above the earth when the big bag suddenly exploded. A great hole was blown in the waistline and the balloon began to fall like a rock. It kept it up for 1,000 feet and we were going down so fast that the sand that Post was throwing out formed a cloud that we passed through. I cut the rope that connected the appendix of the balloon with the basket, hoping that the rush of air would drive the lower part of the canvas to the top of the net and form a parachute. It was our only chance and the canvas responded. Then we began cutting away the sandbags and the result was that, for a moment, after a 1,000-foot fall like a rock, we were safe. But the upward rush of air was too great and the parachute could not withstand the strain. It split in several places and the last 1,000-foot dash to earth began. Bye-bye Forbsie, Post told me as we shook hands. Down we went; however, the parachute broke the fall some. As we climbed up into the rigging the basket went crashing through a roof like a bullet. We were shot into the basket, which had broken the fall, while the balloon caught in the roof. There we were, swinging in a basket in a nicely furnished room belonging to a young lady."[2]

Equally as fascinating was the list of items that the entrants carried with them on their flights. Captain Baldwin explained to the crowd that he would be packing 36 eggs, 40 pieces of fried chicken, 50 slices of buttered bread, ten pies, two dozen oranges, five cans of soup, three loaves of bread, crackers and cheese, apples, lemons, sweet chocolate, cans of fruit, several kinds of prepared foods and gallons of water and coffee. Holland Forbes had a similar fare but also included a German army soup preparation, which had been put in small packages six inches long and one and one-half inches in diameter. It was dissolved in water and weighed one-half pound. He also carried a unique soup stove that used a double-can effect. Inside a large can filled with lime was a smaller one filled with soup. Two holes could be opened in the top of the large can, by pouring water in one hole while letting air escape from the other, the contents became hot almost instantly. This could also keep the hands and feet warm. Another unusual item was included by Mr. Lambert in the *St. Louis 3*. He used an air blower capable of putting 20,000 cubic feet of air per hour into the balloon. Mr. Coey, pilot of the *Chicago* balloon, stocked his basket with enough food for three days. In addition to the food he also took the following items: two guns, a camera, a hunting knife, three big canteens of water, a smaller canteen of spirits, two altitude barometers, a field glass, several kinds of thermometers, two big ocean life protectors, two lamps, a dozen carrier pigeons, heavy overcoats, raincoats, fishing tackle and a hammock. Incredibly, the hammock was hung from the rigging of the balloon!

On Friday, the day before the big balloons took to the air, the entrants and their assistants were at the Speedway from early afternoon to late evening making final preparations for the race. Some of the participants even started to inflate their balloons. While all of this was going on, officials of the Aero Club of America were kept busy answering questions, giving instructions, and planning for Saturday's start. Meanwhile, the Speedway stationed guards to protect the balloons to ensure that nothing went wrong with the supply of gas.

*The scene at the Indianapolis Motor Speedway before the start of the June 1909 balloon races. This picture was likely taken early Saturday morning before the crowd began to arrive as the bleachers to the far left are empty. The St. Louis 3 can be seen at the left while the Indianapolis is the fifth balloon in the same row. The partially inflated balloon in the front of the right row is the University City. (Photo courtesy of the Smithsonian National Air and Space Museum, SI 2004-55415)*

*Moments before the first ascension at the June 1909 balloon races hosted by the Indianapolis Motor Speedway. The third balloon in the left row is the Hoosier and the dark-colored balloon next to it is the University City. The first balloon in the right row is the Indianapolis while the last balloon in the same row is the St. Louis 3. The crowded bleachers can be seen to the far right of the picture. (Photo courtesy of the Indianapolis Motor Speedway)*

*The Indianapolis before the start of the June 1909 balloon races. This picture was taken from the vicinity of the bleachers at the south end of the track. (Photo courtesy of the Indianapolis Motor Speedway)*

*From left to right, the Indiana, Hoosier, New York, University City, and St. Louis 3 before the start of the June 1909 balloon races. This picture was taken from the vicinity of the bleachers at the south end of the track. (Photo courtesy of the Indianapolis Motor Speedway)*

*The Indiana with the Ohio to the left and the Hoosier to the right before the start of the June 1909 balloon races. (Photo courtesy of the Library of Congress, Prints and Photographs Division)*

Although it had rained for several days leading up to the races, a brief shower on Saturday morning gave way to sunshine and a slight breeze that would carry the balloons to the south. All but one of the balloons was fully inflated by 2:00 p.m. at which time the race officials released a group of toy balloons, confirming that the wind was almost due south. John Berry and his team worked until 3:00 p.m. as their balloon the *University City* was the last to be filled. After the inflation was completed, the balloons were balanced and the netting was hooked to the ropes. The assistants held the basket to the ground and loaded as much ballast as possible. More than 20,000 pounds of sand was provided at the Speedway for preparing the ballast. The nine large balloons fully inflated and tugging at their ropes ready to take to the skies made for a spectacular sight! They were all lined up decorated with large flags and pennants, the greenish-yellow *New York*, the chocolate-colored *University City*, the light golden *Cleveland*, the brown *Ohio*, the pearly white, almost transparent balloons of *Indianapolis*, *Indiana*, *Hoosier*, and *St. Louis 3* and towering above them all was the red *Chicago*. The *Chicago*, at 110,000 cubic feet, was the largest balloon in the world and stood as tall as an eight-story building when fully inflated.

Most of the entrants began making their way to the site of the balloons by 3:00 p.m. In the meantime, the event started to take on a military appearance as 100-150 members of Battery A, along with a squad of 20 mounted artillerymen, patrolled the area around the balloons. Additional policemen were stationed around the gates to the Speedway. All were adamant about strictly enforcing the "no smoking near the balloons" rule. By this time the main roads to the Speedway were jammed, making it practically impossible to reach the main gate other than by foot. The road from the Emmerichsville Bridge to the Speedway was one long line of automobiles with horses prancing among them unable to break free. The trains leading to the Speedway were so crowded that several people had taken positions on top of the traction cars. There were only about 3,500 – 4,000 spectators actually inside the grounds. Some spectators apparently favored watching the balloons from outside of the Speedway rather than paying the 50-cent admission price at the east gate or $1.00 at the main gate. Still, others wanted to enter the grounds but found it impossible to do so because of the huge crowds. Many people were perched in trees and on housetops for miles. It was estimated that in excess of 40,000 people were around the Speedway grounds to watch the balloons ascend, causing the Governor himself to miss the start of the national race. He had left his residence around 3:00 p.m. thinking that would be early enough. However, he became caught in all of the traffic, forcing him to abandon his auto and walk the last mile on foot. He arrived at the Speedway in time to see only the final three balloons ascend.

Sharply at 3:50 p.m., amid the burst of patriotic music from the military band and the cheering from the multitude of spectators, the first entrant in the handicap race, the *Ohio*, ascended from the Speedway and began to sail away to the south. The 40,000-cubic-foot balloon left carrying only four bags of sand. The *Indianapolis* with five bags of sand and the mighty *Chicago* with 48 bags of sand followed in five-minute intervals. As the *Chicago* rose to about 500 feet, Mr. Coey unfurled a large silk American flag that prompted the huge crowd to respond with a thunderous ovation.

*Dr. Goethe Link and Russ Irwin ascending in the balloon Indianapolis. (Photo courtesy of the Indianapolis Motor Speedway)*

The start of the national race, the order of which had been determined by a draw the night before, was scheduled for 5:00 p.m. Meanwhile, the national race entrants joined the crowd in watching the handicap race entries sail away to the south as Major Hersey was kept busy providing the pilots with weather updates every few minutes.

The wind had shifted slightly to the southeast at about 20 mph as the official timekeeper, Charles Glidden, counted off the remaining seconds to 5:00 p.m. in a loud voice. The first balloon in the national race, the *New York*, lazily floated from the Speedway and began its drift to the southeast. "Watch us win!"[3] the millionaire Holland Forbes shouted as the big greenish-yellow balloon began its ascent. The *New York*, carrying 48 bags of sand, was the prohibitive favorite primarily because the balloon itself was made of a special, stronger material, putting the cost of the entire vessel at around $4,000. Following the *New York* promptly at 5:05 p.m., Carl Fisher and George Bumbaugh began to rise in the *Indiana* to the delight and cheers of the crowd. The band started to play the Star-Spangled Banner as the crowd saw six big American flags hanging from the netting of the pearly white balloon. As they passed over the crowd, Fisher dropped roses on them as Bumbaugh watched from the load ring above the basket. They left carrying 52 bags of sand. The *New York* may have been the best balloon but the *Indiana* was clearly the crowd favorite with two locals as occupants. There was a slight delay before the *St. Louis 3* with its 50 bags of sand was released, but it was soon off the ground. This particular balloon stirred up the only controversy of the event as some of the entrants thought that it actually had a gas capacity of 80,000 cubic feet, 2,000 cubic feet in excess of the limit for the national race. The race officials responded that they would not make a ruling until after the outcome of the race, perhaps waiting to see if they even needed to address the situation at all. At 5:15 p.m., and right on the heels of the *St. Louis 3*, the light golden *Cleveland* left the ground with A.H. Morgan and J.H. Wade in command. This pair rode in the smallest basket of all the balloons in either race and carried around 15-20 bags of sand. Keeping right on schedule, the *Hoosier* with Captain Thomas Baldwin and Charles Walsh left the Speedway grounds at 5:20 p.m. with about 35-40 bags of sand in tow. Captain Baldwin, who was one of the best-known aeronauts in the country and considered a ringleader among them, stood on the top edge of the basket and shouted farewell through a megaphone to the large crowd below. The spectators roared in amusement as Charles Walsh lost his hat while waving to the masses assembled just outside of the Speedway. Finally, at 5:25 p.m., the last balloon took to the air with John Berry and Paul McCullough riding in the basket accompanied by 26 bags of sand dangling from its sides. The chocolate-colored *University City* slowly drifted forward and upward, though not as high as the others at first.

"On the getaway McCullough and I jockeyed for a start, but could not make headway in the same air strata with the other entrants, who all started ahead of us", pilot John Berry said later. "They were at an altitude of between 1,000 and 2,000 feet and I decided to go higher. Upon reaching an altitude of 10,000 feet, we struck an admirable wind current and rapidly overhauled and passed our rivals. The temperature up there was twenty-nine degrees and, despite our heavy clothing, we were chilled through."[4]

After all of the balloons were in the air, the crowd continued to stay and watch them as they sailed off to the southeast in the blue evening sky. The sun was just starting to set, which caused a faint glow to be cast on the balloons. This provided a magnificent aerial display for those in attendance.

Unlike other races, one had to wait for a few days to learn the outcome of a balloon race. Updates were obtained as the balloon pilots dropped notes from their baskets; however, these notes were sometimes difficult to find. Sunday morning, June 6, the *Indianapolis Star* had these early updates from notes that had been directed to the newspaper since Saturday's launches.

Bargersville, Indiana, June 5 – "We are sailing over Bargersville, Indiana. Time is 5:30 p.m. June 5. Everything seems fine. We are going as far as the wind goes; am out for the distance record." C.A. Coey in the *Chicago*[5]

*Guards around the balloons at the start of the balloon races hosted by the Indianapolis Motor Speedway on June 5, 1909. Note the bags of ballast at their feet. The Cleveland can be seen in the background and the dark-colored balloon in the foreground is the Ohio. (Photo courtesy of the Indiana Historical Society)*

*Guards assist in the efforts to prepare the New York for flight before the start of the balloon races hosted by the Indianapolis Motor Speedway on June 5, 1909. (Photo courtesy of the Indianapolis Motor Speedway)*

23

Nashville, Indiana, June 5 – "The *Ohio* landed one mile west of here tonight at 6:20 p.m. The lack of ballast was the cause for this early descent of the first starter in the handicap race at Indianapolis this afternoon. We had a pleasant, uneventful trip, but regret we were compelled to drop too soon. We landed in a newly plowed Brown County field. Our balloon is being rolled ready to ship home to Salem, Ohio." Dr. H.W. Thompson in the *Ohio*[6]

Franklin, Indiana, June 5 – The balloon *Hoosier* passed eight miles southwest of here at 6:55 p.m.[7]

Edinburgh, Indiana, June 5 – Just at 7:00 p.m. eight balloons were sighted about four miles west of here. They were all going south with the large balloon *Chicago* in the lead.[8]

Trafalgar, Indiana, June 5 at 7:00 p.m. – "Berry (*University City*) very high. Bumbaugh and Fisher (*Indiana*) going up. Lambert (*St. Louis 3*) going up very high. Forbes (*New York*) very low. Morgan (*Cleveland*) still ballooning. All balloons on parallel line except Berry trailing. The *Hoosier* lowest position. *New York* ten miles to the northwest and Fisher south." Captain Baldwin and Charles Walsh in the *Hoosier*[9]

Nineveh, Indiana, June 5 – "We are now talking with Honeywell and Lambert as we are only 800 feet apart. They asked us to come over for supper. It is now 7:15 p.m." Carl Fisher and George Bumbaugh in the *Indiana*[10]

Freetown, Indiana, June 5 – *Hoosier* moving south over Freetown at 9:20 p.m.[11]

Vincennes, Indiana, June 5 – A large balloon was sighted above this city at 9:30 p.m. tonight. Several automobile parties followed it south for 15 miles or more. The name of the bag could not be ascertained as the men were too high to carry on conversation. Flashes from search lights were the only signs received from the flyers. First a red, next a green and then a white light would appear.[12]

Seymour, Indiana, June 5 – Several Indianapolis balloons were seen flying slightly west of here at 10:00 p.m. tonight. They dropped messages.[13]

On Monday evening, June 7 the *Indianapolis News* published the final results of the handicap race. Dr. Goethe Link and Russ Irvin of Indianapolis in the *Indianapolis* had won both the cup offered by the Indianapolis Merchants Association for the farthest distance covered and the cup given by Carl Fisher for the longest time in the air. They cleared the Kentucky-Tennessee line and landed at 11:00 a.m. Sunday morning in Westmoreland, Tennessee, 45 miles northeast of Nashville. Considering that this was the first flight for the duo, it was quite a feat that they piloted the 40,000-cubic-foot balloon over 235 miles for 19 hours. In a telegram sent to Indianapolis after the flight, Mr. Irvin said that their highest altitude was 13,000 feet and that most of the time they maintained an altitude in excess of two miles. He reported that the weather was perfect and the air currents were slow both day and night. He summed it up by saying that they were always in sight of two other balloons and it was a grand trip with the one exception of being shot at twice by angry farmers while passing over Kentucky. The *Chicago* placed second and landed at a fairground in Scottsburg, Kentucky, just 16 miles north of where the *Indianapolis* had landed. The *Ohio* finished third and, as previously reported in the *Indianapolis Star*, landed one mile west of Nashville, Indiana, at 6:20 p.m. Saturday night.

Dr. Thompson of the *Ohio* passed along a humorous story to the newspapers. Since they were about to land in a five-mile wooded area, they had to discard everything from ballast to provisions in an effort to get enough lift to make it to the field that they eventually touched down in. Upon arriving in Helmsburg to

*The Cleveland before the start of the National Championship balloon race from the Indianapolis Motor Speedway on June 5, 1909. The Hoosier is in the foreground and the balloon in the air is the St. Louis 3. (Photo courtesy of the Indianapolis Motor Speedway)*

catch the train home, he was met by a man by the name of Ed Parsley who told him that his wife and four children were setting out sweet potatoes Saturday evening when something landed about six feet from them. "Finest supper I ever had," he told Mr. Thompson, "it was the lunch basket from your balloon!"[14]

The winner of the national race was not so easily determined. The *Indianapolis News* reported in its June 7 edition that the *Indiana* and *St. Louis 3* were battling for honors while the next morning the *Indianapolis Star* published a picture of the *Indiana* stating that it was probably the winner of the national balloon race. As it turned out, these reports were based on incomplete information. These were the only two balloons that had not been heard from recently so it was assumed that they were still in the air. By Wednesday, June 9, all of the balloons had made confirmed landings and the information was beginning to get sorted out as to who would win the two prizes.

The first two balloons to return to earth were the *Cleveland* and the *Hoosier*. The *Cleveland* landed about eight miles west of Columbus, Indiana, around 8:00 p.m. Saturday night. There was some speculation about the balloon receiving bad gas but Mr. Morgan, the balloon's pilot, blamed the short flight on a defect with the balloon. His suspicions were confirmed later as Leo Stevens of Indianapolis, who made the balloon, found a four-inch cut about 20 feet down from the top of the balloon. Mr. Stevens reasoned that since the cut was made under the dipping panel it was made by someone who knew about the construction

*The Hoosier taking to the air at the start of the National Championship balloon race on June 5, 1909. The University City can be seen to the left. (Photo courtesy of the Indianapolis Motor Speedway)*

of balloons. The panel was in a spot that could not be easily seen and the gas pressure was very heavy at that point which would cause the gas to escape quickly. The *Hoosier* came to earth Monday morning around Green Briar, Tennessee, which is within 25 miles of the Kentucky-Tennessee border.

Fisher and Bumbaugh had a very long flight in the *Indiana*. Carl Fisher said that they came down within a few feet of the ground a couple of times but then continued on their way. Despite being in the air for a total of 49 hours, their distance was measured from the first "near landing", giving them a fourth place finish. The pair stressed that these were necessary to replenish their water supply since the cans they used previously held oil or gas. The first touch down was Sunday evening at Shackle Island, Tennessee, about 12 miles north of Nashville as some locals caught their drag rope and lowered them to within about 125 feet of the ground. They lowered their water cans to be filled and once that was accomplished they continued on their way. The second time was early Monday morning at Ashland City which is only about 15 miles west of Shackle Island. Mr. Bumbaugh said that some plantation workers used the balloon's drag rope to pull them down onto a pile of railroad ties about ten feet above the ground. According to him, after they replenished their water Carl Fisher climbed out and walked far away from the balloon to light up a cigar. After about 35 minutes he climbed back in and they continued on their way. They finally decided to land Monday evening after repeatedly getting caught up in revolving air currents that swept along the Cumberland valley. These air currents caused the pair to be carried up two or three miles in as little as a few minutes, spinning like a top. Tired of fighting this on several occasions, they decided to land near Ruskin, Tennessee, which is only about 50 miles from Shackle Island.

The *St. Louis 3* was credited with third place, going a distance of around 320 miles. The balloon landed early Monday morning near Kelso, Tennessee, after 36 hours and 30 minutes. Originally, it was thought that the balloon would make a run for the duration and distance records because it had not been heard from for some time; however, upon landing, it was confirmed that the balloon was not in contention for either award.

"We landed", said Mr. Lambert, "not because we had to but because it seemed wise. We went up to an elevation of 11,500 feet looking for a southern current but this altitude of more than two miles was too much for me. Both Honeywell and I suffered with the cold and I began to feel an awful dizziness toward evening. We thought it best to take what distance we could without running any chance of making it less so after dropping for two miles we picked out a grass plot within a few feet of the railroad station and landed."[15]

Only after determining the precise landing areas of the remaining two balloons and calculating the distances on government maps did the Aero Club of America award the distance prize to the *University City* balloon of John Berry and his aide Paul McCullough. The *New York* was a close second in distance but spent the most time in the air, thus winning the duration trophy. Interestingly enough, Holland Forbes and Clifford Harmon had drifted into Alabama with the *New York* and were headed for Mobile when the wind shifted and began to sail them back to the north. When they finally decided to land to save distance they were about three miles north of Corinth, Mississippi, close to the Mississippi–Tennessee border. Their total distance was 355.5 miles, 26.5 miles short of the 382 miles achieved by the *University City* when Berry and McCullough landed just south of Fort Payne, Alabama. Berry later told of their experience while over Alabama, which was similar to that of the *New York*.

*Sixty-one-year-old pilot John Berry and aide Paul McCullough of the University City. The pair won the National Championship balloon race hosted by the Indianapolis Motor Speedway on June 5, 1909. (Fly magazine, June 1909)*

"Sunday evening, while I was sleeping, McCullough sighted what afterwards proved to be Fort Payne, Alabama, and he woke me up. He got in the basket for a rest and we passed over the town. About two hours later I saw it again and realized that we were drifting back to the north. Then we let the balloon come down, we came down fast without opening the valve, for the gas was contracting as the sun had set. We tried for some time to get a southern current at different altitudes but we could not do it. Finally, we let out the drag rope. A lot of people turned out and three of them caught a hold of the drag rope as we landed on the farm of John Meddaw, who proved to be a preacher and a mighty fine gentleman."[16]

Somehow, it seemed just that the *University City* was the eventual winner in the distance competition because no one gave it much of a chance. The balloon did not arrive at the Speedway until after all of the others were already filling with gas. Berry and McCullough had little help and spent most of Friday night and Saturday until 3:00 p.m. inflating their balloon. Their ascent from the Speedway was the least impressive of all of the balloons as they started slower than the others and the *University City* did not look like it was fully inflated. It was also the oldest balloon in the race and possessed quite a storied history. It had escaped destruction in two previous outings: once when it was shot at after drifting into the Georgia squirrel rifle belt and another time when it narrowly missed being destroyed in a forest fire. H.E. Honeywell, who was the aide in the *St. Louis 3*, had built the balloon but sold it to Berry in favor of the newer *St. Louis 3*. Berry promptly changed the name from *Yankee* to *University City* to honor E.G. Lewis, who was the mayor of University City, a suburb of St. Louis. Ironically, Berry was able to sail the *University City* farther than the balloon that replaced it.

*Chapter 3*

# The Motorcycle Invasion

By Mid-July 1909, Carl Fisher was disappointed with the rate of progress being made on the track. He feared that it would never be completed in time for the motorcycle races, which were only about six weeks away. The primary delay on the track was with the southwest corner where the bridges were being built over the small creek. Carl Fisher asked Mr. Andrews to hire more men so that they could work in shifts around the clock. To make this possible he suggested extending the gas lines used for the balloon races to the inside of the southwest turn and set up open flame burners to provide enough light to work at night. Mr. Fisher also supplied some Prest-O-Lite tanks to use on the outside of the track. These sources provided enough light to work after sunset. Within days after hiring the additional men, there was a dramatic increase in the rate of progress made on the track.

The rest of the Speedway was practically finished, highlighted by the 12,000-seat grandstand on the main straightaway. This grandstand was a covered structure 82 feet wide and 500 feet long and seating was supplemented by two sections of bleachers, one 500 feet by 60 feet and one 350 feet by 65 feet. Additionally, there were 42 other structures, which included: the superintendent's residence, cafés, refreshment stands, garages, stables, the Aero Club clubhouse, press stand and restrooms. A pedestrian bridge spanned across the track near the main grandstand and an auto bridge by the northwest corner.

Meanwhile, the city was busy making final preparations for the motorcyclists. The races to be held at the Speedway were only part of the activities planned in connection with the seventh annual convention of the Federation of American Motorcyclists (F.A.M.). Several hundred motorcyclists were expected to make the trip to Indianapolis to enjoy endurance runs, receptions, a parade, and business meetings. Indianapolis prepared for the four-day event by decorating many downtown buildings and stretching streamers of flags and bunting across all of the main streets at regular intervals. The Indiana Motorcycle Club handled the majority of the arrangements. Started in 1909 with just a few members, the local club had grown to be the second largest in the United States in less than two years time. The complete list of activities planned for the convention were as follows.

- Monday, August 9, all day – Prizes for all of the events were on display at Marott's department store.
- Wednesday, August 11, 4:30 p.m. – The motorcyclists on the endurance run were to begin arriving in the city. The endurance run was scheduled to start Tuesday morning in Cleveland, Ohio, and make an overnight stop in Columbus, Ohio, before heading to Indianapolis. They were to check into the F.A.M. headquarters at the Denison Hotel upon arrival.
- Wednesday, August 11, evening – A reception was scheduled at the clubroom of the Indiana Motorcycle Club at 444 West Vermont Street.
- Thursday, August 12, 9:00 a.m. – A group picture was to be taken of the motorcyclists at Monument Circle and a tour of interesting sights around the city followed the picture.
- Thursday, August 12, 1:30 p.m. – A parade through the city was scheduled. After the parade there was to be a group ride to Riverside Park for afternoon entertainment.
- Thursday, August 12, afternoon – Practice was scheduled at the Speedway.
- Thursday, August 12, afternoon – An endurance run to Kokomo was scheduled.
- Thursday, August 12, evening – A business meeting followed by a reception and vaudeville act at the German House (today known as the Athenaeum) was scheduled.
- Friday, August 13, 1:00 p.m. – Races were scheduled at the Speedway.
- Saturday, August 14, 1:00 p.m. – Races were scheduled at the Speedway.

*The Denison Hotel as it appeared in the early 1900s. The Denison, located at the corner of Ohio and Pennsylvania Streets, served as the headquarters for the Federation of American Motorcyclists for their seventh annual convention during August 1909. (Photo courtesy of the Indiana Historical Society, Bass Photo Co. Collection, negative # 5086)*

Some of the motorcyclists had stopped by the Speedway on Friday, August 6, to get a little practice in for the upcoming races. The riders were on their way to Cleveland to participate in the endurance run. Anxious to get on the track, they had allowed themselves time to stop in Indianapolis along the way. When they arrived at the Speedway, they did not like what they saw. Plus, they were unhappy about not getting some practice time. Convincing the group that the track would be in good shape by the time they returned from their endurance run, Carl Fisher promised that they would have all day on Thursday to practice. Unfortunately, that was not the end of Fisher's problems. The last few tank cars of oil arrived on Tuesday instead of Saturday as scheduled. This meant that, since Monday was lost, the track would likely not be ready until Friday morning. This would set up another confrontation with the motorcyclists on Thursday when Fisher would likely have to go back on his promise and tell them that they couldn't practice until Friday.

*The starting lineup before one of the motorcycle races at the Indianapolis Motor Speedway on Saturday, August 14, 1909. Note the rough, jagged surface of the track. (Photo courtesy of the Indianapolis Motor Speedway)*

Thursday's convention activities started with a group picture of the motorcyclists at Monument Circle followed by a tour of interesting sites around the city. At 1:30 p.m. that afternoon there was a parade through the streets of the city. The parade route was as follows: north on Meridian Street from Monument Circle to Ohio Street, west on Ohio Street to Illinois Street, south on Illinois Street to Washington Street, east on Washington Street to Pennsylvania Street, then north on Massachusetts Avenue to the German House. From the German House the route continued west to Delaware Street, north on Delaware Street to Twenty-fifth Street, then to Meridian Street, north on Meridian Street to Thirtieth Street, from there to Capitol Avenue, south on Capitol Avenue to Vermont Street, west on Vermont Street to the home of the

Indiana Motorcycle Club. Several members of the group then went on to Riverside Park for an afternoon of fun. The Thursday endurance run to Kokomo was cancelled due to bad road conditions caused by the recent rains; however, a special interurban car carried 68 of the F.A.M. delegates to the city where they were given a banquet at the country club.

Somehow, Carl Fisher had the track in good condition late Thursday afternoon as Ed Lingenfelder, a professional rider from California, rode 25 miles in 25 minutes. The world record for this distance was set by Jake De Rosier in Springfield, Massachusetts, at a little over 20 minutes. Concerns stirred among the riders that the track was unsafe as they complained to Chicago's Earle Ovington, president of the F.A.M., of exposed sharp edges from the crushed stone. Therefore, many of the riders did not want to race on the track. Some suggested moving the races to the Indiana State Fairgrounds track but the F.A.M. decided in a meeting late Thursday night to go ahead with the races at the Speedway.

Carl Fisher had responded to the criticism by empathetically stating that the Speedway would be in excellent condition in time for the races. "The Speedway will positively be in finished condition and ready for record time. The track is better now than the Brooklands track ever was. We have double the force of men working day and night smoothing out the remaining defects, and there is no reason why records cannot be broken. The races on the track tomorrow will demonstrate the truth of this assertion, as the practices have already done."[1]

The inner two-and-a-half mile road course was not complete; therefore, the motorcycle races and the automobile races the following week would only use the outer two-and-a-half mile course.

The paper listed more than 300 entries for the races in the two-day program. There were a total of 15 events as listed below.

Friday, August 13

- 🏁 Event No. 1 – Five-mile race, limited to private owners
- 🏁 Event No. 2 – One-mile race for the F.A.M. National Championship
- 🏁 Event No. 3 – Five-mile handicap race, limited to members of the Indiana Motorcycle Club
- 🏁 Event No. 4 – Ten-mile race for the F.A.M. amateur national championship
- 🏁 Event No. 5 – Five-mile race for motorcycles with engines of less than 55 cubic inches of piston displacement (CID) without auxiliary exhaust ports
- 🏁 Event No. 6 – Ten-mile race for professionals
- 🏁 Event No. 7 – Five-mile handicap race open to all
- 🏁 Event No. 8 – 25-mile race open to motorcycles with engines of less than 30.5 CID

Saturday, August 14

- 🏁 Event No. 1 – Two and one-half mile handicap race, limited to private owners
- 🏁 Event No. 2 – Five-mile national championship race
- 🏁 Event No. 3 – One-mile time trials with a flying start
- 🏁 Event No. 4 – Ten-mile handicap race
- 🏁 Event No. 5 – Five-mile professional race
- 🏁 Event No. 6 – Ten-mile race open to motorcycles with engines of less than 30.5 CID
- 🏁 Event No. 7 – One hour race for the F.A.M. national championship

A light rain most of Friday morning forced the officials to postpone the day's races until Saturday, moving Saturday's races to Monday. Saturday turned out to be a very hot day, which may have contributed to the disappointing crowd of around 3,500 people. The riders had a brief practice period before the races started, but it appeared that many of them were taking it easy as they were still getting used to the track. Many more riders continued to complain about the exposed sharp edges on the track's surface and that the turns were not banked enough to obtain a high rate of speed. As a result, many of the riders entered in the races declared that they were not going to run on the track. This brought charges of "being yellow" and having "cold feet" from some of the other riders but most stood by their conviction that they were not going to race.

The first race of the day started at 2:00 p.m. Only nine of the original 13 entrants decided to run the five-mile race, which was limited to private owners. Made in Springfield, Massachusetts, the Indian motorcycle dominated the event with the top three finishers. The winner was A.G. Chapple of New York in a time of 4:53.20, well off of the record for this distance. Nelson J. Hodgin of Indianapolis placed second and Tim Bahnsen of St. Louis was third.

The second race was for the one-mile F.A.M. national championship. A low number participated as only ten of the original 29 entrants lined up at the mile marker at the north end of the track. In what proved to be a terrific finish, Fred Huyck of Chicago, riding an Indian, came up on the Merkel of Stanley Kellogg with a burst of speed just as the riders passed the bridge going over the track, charging ahead for the win. The timers at the finish line, who received their start cue by telephone, clocked Huyck with a time of 1:05.20. Again, the winning time was well off of record pace. Stanley Kellogg of New York hung on for second place on his Milwaukee-made Merkel, and Raymond Seymour finished third riding a Reading-Standard, a product from Reading, Pennsylvania.

The five-mile handicap race for members of the Indiana Motorcycle Club was the next race on the schedule. The trend of a decreased number of participants continued as only nine of the original 15 entrants lined up for the start of this race. It was a competitive race, making the rest of the country take notice that Indianapolis had a very talented group of riders despite the times not being up to record pace. Paul E. Koutowski rode a Minneapolis to victory in a time of 5:17.00. Nelson J. Hodgin rode his Indian to second, and John McCarver was third on his Excelsior, a product of the Excelsior Supply Company of Chicago, Illinois.

Chicago's Fred Huyck picked up his second win of the day in the next event which was the five-mile race for motorcycles with engines of less than 55 cubic inches of piston displacement and without auxiliary exhaust ports. In a thrilling race, he rode his Indian to a win by only a few feet over A.G. Chappel in a time of 5:24.40. The close finish had the small but boisterous crowd on their feet cheering on the riders. This fourth event, originally scheduled as the seventh, was moved up in the program moving the rest of the events back a place.

*A 1909 N.S.U. motorcycle with rider Arthur Mitchell (not entered in the races at Indianapolis). Ed Lingenfelder rode the same model during the August 1909 races at the Indianapolis Motor Speedway. (Photo courtesy of Megden Publishing Company)*

A lengthy delay after the fourth race due to the condition of the track prompted some of the people in the grandstands to leave as the discussion continued. Apparently, the delay had been caused by the F.A.M. officials who were considering calling off the rest of the races because many of the riders refused to race on what they felt was an unsafe track, preventing them from breaking any records. Carl Fisher convinced them to continue the races after telling them not to disappoint the fans who had paid to see the riders give it their all. After a few more minutes of delay, it was finally decided that the champion of the West, Ed Lingenfelder from California, would race the champion of the East, French-Canadian Jake De Rosier from Massachusetts in a ten-mile race for professionals.

The crowd began to buzz with excitement and the band started to play as E.A. Moross, who served as the starter for the meet, announced the pairing for the race. Ed Lingenfelder was the first man to ride out on the track wearing a pure white uniform as he rode his N.S.U. motorcycle before stopping to direct the attendants to secure his feet to the pedals with straps. The N.S.U. was made in Germany by the Neckarsulm Strickmaschinen Union Company. Jake De Rosier, wearing bright red tights with a silk United States flag on his back, then pushed his American-made Indian motorcycle to the starting line alongside Lingenfelder. Charlie Merz of Indianapolis was also originally entered in this event but withdrew.

*Jake DeRosier on a 1909 Indian at an unidentified board track. (Photo courtesy of Megden Publishing Company)*

The small crowd was cheering wildly as the two were sent off into the first turn. The pair stayed close throughout the first lap on the big track. The N.S.U. of Lingenfelder barely led De Rosier's Indian as they crossed the line after the first lap. The two remained close to one another but in the middle of the far straightaway on the second lap De Rosier passed Lingenfelder in a burst of speed. The move caught Lingenfelder by surprise but he responded by eventually catching De Rosier and passing him as they came out of the final turn on the second lap. Just before the riders passed under the bridge, about 250 yards from the main grandstand, De Rosier's front tire blew. The tire wedged in the front fork of his motorcycle throwing him into the air. His motorcycle continued to slide down the track in front of him as he slid along the track for about 30 yards. The crushed stone surface of the track cut him up from head to toe. When he finally came to a rest, he staggered to his feet and managed to make it to a ditch on the side of the track where he fell unconscious. Lingenfelder began to slow down as if he knew something had happened to De Rosier but went on to finish the event in a time of 10:51.80. He said later that he knew something happened to De Rosier, not because he looked back, but because he could hear his ear-piercing screams even over the roar of the motorcycles. Meanwhile, the crowd had become hysterical at the sight of the violent crash that had unfolded nearly in front of them.

After a few minutes the ambulance arrived and carried De Rosier away on a stretcher. Lingenfelder was later quoted saying that about half way around the track on the second lap De Rosier yelled for him to "take it easy"[2] and Lingenfelder responded by asking, "Are you getting cold feet?"[3] Apparently, De Rosier answered back with some sort of challenge prompting the pair to go all out for the win. Ironically, if Lingenfelder had been the one to wreck, he most likely would have been killed since he had his feet strapped to his motorcycle.

After the crowd was quieted down, the officials began to get the entrants for the five-mile open handicap race to the starting line. There were nine starters, far fewer than the original number of entrants, and Fred Huyck picked up his third win of the day. He rode his Indian to the finish in 4:36.60 and was followed by Charles Balke of Los Angeles in second and J.A. Turner of Chicago in third, both riding Merkels.

*Chicago's Fred Huyck on a 1909 Indian. Huyck won three of the seven motorcycle races held at the Indianapolis Motor Speedway on August 14, 1909. (Photo courtesy of Megden Publishing Company)*

The seventh event started with only four of the original 46 entrants placing their motorcycles on the line to try for the ten-mile F.A.M. amateur national championship. Indianapolis riders took the top three spots as Erwin G. Baker (this was a few years before he became known as "Cannonball" Baker) on an Indian won the event in a time of 11:31.20 followed by H. R. Bretney and John Merz, both riding Thors. The Thor was produced by the Aurora Automatic Machinery Company of Aurora, Illinois, who ironically, supplied engines to Indian until 1907. J.F. Torney of Chicago, the fourth rider in the event, was involved in

*Indianapolis native Erwin "Cannonball" Baker on an Indian. (Photo courtesy of Megden Publishing Company)*

*Baker's motorcycle that he rode during the August 1909 races at the Indianapolis Motor Speedway as on display at the Speedway Museum. (Photo taken by Ron McQueeney of the Indianapolis Motor Speedway)*

the second accident of the day though not as serious as De Rosier's. He was rounding the fourth turn behind the woods when his back tire blew. He quickly turned his motorcycle to the inside of the track and landed on the soft ground – allowing him to walk away unharmed.

F.A.M. President Earle Ovington promptly called off the final event of the day, the 25-mile race open to all motorcycles with engines of less than 30.5 cubic inches of piston displacement, due to a lack of entries. He also made the decision to cancel all of the events rescheduled for Monday afternoon as well. Mr. Ovington said that he called off the races because "he did not care for the Speedway, or the disappointed crowds, or anything else, but wanted to protect the lives of the riders"[4]. He added that the riders refused to enter the races anyway.

Some of the newspapers referred to the event as a complete fiasco, but many people thought that the races of the first day were a success hampered only by trade jealousy and disorganization among F.A.M. officials. Nowhere was this more apparent than late into the evening before the races as the officials argued among themselves about how the three classes of riders should be setup. They eventually agreed upon professional, amateur, and trade rider but continued arguing about the definition of an amateur. Adding to the controversy was certainly the refusal of many of the motorcyclists to race on the Speedway's track. They were used to racing on smooth beach straights so the sight of the big Speedway with its huge turns was unlike anything that they had ever seen before and probably overwhelmed the motorcyclists. Despite the events of the week, interest in the Indianapolis Motor Speedway was high as the automobiles were ready to begin practice for the following weekend's races.

*Chapter 4*

# Tragedy Strikes First Auto Races

Just two days after the motorcyclists finished at the Speedway the automobiles began practicing for the upcoming auto races. The entry list included an astounding 65 entries representing over 15 different car manufacturers. Almost half of these companies were located in Indiana or Michigan. Far different than today's arrangements, the drivers were usually employed by the car manufacturers in one capacity or another, such as an engineer or a mechanic. However, there were some drivers known throughout the country as strictly race car drivers.

The Buick Motor Company of Flint, Michigan, had a trio of such drivers. One of the most famous of all was Bob Burman. He first became interested in racing in 1906, signing on to drive with the Buick team in 1908. He was fearless and had a reputation of driving wide-open at all times. Teammate Lewis Strang was a New Yorker with a flair for the dramatic. Similar to Burman, he drove every race like it was his last. The third member of the team, Louis Chevrolet, was a big man physically with a dynamic and powerful personality. Born in Switzerland and educated in France, he came to America in 1900 and began racing five years later. He drove for the Matheson Automobile Company in 1908 before joining Buick a year later. Chevrolet, an expert mechanic, was known by his fellow drivers as one of the most intense competitors in a race car. Then of course there was Barney Oldfield. Probably the most recognized name of the time, he was the ultimate showman. Many would debate the level of his talent but no one disputed the fact that he attracted the fans. Two Indianapolis drivers who would play a big role at the Indianapolis Motor Speedway, not only during 1909 and 1910 but also in the years to follow, were Ray Harroun and Johnny Aitken. Harroun was known as a brilliant engineer at Nordyke & Marmon. He was a few years older than most of the drivers of the time (as was Chevrolet) but was just as tenacious, although this was somewhat concealed by his even-tempered, methodical approach behind the wheel of a race car. Another engineer, Aitken was employed by the National Motor Vehicle Company of Indianapolis. Always quick with a joke, he was more outgoing than Harroun and could be a real clown at times. Because of this, he was known to many as "Happy Johnny".

Flint, Michigan,
June 8th, 1908.


Buick Motor Company,

Flint, Michigan.

Gentlemen,-

I hereby agree to enter your employ for the purpose of driving automobiles furnished by you, in such hill-climbing and racing contests as I may be directed to enter, for and in consideration of the sum of Fifty Dollars ($50.00) per week, commencing this day, June 8th, together with traveling expenses, such services to continue until I am notified to the contrary by you; also in consideration of payment by you of any and all physicians, surgeons, medical and hospital bills incurred by me, as the result of any accident which I may sustain while in the discharge of my duties, which may accrue within _60_ days of the time of such accident.

This will certify that I enter your employ as above, with a full and complete understanding of the dangers and extra hazardous nature of my employment, and agree and do hereby accept of the above consideration in full for any and all personal injuries which I may receive in the future while in your employ and in the discharge of my duties for the purposes named; such consideration shall also be in full of any and all injuries, personal or otherwise, which I may sustain while driving automobiles belonging to you, in any such contests, which injuries or damages may arise either from my own carelessness or that of a fellow-employe, or any defective workmanship or materials used in the construction of the automobiles in question.

*[signature: Burman]*

We hereby accept the above proposition.

BUICK MOTOR COMPANY,

By *[signature]*
Sales Manager

*The contract between the Buick Motor Company and Bob Burman, signed in June of 1908. (Courtesy of the Alfred P. Sloan Museum, Flint, Michigan)*

Len Zengel was one of the first drivers on the track, having made a practice lap in 2 minutes and 2 seconds for a speed of 73.74 mph in a Chadwick. By the end of the day on Tuesday, all 65 entries had been on the track. On Wednesday, Barney Oldfield became the first driver to break the two-minute barrier by turning a lap in 1:58 for a speed of 76.26 mph. Based on the practice times, Barney Oldfield in his Blitzen Benz, Ralph DePalma in his Fiat, and John Walter Christie in his front-wheel drive Christie positioned themselves as the drivers to beat.

As practice continued, it soon became evident that there were problems with the racing surface. One problem experienced by the drivers and riding mechanics was dealing with all of the dust thrown up as the cars raced around the track. They quickly became covered in dirt, oil, and tar from head to toe. Then ruts and chuckholes began to form on the track, particularly in the turns. The drivers complained that as the track was breaking up, they were getting hit by flying pieces of gravel. Driving on the track was like flying through a meteor shower. Several drivers came into the pits with broken goggles or bloody cheeks as the result of being hit by flying debris. To help reduce the problem, Carl Fisher had the workmen continually making repairs when the cars were not practicing. He agreed that it was not as smooth as he wanted it, but that it would surpass the Brooklands track when completed.

The *Indianapolis News* featured a story about the riding mechanics, many times the forgotten part of the team. Besides alerting the driver to the traffic around him, they also monitored the oil pressure and took care of any emergencies that arose. There have been some colorful stories over the years about riding mechanics climbing out on cars to put out fires or even acting as a relief driver at a moment's notice. Additionally, it was too noisy for the two men to talk to one another while on the track so they had to rely on hand signals to communicate. One finger meant that a car was coming; two fingers meant that a competitor was close behind; three fingers meant that a car was very close and four fingers meant that someone wanted to pass. The riding mechanic would also watch the oil gauge and signal if the car was out of oil by holding his thumb and first finger in the shape of an "O".

The papers also reviewed the meanings of the different flags used in auto racing at the time. A red flag meant the start of the race, a yellow flag meant to stop immediately, a green flag signaled the start of the last lap, the white flag signaled to stop for consultation, and the blue flag signaled an accident on the course. One thing that hasn't changed through the years, the checkered flag signaled that the driver had completed the race.

Several fans were in attendance early in the week to watch the drivers practice. Publicity for the races was given a boost when Bob Burman took Betty Blythe, a female reporter, for a few laps around the Speedway in his Buick at about 60 mph. She published her thoughts about the ride in the *Indianapolis Star*.

"Don't get the notion that riding in a racer is anything like gentle dalliance in a touring car," Blythe reported. "First you hold hard and guess if you will land on the biggest pile of rocks. You turn up a disgusted nose at the oil that rains from the machine and wraps you in a cloud. You try to find another foothold for the foot that you are sure the red-hot engine is burning to a cinder. You observe with deep distaste that your hand is reeking with nasty oil and you suspect that what is left of your face is likewise decorated. You find yourself inquiring sarcastically of the driver how he knows precisely where all the roughest spots are. The fact that the driver is completely oblivious to the fact that you are talking at all does not make any difference."[1]

Besides the local spectators, many made the trip to the Speedway from out of town, flooding the city with cars. The Chicago Auto Club sponsored an endurance run of over 100 cars to the Speedway and set up its temporary headquarters at the Claypool Hotel. The trains also brought in spectators from most of the larger cities in the Midwest and as far away as New York.

One of the attendees from New York, a gentleman by the name of Lynn Skeels, was a photographer for the Stereo-Travel Company. He documented the events during the three-day racing program by producing a series of 40 stereoscopic photographs. A very common form of photography during the late eighteenth and early nineteenth centuries, a three-dimensional effect was created when the photos were viewed with a stereo viewer. (Please refer to the section titled *August 1909 Stereoscopic Photographs* near the end of this book for the original version of these photographs along with additional information.) The photos from the three-day program are a very rare find today; however, the majority of them have been included in this chapter to provide a greater appreciation for these history-making races.

By Wednesday night, practice had been completed and most of the spectators had descended upon the city, setting the stage for the first auto races to be held at the Speedway. The whole grounds looked like a carnival with hundreds of flags of all colors waving from the roofs of the grandstands, judges' stands, press boxes, and garages. Visitors arriving at the Speedway through the main entrance saw a row of tents that housed cars on exhibit by the various auto manufacturers. The tents were nicely decorated with potted plants, ferns, palms, and chairs for the visitors. One feature of the Overland Automobile Company's exhibit was a gold-plated automobile. The company was awarding it to the driver with the fastest mile time obtained during 1909. The drivers would be permitted to make two attempts, electronically timed, for the kilometer and mile records on Friday and Saturday. The entire schedule of events for the three-day spectacle was as follows.

### Thursday, August 19

- Event 1 – Five-mile race open to stock chassis with engines of 161 – 230 cubic inch piston displacement (CID)
- Event 2 – Ten-mile race open to stock chassis with engines of 231 – 300 CID
- Event 3 – Five-mile race open to stock chassis with engines of 301 – 450 CID
- Event 4 – Ten-mile free-for-all handicap race
- Event 5 – 250-mile race for the Prest-O-Lite trophy open to stock chassis with engines of 301 – 450 CID

### Friday, August 20

- Event 1 – Trials to lower the world's track records, free for all cars. Each car will be permitted to make two attempts, electronically timed, for the kilometer and mile records.
- Event 2 – Five-mile race open to stock chassis with engines of 231 – 300 CID
- Event 3 – Ten-mile race open to stock chassis with engines of 301 – 450 CID
- Event 4 – Ten-mile race open to stock chassis with engines of less than 600 CID
- Event 5 – 50-mile race open to stock chassis with engines of 161 – 230 CID
- Event 6 – Ten-mile free-for-all race for the Ford trophy
- Event 7 – Five-mile free-for-all handicap race
- Event 8 – 100-mile race for the G & J trophy open to stock chassis with engines of 231 – 300 CID

### Saturday, August 21

- Event 1 – Trials to lower the world's track records, free for all cars. Each car will be permitted to make two attempts, electronically timed, for the kilometer and mile records.
- Event 2 – 15-mile free-for-all handicap race
- Event 3 – Ten-mile race for the Amateur Championship of America
- Event 4 – 25-mile free-for-all race for the Remy Grand Brassard
- Event 5 – 300-mile race for the Wheeler-Schebler trophy open to all stock chassis with engines of less than 600 CID

Thursday started off with a practice session held between 8:00 a.m. and 8:30 a.m. After the practice session, workers resumed applying oil to the track in an effort to reduce dust. Big steamrollers also toiled in an attempt to smooth the racing surface. This even continued past 9:00 a.m. when the gates opened to the public.

Special trains were run to accommodate the mass of people that descended upon the Speedway. One train brought about 500 workers from the Nordyke & Marmon plant. Another one ran from the Stoddard-Dayton factory in Dayton, Ohio, transporting about 1,200 employees to the Speedway. The Big Four ran special trains on a 15 minute schedule to and from Union Station while the Ben-Hur traction line had a string of cars in service all of the time. Parking accommodations consisted of almost 10,000 spaces for cars and close to 3,000 hitching posts for horses. Tickets were $1.00 at the main gate; however, spectators could enter the east gate for 50 cents and sit in the "balloon" bleachers at the south end of the track.

*View looking down the front stretch towards turn one of the Indianapolis Motor Speedway during the August 1909 auto races. Note the cars along the fence on the right side of the photo. The corner of a café can also be seen just before the main grandstand. (Stereoscopic photo courtesy of Grant Meitzler)*

The grandstands began to fill rapidly long before the noon start time of the first race. Hundreds brought lunch baskets, and the ones who didn't took advantage of the many concession stands on the grounds. Some spectators complained about the exorbitant price of pop for 10 cents, but Ernest Moross put a stop to this when he exercised his authority as the Director of Events and announced that no more than 5 cents could be charged for pop. In addition to the many spectators in the grandstands, there were also around 1,000 automobiles that entered the infield of the Speedway with nearly three times as many occupants. Sharply at 11:30 a.m. the Indianapolis Military Band entered the grandstand and played music right up until the start of the first race – at which time the crowd had swelled to somewhere between 15,000 – 20,000 anxious spectators.

The first event of the day, a five-mile race open to stock chassis with engines of 161 – 230 CID, started at noon. The five entrants assembled at the bridge 200 yards north of the main grandstand prior to attempting a flying start. However, the cars were not in good alignment as they approached the starting line, forcing starter Fred "Pop" Wagner to wave the yellow flag to stop the field and subsequently begin the race from a standing start.

When the red flag finally waved to start the race, Louis Schwitzer in a Stoddard-Dayton led the charge into the first turn followed closely by his teammate Carl Wright. George DeWitt positioned his Buick in third and John Stickney's Velie fell in behind DeWitt. The fifth starter, John Ryall in a Buick, had engine trouble, which eliminated him from the race soon after entering the first turn. As they continued in that order for the remainder of the first lap, the cars went flying by the main grandstands in a cloud of dust while the loud roar of the engines drowned out the applause of the crowd. Schwitzer continued to hold off the pack throughout the second lap with his teammate close behind. He drove his Stoddard-Dayton to the checkered flag to become the first driver to win an auto race at the Indianapolis Motor Speedway. The five-mile race was completed in 5 minutes and 18.40 seconds for an average speed of 57.43 mph. As Schwitzer crossed the finish line about 150 feet in front of his Stoddard-Dayton teammate, the contingent from Dayton was on its feet cheering madly for their drivers. The final results of the first auto race at the Indianapolis Motor Speedway were as follows.

*Race starter Fred "Pop" Wagner. (Chicago Daily News negatives collection, SDN-058713.Courtesy of the Chicago Historical Society)*

| Place | Car # | Driver | Car | Laps | Led |
|---|---|---|---|---|---|
| 1 | 19 | Louis Schwitzer | Stoddard-Dayton | 2 | 2 |
| 2 | 18 | Carl Wright | Stoddard-Dayton | 2 | 0 |
| 3 | 30 | George DeWitt | Buick | 2 | 0 |
| 4 | 49 | John Stickney | Velie | 2 | 0 |
| 5 | 33 | John Ryall | Buick | 0 | 0 |

The ten-mile race for stock chassis with engines of 231 – 300 CID was the next contest of the day. Among the eight starters for this event were two Marmons driven by Harry Stillman and Ray Harroun and the Buicks of Louis Chevrolet and Bob Burman. Again, a flying start was tried, but as the cars neared the judges' stand; Louis Chevrolet and Ray Tinkler were ahead of the rest of the field so Wagner, waving the yellow flag, brought them back to a standing start.

As the race began, Lewis Strang flew into the first turn with a big lead on the rest of the field. Strang was easy to spot with his trademark long strip of red cloth blowing in the wind straight back from his helmet. He battled with Chevrolet and Burman for most of the first two and a half miles until Chevrolet wrestled away control of the race just before the end of the lap. The Marmons of Stillman and Harroun followed the three Buicks while the three Marions driven by Steity, Tinkler, and Adolph Monson rounded out the field.

*Racing action during a 10-mile race on August 19, 1909. Cars pictured from left to right are; Louis Chevrolet in the #34 Buick, (eventual winner), Ray Harroun in the #16 Marmon, Harry Stillman in the #15 Marmon, Lewis Strang in the #33 Buick, and Steity in the #11 Marion. (Stereoscopic photo courtesy of Joe Freeman)*

The Marions of Tinkler and Adolph Monson retired from the race early on the second lap. Soon afterward, Chevrolet had built an insurmountable lead as Strang, Burman, Stillman, Harroun, and Steity followed in that order. On the third circuit around the track, Steity passed Harroun for fifth place just prior to Chevrolet lapping both of them in front of the main grandstand. Chevrolet cruised to the easy win by more than a mile over the second place car of Lewis Strang in a time of 8:56.40 for an average of 67.114 mph. This broke the world's record of 9:12.00 set in October 1904 by Barney Oldfield. Burman held on for third place to give Buick a one-two-three sweep. Following are the results of the race.

| Place | Car # | Driver | Car | Laps | Led |
|-------|-------|--------|-----|------|-----|
| 1 | 34 | Louis Chevrolet | Buick | 4 | 4 |
| 2 | 33 | Lewis Strang | Buick | 4 | 0 |
| 3 | 32 | Bob Burman | Buick | 4 | 0 |
| 4 | 15 | Harry Stillman | Marmon | 4 | 0 |
| 5 | 11 | Steity | Marion | 4 | 0 |
| 6 | 16 | Ray Harroun | Marmon | 4 | 0 |
| 7 | 14 | Ray Tinkler | Marion | 1 | 0 |
| 8 | 12 | Adolph Monson | Marion | 1 | 0 |

*The #15 Marmon of Harry Stillman in the pits for repairs during the August 1909 automobile races at the Indianapolis Motor Speedway. (Stereoscopic photo courtesy of Joe Freeman)*

The most exciting event of the day proved to be the five-mile race open to stock chassis with engines of 301 – 450 CID. Nine cars started the contest, which featured a dazzling race-long battle between Bob Burman and Wilfred Bourque. Consistent with the previous two races, the flying start proved to be a failure. This prompted "Pop" Wagner to declare that the race, and all future races, would utilize a standing start. Burman's white Buick and Bourque's big brown Knox were literally side-by-side throughout the entire first lap. Burman had managed to edge into the lead by a half a car length as the two headed into turn one for the second time. Bert Miller positioned his Stoddard-Dayton in third just ahead of Louis Chevrolet's Buick as the rest of the field trailed further behind. The Stoddard-Dayton of Jap Clemens retired with engine problems as he completed the first lap. Meanwhile, Bourque and Burman maintained a fierce, wheel-to-wheel battle as they approached the finish line in a dead heat. Bourque suddenly forged ahead as they raced under the pedestrian bridge. At the line Bourque edged out Burman by the narrowest of margins in 4:45.50 while Chevrolet had passed Miller for third. The final results of the race follow.

| Place | Car # | Driver | Car | Laps | Led |
|-------|-------|--------|-----|------|-----|
| 1 | 3 | Wilfred Bourque | Knox | 2 | 1 |
| 2 | 35 | Bob Burman | Buick | 2 | 1 |
| 3 | 37 | Louis Chevrolet | Buick | 2 | 0 |
| 4 | 20 | Bert Miller | Stoddard-Dayton | 2 | 0 |
| 5 | 45 | Lewis Strang | Buick | 2 | 0 |
| 6 | 52 | Leigh Lynch | Jackson | 2 | 0 |
| 7 | 53 | Fred Ellis | Jackson | 2 | 0 |
| 8 | 20 | Tobin DeHymel | Stoddard-Dayton | 2 | 0 |
| 9 | 21 | Jap Clemens | Stoddard-Dayton | 1 | 0 |

*Cars waiting for the start of a 5-mile race on August 19, 1909. The first two cars in line are Louis Chevrolet in the #37 Buick and Bob Burman in the #35 Buick. (Stereoscopic photo courtesy of Joe Freeman)*

After the exciting conclusion to the last event, 16 entries lined up for a ten-mile handicap contest. Each driver was given a handicap to start the race based on the size of the car's engine. Accordingly, Ray Harroun and Bruce Keen in the Marmons, Leigh Lynch in a Jackson, Carl Wright in a Stoddard-Dayton, and Ray Tinkler in a Marion were the first five cars off the line. The Jackson of Fred Ellis and the Stoddard-Dayton of Tobin DeHymel started 15 seconds later. A full 50 seconds after the second group of cars had started, Bert Miller in a Stoddard-Dayton, William McCulla in an Apperson, and George Dewitt in a Buick began their ten-mile trek. Finally, one minute and 25 seconds after the initial start of the race, the remaining six entrants left the starting line. This group included: Bob Burman and Louis Chevrolet in Buicks, Al Dennison in a Knox, William Heina in a Lozier, Ford in a Stearns, and 21-year-old Indianapolis resident Charlie Merz in a National. Merz's father, who was an Indianapolis policeman, was stationed at the Speedway for the races and tried to keep an eye on his son as well as the crowd.

Ray Harroun took advantage of the handicap, dominating the four-lap race to give the Marmon team its first victory at the Indianapolis Motor Speedway in 8:22.50. Leigh Lynch kept a consistent pace to finish second just barely ahead of a hard-charging Charlie Merz in a National. Merz was in tenth place after the first lap but continued to charge up through the field to make up tremendous ground over the next three circuits. Likewise, Louis Chevrolet hooked up with Merz and followed him through the field to a fourth place finish in his Buick. Fred Ellis had controlled second place for most of the race before yielding the two places to Merz and Chevrolet at the end. The final results of the race follow.

| Place | Car # | Driver | Car | Laps | Led |
|-------|-------|--------|-----|------|-----|
| 1 | 15 | Ray Harroun | Marmon | 4 | 4 |
| 2 | 51 | Leigh Lynch | Jackson | 4 | 0 |
| 3 | 8 | Charlie Merz | National | 4 | 0 |
| 4 | 37 | Louis Chevrolet | Buick | 4 | 0 |
| 5 | 52 | Fred Ellis | Jackson | 4 | 0 |
| 6 | 5 | William Heina | Lozier | 4 | 0 |
| 7 | 22 | Bert Miller | Stoddard-Dayton | 4 | 0 |
| 8 | 35 | Bob Burman | Buick | 4 | 0 |
| 9 | 4 | Al Dennison | Knox | 4 | 0 |
| 10 | 18 | Carl Wright | Stoddard-Dayton | 4 | 0 |
| 11 | 66 | Ford | Stearns | 4 | 0 |

Five other cars were out of the race before the four laps were complete: Bruce Keen in a Marmon, William McCulla in an Apperson, Ray Tinkler in a Marion, Tobin DeHymel in a Stoddard-Dayton, and George DeWitt in a Buick. Consequently, they were not placed in the final race summary.

After the fourth race, an exhibition was held for attempts to break the world's mile record. Barney Oldfield took to the track in his Blitzen Benz and was timed in 43.10 seconds, shattering the old record of 48.20 seconds set by Webb Jay. No other drivers approached Oldfield's time.

*Louis Chevrolet and his riding mechanic in the #37 Buick during the August 1909 automobile races at the Indianapolis Motor Speedway. (Stereo-scopic photo courtesy of Joe Freeman)*

The fifth and final event of the day was a 250-mile race open to stock chassis with engines of 301-450 CID for the Prest-O-Lite trophy. The crowd buzzed with excitement as nine cars were placed into position in front of the main grandstand in preparation for the big finale of the day.

At the start, Louis Chevrolet drove his Buick into the lead before battling teammate Bob Burman for much of the first 125 miles. Lewis Strang joined the duo – opening the possibility for another Buick sweep. However, things began to fall apart for Buick when Lewis Strang flew into the pits with flames shooting from the back of his car. They were extinguished, but not without help from others. Because of this, the officials ruled that Strang was out of the race. After arguing the point, he was eventually allowed to continue but by then was several laps behind. The Buick team suffered another blow when Chevrolet, after controlling the first 125 miles, brought his Buick to a stop on the far side of the track. He was forced to abandon the race after being hit in the goggles by a stone. His riding mechanic led him to the track hospital half a mile away where he had dust, tar, and slivers of glass removed from his eyes.

*Louis Chevrolet in the #37 Buick during the 250-mile Prest-O-Lite trophy race on August 19, 1909. (Stereoscopic photo courtesy of Joe Freeman)*

Immediately after Chevrolet's retirement, tragedy struck the Indianapolis Motor Speedway for the first time in its brief history. Wilfred Bourque had brought his big Knox around the fourth turn when the car started to slide just above the bridge about 200 feet before the main grandstand. The car darted into a ditch beside the track, violently flipped end over end, slammed against a fence post, and came to rest upside down on the ground. Hundreds of people rushed to the scene; however, the police did a good job of keeping everyone back as the two ambulances arrived from the track hospital. After a hole was cut in the fence big enough to get through, the physicians carried Bourque and riding mechanic Harry Holcomb across the track on stretchers and dodged the speeding cars that continued to race. Confusion remained at the scene for some time. It appeared that the car's rear axle had snapped, and this seemed to be substantiated by

Wilfred Bourque and riding mechanic Harry Holcomb before the start of the Prest-O-Lite trophy race on August 19, 1909. Bourque and Holcomb were killed during the race shortly after this photograph was taken. (Stereoscopic photo courtesy of Joe Freeman)

Cars lined up before the start of the 250-mile Prest-O-Lite trophy race on August 19, 1909. Tom Kincaid can be seen in the #6 National. The #36 Buick of Lewis Strang is next to Kincaid. (Stereoscopic photo courtesy of Joe Freeman)

several eyewitnesses who had seen the two turn and look behind them just before the car started to slide. Twenty-two year old Harry Holcomb was thrown from the car and killed instantly when his head hit a fence post. Wilfred Bourque, twenty-six years old, pinned under the car and still alive when the emergency crew arrived, succumbed to his injuries before he could be rescued.

"I was watching the car," said patrolman John Weaver, "and I saw the driver look back. It seemed that his car was unsteady. When he looked back, he turned his wheel and the car shot into the ditch, turning turtle and landing against the fence. The two men were hurled aside. It was so sudden that I do not know which was which, but one of the men struck a fence post with his head and the other landed under the car. Both axles were torn from the machine; one wheel went flying into the track, together with a shoe of one of the men. One of the axles was thrown toward the ditch."[2]

Meanwhile, Burman kept a tight grip on control of the race before making a pit stop just after the 200-mile mark. Fred Ellis then assumed the lead in a Jackson as Jap Clemens pulled his Stoddard-Dayton into second place. Ellis kept the lead until around lap 90 when he came into the pits. After the pit stop was finished, the car stalled so Ellis and his mechanic, A.J. House, got out to crank it in an attempt to restart the machine. As a result of fatigue, combined with the heat of the day, both men collapsed to the ground. They were taken to the track hospital where they were both revived. Ellis was treated for a badly blistered hand from holding on to the vibrating steering wheel and both men had to have sand and gravel removed from their eyes.

Bob Burman retook the lead after Ellis dropped out and never relinquished it. He won the race in 4 hours, 38 minutes, and 57.40 seconds for an average speed of 53.77 mph. Meanwhile, Jap Clemens drove his Stoddard-Dayton to a surprising second place finish. Local driver Tom Kincaid was headed for a third place finish but had trouble with his gas tank, which allowed Charlie Merz to slip by him to claim the spot, relegating Kincaid to fourth. The final race summary follows.

| Place | Car # | Driver | Car | Laps | Led |
|---|---|---|---|---|---|
| 1 | 35 | Bob Burman | Buick | 100 | 43 |
| 2 | 61 | Jap Clemens | Stoddard-Dayton | 100 | 0 |
| 3 | 7 | Charlie Merz | National | 100 | 0 |
| 4 | 6 | Tom Kincaid | National | 99 | 0 |
| 5 | 21 | Bert Miller | Stoddard-Dayton | 98 | 0 |
| 6 | 53 | Fred Ellis | Jackson | 88 | 8 |
| 7 | 3 | Wilfred Bourque | Knox | 58 | 0 |
| 8 | 37 | Louis Chevrolet | Buick | 58 | 49 |
| 9 | 36 | Lewis Strang | Buick | 36 | 0 |

It was around 7:00 p.m. when the final race of the day concluded. If it had not been for the two fatalities in the last race, the day probably would have been considered a resounding success as two new world records were established. A major part of the success was the way the program was run without delays; likewise, the organizers kept the crowd well informed. The progress of the drivers was not only posted on a big scoreboard opposite the main grandstand but the announcers with megaphones also gave the crowd additional details as they developed. However, by the end of the day the track had broken up badly in various places and the officials from the American Automobile Association considered canceling Friday and Saturday's events. Not to be denied, Carl Fisher used his promotional skills to convince them that he would have workers on the track all night making it suitable for the remaining races. The officials sided in Mr. Fisher's favor; thus, the workmen immediately began repairing the track.

True to his word, Carl Fisher had the track in fine shape for Friday's events which attracted a crowd of 20,000 – 25,000. As a result of the deaths of Bourque and Holcomb, the Knox company withdrew its entries for the rest of the events saying that they would likely discontinue their racing program altogether. Buick driver Bob Burman decided to sit out the day's contests as well to recover from the effort that he put in to win the 250-mile Prest-O-Lite trophy race on Thursday. Nonetheless the crowd was treated to the Speedway debut of another favorite, Ralph DePalma.

The day started out with several drivers participating in trials to lower the kilometer and mile world records. Barney Oldfield set the fastest pace in his Blitzen Benz but could do no better than the 43.10 second world record that he established on Thursday. Ralph DePalma was timed in his Fiat in 46.60 seconds and Len Zengel's Chadwick ran 49.30 seconds.

*Crowds in the bleachers during the August 1909 automobile races at the Indianapolis Motor Speedway. (Stereoscopic photo courtesy of Grant Meitzler)*

The first race of the day was a five-mile contest open to stock chassis with engines of 231 – 300 CID. In an uneventful race, Lewis Strang, driving his Buick without a mechanic, took control from the start to easily win in 4:45.00. His Buick teammate, Louis Chevrolet, finished in second place about an eighth of a mile back while the Marion cars of Harry Stutz and Adolph Monson finished a distant third and fourth respectively. The race summary follows.

| Place | Car # | Driver | Car | Laps | Led |
|-------|-------|--------|-----|------|-----|
| 1 | 33 | Lewis Strang | Buick | 2 | 2 |
| 2 | 34 | Louis Chevrolet | Buick | 2 | 0 |
| 3 | 12 | Harry Stutz | Marion | 2 | 0 |
| 4 | 14 | Adolph Monson | Marion | 2 | 0 |

The third event provided the most popular winner of the day when Indianapolis native Charlie Merz drove his National to victory in the ten-mile race for stock chassis with engines of 301 – 450 CID. Surprisingly, this would be the popular driver's only victory of his career at the Speedway. He did however go on to be very competitive in future races, including four Indianapolis 500s.

On the first lap, Jap Clemens had trouble with his Stoddard-Dayton which put him out of contention. It likely did not make a difference in the race as Merz drove uncontested the entire way winning by a big margin over Louis Chevrolet in a time of 9:16.30. Tobin DeHymel in a Stoddard-Dayton finished third. Lewis Strang and Leigh Lynch entered the event but withdrew due to mechanical problems with their cars. Likewise, Tom Kincaid did not start the race because he was late getting his National to the starting line. The results of the four drivers who made the race follow.

| Place | Car # | Driver | Car | Laps | Led |
|-------|-------|--------|-----|------|-----|
| 1 | 7 | Charlie Merz | National | 4 | 4 |
| 2 | 37 | Louis Chevrolet | Buick | 4 | 0 |
| 3 | 20 | Tobin DeHymel | Stoddard-Dayton | 4 | 0 |
| 4 | 61 | Jap Clemens | Stoddard-Dayton | 1 | 0 |

*Inside view of a 1909 Stoddard-Dayton race car. This photo of auto mechanic John Harcombe was taken during the 1909 Cobe Cup race held at Crown Point, Indiana, during June. (Chicago Daily News negatives collection, SDN-055212. Courtesy of the Chicago Historical Society)*

The fourth event was the most competitive contest during the first two days of racing. Adding to the excitement was the notoriety of the drivers. Chicago's Eddie Hearne and Indianapolis favorite Johnny Aitken, both of whom would figure prominently in the Indianapolis events during 1909 and 1910, were making their racing debuts at the Speedway in the ten-mile contest for stock chassis with engines of less than 600 CID. The multitude of auto enthusiasts was equally as anxious to witness the Speedway racing debut of Barney Oldfield. He would be driving his National with "Old Glory" painted on the hood but only after some deliberation. Some had questioned whether or not he should be allowed to have the American flag painted on the car. Attorney General James Bingham had finally ruled Thursday night that since Oldfield owned the car, it did not fall under the merchandising statue. This decision cleared the way for him to race the National while proudly displaying the American flag.

When "Pop" Wagner dropped the red flag to start the race, Eddie Hearne bolted to the front in his Fiat – a position that he held well into the second lap – followed by the Stoddard-Daytons of Tobin DeHymel and Jap Clemens. Aitken, on the other hand, got off to a slow start and initially ran last in the procession of eight cars. The crowd's thrill of seeing Barney Oldfield compete in his first race at the Speedway was short lived as he had an incident that could have been much worse than it was. The technical committee had the drivers put reflectors on their hoods, which forced the fire from the exhaust up into Oldfield's carburetor and set the car on fire. This burnt the leather straps holding the hood, causing it to fly back and strike him in the right arm as he was protecting his head. He dropped out of the race before the end of the first lap to have the cut on his arm attended to by the staff at the track hospital.

As Hearne started to falter, DeHymel assumed the lead by the end of the second lap. Meanwhile, Aitken was engineering a steady climb to the front, moving into fifth position. Hearne eventually retired from the race just before Clemens forged ahead of teammate DeHymel as the cars thundered down the front stretch to complete the third lap. The fans shouted their approval as Aitken swung around the Apperson of Herbert Lytle to fall in behind the leader. Incredibly, both Stoddard-Dayton cars dropped out of the race on the final lap opening the door for Aitken to storm into the lead and take the win over Herbert Lytle in 9:26.60 to the delight of the spectators. The final race summary follows.

| Place | Car # | Driver | Car | Laps | Led |
|-------|-------|--------|-----|------|-----|
| 1 | 8 | Johnny Aitken | National | 4 | 1 |
| 2 | 1 | Herbert Lytle | Apperson | 4 | 0 |
| 3 | 5 | Ralph Mulford | Lozier | 4 | 0 |
| 4 | 6 | Tom Kincaid | National | 4 | 0 |
| 5 | 62 | Tobin DeHymel | Stoddard-Dayton | 3 | 1 |
| 6 | 22 | Jap Clemens | Stoddard-Dayton | 3 | 1 |
| 7 | 24 | Eddie Hearne | Fiat | 2 | 1 |
| 8 | 9 | Barney Oldfield | National | 0 | 0 |

*The Stoddard-Daytons of Jap Clemens (#22) and Tobin DeHymel (#62) during a 10-mile race on August 20, 1909. (Stereoscopic photo courtesy of Joe Freeman)*

There were five cars entered in the fifth event of the day, a 50-mile race for stock chassis with engines of 161 – 230 CID. This contest turned out to be a battle between the Stoddard-Daytons of Carl Wright and Louis Schwitzer. Wright controlled the race for the first lap then fell to third as Schwitzer and the Buick of George DeWitt passed him. After Schwitzer lead the second lap, DeWitt briefly grabbed the lead on lap three before Schwitzer fought back to regain the lead and hold it until lap eight. Wright, ever determined, regained the lead on lap nine and never relinquished it. At the end of the race, Wright and Schwitzer were alone on the track as the others had dropped out for various reasons. The race summary follows.

| Place | Car # | Driver | Car | Laps | Led |
|---|---|---|---|---|---|
| 1 | 18 | Carl Wright | Stoddard-Dayton | 20 | 14 |
| 2 | 19 | Louis Schwitzer | Stoddard-Dayton | 20 | 5 |
| 3 | 30 | George DeWitt | Buick | 17 | 1 |
| 4 | 31 | John Ryall | Buick | 15 | 0 |
| 5 | 49 | Merritt | Velie | 6 | 0 |

Ralph DePalma and Barney Oldfield highlighted the next race, a ten-mile free-for-all for the Ford trophy. The two great stars were joined by four others including Johnny Aitken, who already had one victory for the day.

To no one's surprise, Barney Oldfield blasted his Blitzen Benz into the lead with Len Zengel not far behind. A gasp surged from the grandstand as Ralph DePalma's Fiat suddenly stopped on the far side of the track. His race was over. Before the spectators had a chance to catch their breath, Oldfield shocked them as he slid off the track coming around to lead his second lap. Because of the injury that he had suffered to his arm earlier in the day, Oldfield had trouble controlling the big Benz, resulting in the accident. Zengel, seizing the opportunity with the two big stars out of the race, snatched the lead and never looked back. He held off Aitken and went on to win the race in 8:32.20. His average of over 73 mph was the fastest pace ever run by a stock car on a circular track in America. To add insult to injury, he broke Barney Oldfield's record of 9:12.60 set in New York in October of 1904. Ironically, Oldfield and DePalma, arguably the two biggest stars in the race, finished fifth and sixth. The final results of the race follow.

| Place | Car # | Driver | Car | Laps | Led |
|---|---|---|---|---|---|
| 1 | 50 | Len Zengel | Chadwick | 4 | 3 |
| 2 | 8 | Johnny Aitken | National | 4 | 0 |
| 3 | 66 | Ford | Stearns | 4 | 0 |
| 4 | 5 | William Heina | Lozier | 4 | 0 |
| 5 | 27 | Barney Oldfield | Benz | 2 | 1 |
| 6 | 24 | Ralph DePalma | Fiat | 1 | 0 |

After the race, a feeling of disappointment quickly spread around the Speedway grounds. People assumed that Oldfield was likely finished for the meet, since his arm was too weak to allow him to handle his big racing machine.

The sixth event on the schedule was supposed to be a formality before the big finale of the day, but it produced some unexpected controversy. A total of 14 cars participated in the free-for-all handicap race. As with the previous day, the handicaps – based on the size of the car's engine – were assigned to the best of the official's ability. The first four cars to start consisted of the two Marions driven by Harry Stutz and Adolph Monson, the Jackson driven by Leigh Lynch, and the Stoddard-Dayton driven by Tobin DeHymel. Ten seconds later, five more cars were released at the line: the Marmons of Bruce Keen and Harry Stillman, the Jacksons of D. Bisbee and Fred Ellis, and the Stoddard-Dayton of Bert Miller. After another ten second wait the Nationals of Tom Kincaid and Charlie Merz were thrown into the mix. Finally, the trio of Johnny Aitken's National and the Appersons of Herbert Lytle and William McCulla entered the race an additional ten seconds later.

Aitken and Merz made up the handicap quickly but Miller was able to hold them off in his Stoddard-Dayton to lead the first lap. As the second circuit unfolded, teammates Aitken and Merz flew by Miller to begin a furious dual that lasted all the way to the checkered flag, resulting in a dead heat at the line. After some discussion, the timers gave Aitken the win by one hundredth of a second – although this was openly questioned by many in the crowd. Adding to this controversy were the handicaps. Many, including Harry

*The #31 Buick of John Ryall during the 50-mile race on August 20, 1909. (Stereoscopic photo courtesy of Joe Freeman)*

*Louis Schwitzer in the #19 Stoddard-Dayton during the 50-mile race on August 20, 1909. Schwitzer won the very first auto race at the Indianapolis Motor Speedway the day before in the same car. (Stereoscopic photo courtesy of Joe Freeman)*

Stutz, thought that they were not assigned fairly. Critics pointed out that the four cars only receiving a 40-second head start finished in the last four positions. Regardless of the handicaps, Aitken's time of 4:25 broke the world record of 4:26 set by Ralph DePalma at Providence, Rhode Island, in 1908. The complete race results follow.

| Place | Car # | Driver | Car | Laps | Led |
|---|---|---|---|---|---|
| 1 | 8 | Johnny Aitken | National | 2 | 1 |
| 2 | 7 | Charlie Merz | National | 2 | 0 |
| 3 | 22 | Bert Miller | Stoddard-Dayton | 2 | 1 |
| 4 | 52 | D. Bisbee | Jackson | 2 | 0 |
| 5 | 53 | Fred Ellis | Jackson | 2 | 0 |
| 6 | 1 | Herbert Lytle | Apperson | 2 | 0 |
| 7 | 2 | William McCulla | Apperson | 2 | 0 |
| 8 | 6 | Tom Kincaid | National | 2 | 0 |
| 9 | 16 | Bruce Keen | Marmon | 2 | 0 |
| 10 | 15 | Harry Stillman | Marmon | 2 | 0 |
| 11 | 14 | Harry Stutz | Marion | 2 | 0 |
| 12 | 20 | Tobin DeHymel | Stoddard-Dayton | 2 | 0 |
| 13 | 12 | Adolph Monson | Marion | 1 | 0 |
| 14 | 51 | Leigh Lynch | Jackson | 1 | 0 |

The final event of the day, the 100-mile race open to stock chassis with engines of 231 – 300 CID, featured six drivers competing for the G & J trophy. Given the length of the contest, many people expected a repeat of Thursday's tragedy; however, the track held up very well and several of the participants drove more cautiously as a result of Thursday's incident.

Lewis Strang, winner of the first race of the day, capped off Friday's festivities by also winning the last race of the day. The event was a safe one but unfortunately a boring one. Strang immediately established his presence by blasting into the lead at a record-setting pace and never looked back as he led all 40 laps! He set world records from the 20-mile mark through the end of the race finishing in a time of 1 hour 32 minutes and 47.08 seconds. Strang's performance was so dominant that George DeWitt, who earned second place, finished 8 minutes and 45 seconds behind Strang! Louis Chevrolet, trying to make it a Buick sweep, worked his way up from last to third before going out of the race on the eleventh lap. The two Marmons tagged together and swapped places throughout the race before Harroun finally held on for third with Stillman right behind in fourth. The final results of the race follow.

*Johnny Aitken in the #8 National during the auto races at the Indianapolis Motor Speedway on August 20, 1909. (Stereoscopic photo courtesy of Grant Meitzler)*

| Place | Car # | Driver | Car | Laps | Led |
|-------|-------|--------|-----|------|-----|
| 1 | 32 | Lewis Strang | Buick | 40 | 40 |
| 2 | 33 | George DeWitt | Buick | 40 | 0 |
| 3 | 15 | Ray Harroun | Marmon | 40 | 0 |
| 4 | 16 | Harry Stillman | Marmon | 40 | 0 |
| 5 | 34 | Louis Chevrolet | Buick | 10 | 0 |
| 6 | 12 | Adolph Monson | Marion | 4 | 0 |

The second day of racing concluded just after 5:30 p.m. Lewis Strang was the talk of the day with his record-breaking performance in the G & J trophy race, and the Speedway management was relieved that there were no serious accidents. An even larger crowd was expected for Saturday's races as the spectators were eagerly anticipating the big 300-mile race for the $10,000 Wheeler-Schebler trophy. This event, the finale for the three days of racing, featured a large field that included all of the well-known drivers.

Despite the hot, humid conditions, a crowd of over 35,000 assembled for the final day of racing at the Speedway. A big throng was waiting to get into the track when the gates opened at 9:00 a.m., and the mass continued to grow right up to the start of the first event. There was standing room only in the main grandstand and the overflow crowd spilled out into the paddock area where people lined the fence four to

*The start of the G & J trophy race on August 20, 1909. Eventual winner Lewis Strang can be seen in the #33 Buick alongside Louis Chevrolet in the #34 Buick. (Photo courtesy of the Indianapolis Motor Speedway)*

*A guard stationed along the track during the August 1909 automobile races. (Stereoscopic photo courtesy Grant Meitzler)*

*Members of the Marmon team waiting for the next race during the August 1909 auto races at the Speedway. (Stereoscopic photo courtesy of Grant Meitzler)*

*View looking down the front stretch towards the first turn at the Indianapolis Motor Speedway during the August 1909 automobile races. (Stereoscopic photo courtesy of Grant Meitzler)*

*Action during the 100-mile G & J trophy race on August 20, 1909. (Stereoscopic photo courtesy of Grant Meitzler)*

*A guard stationed on the outside of the Speedway during the August 1909 auto races. (Stereoscopic photo courtesy of Grant Meitzler)*

*Armed guards along the back stretch during the August 1909 automobile races at the Indianapolis Motor Speedway. (Stereoscopic photo courtesy Joe Freeman)*

*Crowds jammed along the fence down the front stretch at the Indianapolis Motor Speedway during the August 1909 automobile races. (Stereoscopic photo courtesy of Grant Meitzler)*

eight deep for a half a mile north of the main grandstand. The private boxes reserved for the various automobile companies were packed, as were the rest of the bleachers. The Speedway estimated that there were close to 6,500 cars in and around the grounds for the last day of events. This was almost double the previous day's estimate. Those spectators who arrived early entertained themselves by watching the workmen oil the track, particularly in front of the main grandstand. The workmen used large tanks of oil each drawn by four horses.

Walter Christie started things off at 11:45 a.m. when he rolled his Christie out on the track to take a shot at the world's kilometer record. Christie was timed in 28.70 seconds, just a second faster than the next driver, Len Zengel in a Chadwick at 29.90 seconds. But the event belonged to Barney Oldfield, bandaged arm and all, who drove his Benz to a new world record for the kilometer in 26.20 seconds at a speed of 86.5 mph. The roar of the crowd shook the grandstand when Oldfield took to the track since many assumed that he would not be driving as a result of the arm injury that he sustained on Friday.

The first race of the day was a 15-mile free-for-all handicap contest with four entries. The Buick of George Dewitt was first off the line followed one minute later by the Marmon of Harry Stillman. Wagner then waved the red flag to start the National of Tom Kincaid 15 seconds after Stillman entered the race. The final entrant, Ralph DePalma's Fiat, joined the procession two minutes and 15 seconds after Dewitt had initially started the race. By the time the big Fiat moved away from the main grandstand, a small cloud of dust could be seen at the northwest corner of the track making its way toward the judges' stand. It was Dewitt's Buick.

DeWitt took full advantage of the handicap granted to him by leading the first three laps of the race. Time had run out on the Buick however as the other three cars eventually caught and passed Dewitt – leaving him destined for a last place finish. Kincaid piloted his big blue National around the two-and-a-half-mile oval at a rapid pace; but by this time, DePalma was up to speed and really flying in an all-out effort to erase the handicap levied against his big machine. In the end, Kincaid crossed the finish line first in 13:23.50 as he gave a wave to the crowd. DePalma actually had a quicker overall time for the distance, but the results were based on how they crossed the line. The final results follow.

| Place | Car # | Driver | Car | Laps | Led |
|-------|-------|--------|-----|------|-----|
| 1 | 6 | Tom Kincaid | National | 6 | 3 |
| 2 | 24 | Ralph DePalma | Fiat | 6 | 0 |
| 3 | 17 | Harry Stillman | Marmon | 6 | 0 |
| 4 | 30 | George Dewitt | Buick | 6 | 3 |

The ten-mile amateur championship of America was the next event. All of these drivers were wealthy enough to have their own cars, allowing them to keep their amateur status rather than driving for one of the car manufacturers. This was a close, competitive race that saw three lead changes among three drivers. Arthur Greiner darted into the lead driving a Thomas while John Ryall's Buick maintained a close second. Meanwhile, Eddie Hearne's Fiat suffered from an uncharacteristically slow start but held down third place as the Stearns driven by Cameron failed to complete a lap. Unfortunately for Greiner, his car started to slow near the end of the second lap forcing him to retire from the race just past the judges' stand. Ryall flashed past him to lead the second lap and continued to press on into the fourth lap. He looked like a certain victor until Hearne guided his trusty Fiat past him during the last half of the final lap to take the win in 9:44.30. The race summary follows.

| Place | Car # | Driver | Car | Laps | Led |
|-------|-------|--------|-----|------|-----|
| 1 | 24 | Eddie Hearne | Fiat | 4 | 1 |
| 2 | 47 | John Ryall | Buick | 4 | 2 |
| 3 | 29 | Arthur Greiner | Thomas | 2 | 1 |
| 4 | 67 | W. W. Cameron | Stearns | 0 | 0 |

*Harry Stillman driving the #17 Marmon during the 15-mile free-for-all handicap race on August 21, 1909. (Stereoscopic photo courtesy of Joe Freeman)*

*Tom Kincaid crosses the finish line in the #6 National to claim victory in the 15-mile free-for-all handicap race on August 21, 1909. (Stereoscopic photo courtesy of Joe Freeman)*

Crank starting the Fiat of Eddie Hearne (#24), the Buick of John Ryall (#47), and the Thomas of Arthur Greiner (#29) before the start of the 10-mile amateur race on August 21, 1909. (Stereoscopic photo courtesy of Joe Freeman)

Eddie Hearne and crew moments before the start of the 10-mile amateur race on August 21, 1909. (Stereoscopic photo courtesy of Joe Freeman)

*Arthur Greiner in the #29 Thomas during the 10-mile amateur race on August 21, 1909. (Stereoscopic photo courtesy of Joe Freeman)*

*Eddie Hearne driving the #24 Fiat on his way to victory in the 10-mile amateur race on August 21, 1909. (Stereoscopic photo courtesy of Joe Freeman)*

The noise from the grandstand rose to a feverish pitch as three cars were brought out on the track to do battle in a 25-mile race for the Remy Grand Brassard. To the delight of many, Barney Oldfield, with his trademark cigar clinched in his teeth, returned to the track with his Blitzen Benz in an attempt to capture the coveted prize. Ralph DePalma, unfazed by all of the commotion, lined up his Fiat next to Oldfield with Len Zengel's Chadwick on the other side of him.

The Remy Grand Brassard was one of the most unique prizes ever offered in auto racing. It was an arm shield made of silver and the winner received a cash bonus of $75 a week until it was contested for again. The donor and originator of the prize, millionaire magneto manufacturer Frank Remy of Anderson, Indiana, conceived the idea of the Brassard, which is a French word to signify an arm shield. It was an effort to offer a unique award that would appeal to the driver rather than the manufacturer. He had hoped that this would promote the sport of auto racing rather than the commercialism.

The enthusiasm of the crowd was suppressed somewhat by the way Oldfield's Benz overpowered the other two cars. He led Zengel by 50 yards over the first two laps. Zengel then began to lose ground and was passed by DePalma as they started the sixth circuit. However, DePalma was no match for the record-smashing pace set by Oldfield. At the end of the ninth lap Oldfield was over a mile ahead of DePalma and eventually won by three-quarters of a lap. He led the entire race, establishing world records at every five-mile increment, enroute to winning with a time of 21:21.70. The race summary follows.

| Place | Car # | Driver | Car | Laps | Led |
|-------|-------|--------|-----|------|-----|
| 1 | 27 | Barney Oldfield | Benz | 10 | 10 |
| 2 | 24 | Ralph DePalma | Fiat | 10 | 0 |
| 3 | 50 | Len Zengel | Chadwick | 10 | 0 |

*Barney Oldfield in the #27 Benz winning the 25-mile Remy Grand Brassard race on August 21, 1909. (Stereoscopic photo courtesy of Joe Freeman)*

The grand finale for the three days of racing was the 300-mile contest for the Wheeler-Schebler trophy open to stock chassis with engines of less than 600 CID. Frank Wheeler designed the 7 ½-foot trophy then commissioned Tiffanys to craft it out of silver at a price of around $10,000. It was a beautiful trophy, which brought out a huge field with all of the top drivers included. No one could have imagined, however, the terrible tragedy that would come to the Speedway in just a little over four hours.

The 19 entrants stormed away at 1:25 p.m. with Johnny Aitken's National leading the thundering herd of machines into the first turn. By the end of the first 25 miles, the cars had strung out all around the track, as Aitken held the advantage on the rest of the field. At the 50-mile mark Aitken was still in the lead with the Apperson of Lytle and the Buick of Burman running second and third. Shortly before the 75-mile mark, Herbert Lytle provided the first excitement of the race when a broken steering arm sent his Apperson careening straight for the south grandstand. Within a few feet of the grandstand, Lytle somehow managed to steer his car the other way where it eventually ran into the dirt mounds on the inside of the track. The car straddled the embankment as it came to an abrupt stop, throwing riding mechanic Joe Betts of Kokomo from the car. Lytle quickly jumped from the car, grabbed a shovel from a nearby attendant, and started to dig the car out. Betts, who was uninjured, joined him; thus, they eventually continued on their way several laps later.

*The crowd along the frontstretch during the races at the Indianapolis Motor Speedway on August 21, 1909. (Stereoscopic photo courtesy of Joe Freeman)*

Aitken was setting a furious pace, leading the field across the starting line at the end of 100 miles as he set a new world record for the distance in one hour 31 minutes and 41.90 seconds. Bob Burman had taken over second place while Ralph DePalma was biding his time in third place. Suddenly, Aitken experienced engine trouble just before the end of lap 41 and struggled to nurse his car into the pits before abandoning the race. After emerging from his car, he predicted that someone would surely get killed because the track was breaking up badly. He complained how hard it was to stay in the seat and that the dust was so bad at times he could not tell if anyone was in front or behind him. He fully expected to run into someone's wreck. Johnny Aitken couldn't have been more accurate in his prediction.

With Aitken now sidelined, the Buick of Bob Burman gained control of the race but his time at the front was brief. He was forced to retire from the race with a cracked cylinder. Leigh Lynch was there to pick up the lead as Burman went out, but Ralph DePalma lurked in second place. Meanwhile, the three Marmon cars stayed out of trouble and held down the third through fifth positions.

Then it happened. After 175 miles, as his National rounded the south turn by the "balloon" bleachers, Charlie Merz blew a right front tire, sending his car straight for the outer fence. His car sailed through the air for over 100 feet, ripping through five fence posts, and trampling the crowd that was standing along the fence. As the car flew across the track about 50 feet in the air, a spectator who had been pinned to the radiator, dropped to the ground before the car landed upside down on the far side of the creek. Merz's riding mechanic was fatally injured as he was thrown from the car, yet Merz miraculously crawled out from underneath the big machine with only minor injuries.

"I think I am the luckiest man on earth this day," Merz said after the race. "As soon as my tire blew out, I knew I would have to check my speed, but it was all so quick I was helpless and had it been any other spot in the whole track we would have escaped with less fatal results most probably. But it was the most dangerous site on the entire course, just by that high embankment and stone culvert. I remember my car hitting the fence, there was a blurred vision of men falling beneath us as we swept through the air. Then the rest came in an instant, the car turned over and I found myself under it on the other side of the creek."[3]

Confusion ruled the scene long after the accident occurred as the final count of victims included: the riding mechanic, spectators James West of Indianapolis, and Homer Jolliff of Franklin. Several other spectators received minor injuries. Afterwards, local aeronaut George Bumbaugh said that he felt the heat of the car along with the rush of a mighty wind that almost swept him off his feet as it barely missed him. It was his feeling that if the car had come into the crowd just one more foot, the list of victims would have been four times as many.

Meanwhile, amid all of the confusion at the accident scene and just ten laps later, Marmon driver Bruce Keen rounded a corner of the track and hit a hole, which spun his car against one of the supports for the pedestrian bridge. He remained in the car and was unhurt; however, his riding mechanic Jim Schiller, had jumped from the car and received lacerations to his scalp and a possible fractured skull. He was able to walk to the ambulance and was treated at the track hospital. Those on the bridge at the time of the accident reported that the car's rear end rose up after hitting a hole in the track which spun the car around backwards, throwing it into a support on the bridge.

*Indianapolis native and driver for the National team, Charlie Merz. (Photo courtesy of the Indianapolis Motor Speedway)*

*The start of the 300-mile Wheeler-Schebler race at the Indianapolis Motor Speedway on August 21, 1909. The #8 National of Johnny Aitken is shown jumping out to the early lead. Aitken led the first 40 laps before retiring with engine trouble. (Stereoscopic photo courtesy of Grant Meitzler)*

*An Apperson driven by Herbert Lytle races against one of the Buick cars during the 300-mile Wheeler-Schebler race at the Indianapolis Motor Speedway on August 21, 1909. (Stereoscopic photo courtesy of Joe Freeman)*

*The #37 Buick of Louis Chevrolet rushing down the front stretch during the 300-mile Wheeler-Schebler race at the Indianapolis Motor Speedway on August 21, 1909. (Stereoscopic photo courtesy of Grant Meitzler)*

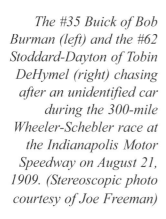

*The #35 Buick of Bob Burman (left) and the #62 Stoddard-Dayton of Tobin DeHymel (right) chasing after an unidentified car during the 300-mile Wheeler-Schebler race at the Indianapolis Motor Speedway on August 21, 1909. (Stereoscopic photo courtesy of Joe Freeman)*

*A Marmon and two Buicks racing down the stretch during the auto races at the Indianapolis Motor Speedway in August 1909. (Stereoscopic photo courtesy of Joe Freeman)*

*A Jackson, two Buicks, and a Stoddard-Dayton racing during the 300-mile Wheeler-Schebler race on August 21, 1909. (Stereoscopic photo courtesy of Joe Freeman)*

By this time starter "Pop" Wagner had seen enough and stopped the race and declared it no contest. He grabbed the checkered and yellow flags and waved them to Leigh Lynch who had a one lap lead over Ralph DePalma as he completed 235 miles in a time of 4 hours, 13 minutes, and 31.40 seconds for an average speed of 55.61 mph. Since the race was stopped early, no awards were given out. However, the race officials did recommend to the Speedway management that suitably engraved certificates be awarded to all active participants in the race at the time it was stopped. The final results of the race follow.

| Place | Car # | Driver | Car | Laps | Led |
|---|---|---|---|---|---|
| 1 | 52 | Leigh Lynch | Jackson | 94 | 47 |
| 2 | 24 | Ralph DePalma | Fiat | 93 | 0 |
| 3 | 75 | Bruce Keen | Marmon | 80 | 0 |
| 4 | 17 | Harry Stillman | Marmon | 80 | 0 |
| 5 | 58 | Ray Harroun | Marmon | 80 | 0 |
| 6 | 9 | Barney Oldfield | National | 70 | 0 |
| 7 | 62 | Tobin DeHymel | Stoddard-Dayton | 70 | 0 |
| 8 | 23 | Bert Miller | Stoddard-Dayton | 70 | 0 |
| 9 | 10 | Charlie Merz | National | 70 | 0 |
| 10 | 53 | Fred Ellis | Jackson | 60 | 0 |
| 11 | 35 | Bob Burman | Buick | 50 | 7 |
| 12 | 22 | Jap Clemens | Stoddard-Dayton | 50 | 0 |
| 13 | 1 | Herbert Lytle | Apperson | 50 | 0 |
| 14 | 37 | Louis Chevrolet | Buick | 40 | 0 |
| 15 | 8 | Johnny Aitken | National | 40 | 40 |
| 16 | 55 | Harry Stutz | Marion | 30 | 0 |
| 17 | 76 | Robert Drach | American | 20 | 0 |
| 18 | 36 | Lewis Strang | Buick | 10 | 0 |
| 19 | 2 | William McCulla | Apperson | 10 | 0 |

In a strange twist of fate, Charlie Merz's riding mechanic, Herbert Lyme, was not the one killed. Rather it was Claude Kellum who was Johnny Aitken's riding mechanic. Earlier in the race when Merz's battery failed while he was on the backstretch, Herbert Lyme ran across the infield to get a new battery for him. By the time he arrived in the pits, he was so out of breath that Claude Kellum delivered the new battery to Merz and had continued with him for the rest of the race.

Emotions about the Speedway were mixed. Several world records were established and the crowds grew everyday to the point where the final day's attendance overflowed. Yet, the races claimed five lives, in part because the track did not hold up well at all. The Knox team had pulled out of the races after the deaths of Wilfred Bourque and Harry Holcomb on Thursday, and Arthur Newby declared that National would no longer participate in auto racing because the deaths were too high of a price to pay. This decision was later reversed, but Newby's reaction made for a controversial situation since he was one of the four founders of the Speedway. Additionally, the American Automobile Association was threatening to boycott all future races at the Speedway unless management addressed the safety of the race drivers and spectators.

The press had its share of thoughts on the tragedies as well. The *Indianapolis Star* published photographs of the tragic accident scene from the Wheeler-Schebler race while the *Indianapolis News* ran excerpts of editorials from several national newspapers condemning the deaths at the Speedway and suggesting a ban be placed on all auto racing. The *Indianapolis News* even published a cartoon implying that auto racing would be responsible for widows and orphans.

## THE MARMON
"The Easiest Riding Car In The World"

## Mile - a - Minute Reliability

The success of the Marmon "Thirty-two" stock cars in the big race event of the year is still the talk of motordom. In the Vanderbilt, won the Wheatley Hills Trophy—190 miles in 190 minutes—*without a stop.* Won the Atlanta Speedway Trophy, 120 miles in 109 minutes, *without a stop and without a mechanician.* At New Orleans, won the 20, 50, and 100-mile events at practically a mile a minute on a one-mile track—*all without a stop.* In Indianapolis Speedway Races, made mile-a-minute runs of 100 and 225 miles *without a stop.*

*No other car has ever shown such stability under the merciless strain of long continued high speed.*

The Marmon is manufactured (not merely assembled) by a company known to buyers of high-grade machinery, the world over, for more than fifty years.

It is pre-eminently the safe choice for the buyer who seeks absolute certainty of service, style, comfort and value.

One chassis only—the "Thirty-two." 32-40 H. P. Option of body. Weight 2300 lbs. Complete high-class equipment. **$2650**

### Nordyke & Marmon Co.

(Estab. 1851)          Indianapolis, Ind.

*A 1909 magazine ad for Nordyke & Marmon publicizing the racing success of the Model 32. Ads such as these were commonly used by car manufacturers to help sell their cars to the public. (Scribner's magazine, 1909)*

The *Detroit News* published quite a stirring editorial of its own. "What then is the significance of these several deaths? It is the final proof that track racing will never do. For a long time now, many manufacturers have been decrying this phase of the great sport as more brutal than bull fighting, gladiatorial combats or prize fighting. During the Glidden tour a man prominently identified with motor racing said that he would as soon ask a man to stand against a wall and be shot at with a Winchester as ask him to drive in a track race. Spectators of these events have time and again demonstrated that it is the human lust for blood that calls them to the big track meets. This is the final straw. The blood of the Indianapolis Motor Speedway has probably rung the knell on track racing in the United States."[4]

*Chapter 5*

# The Speedway Becomes the Brickyard

Carl Fisher wasted little time in expressing his opinion on the tragic events of August. He declared that all future races should be cancelled until the racing surface could be upgraded and improved safety features installed. He believed that auto racing was a great spectator sport, and was prepared to spend any amount of money necessary to provide a first class facility for the drivers and spectators. The Speedway partners agreed to hire P.T. Andrews, the New York engineer who had served as the original Superintendent of Construction for the Speedway, to make recommendations for the surface to be used.

Mr. Andrews immediately met with the four men to share his thoughts on the project. He believed that the existing track would serve as a good base for the two best choices, concrete or brick. He estimated that they could have a concrete surface for approximately $110,000 but that a brick surface would cost about twice as much. When asked the difference between the two, Mr. Andrews reported that brick would last longer and give the cars a better grip. Thus, resulting in faster speeds by a couple of miles an hour; but they would have to decide if it was worth the additional money.

For testing purposes, the partners made arrangements in early September for several hundred yards of brick to be laid on the Speedway's racing surface as well as wood blocks that had been treated with creosote, an oily liquid obtained by the distillation of coal tar. Local driver Johnny Aitken used a National to make several high-speed runs over the bricks. To further monitor their durability, the wheels of Aitken's National were secured by a rope to two posts (one behind the car and one in front) anchored into the ground by concrete. With the car sitting on the bricks, he ran the machine at full throttle, causing the wheels to churn on the brick surface. The car swayed from side to side until the odor of burning rubber filled the air but even then the bricks did not break loose. He also tried several fast standing starts. All of these experiments were repeated with successful results after wetting the surface, proving that races could potentially be run on wet bricks if necessary. Various kinds of bricks were tried over the next several days.

The interest generated by the tests proved phenomenal. A number of parties were on hand to study the results. Many were interested in what kind of surface could best handle automobile traffic, not just for racing but for everyday driving. After the tests were completed, the Speedway partners quickly decided that brick was the better choice despite the additional cost. Further, they agreed to construct a concrete wall on the outside of the track to protect the spectators. Mr. Andrews estimated the work would take two to three months to complete, so the partners gave him approval to start on September 16.

Not long after that, the four partners debated over a suitable schedule for the reopening of the track. Originally, they decided on a November 1 date; however, that changed once it became apparent that the brick paving would not be completed in time. Carl Fisher then wanted to have an event in mid-December so that new speed records could be established before the racing season started in 1910. The others protested that it would be too cold for the spectators and could possibly prevent new records from being set. After much discussion, James Allison suggested that they invite the auto manufacturers to the track in mid-December to set some records but not offer any prize money. He thought they could invite the public for a minimum fee and reasoned that as long as they received some press coverage the Speedway would benefit from it. The others agreed with the idea and set Friday and Saturday, December 17 and 18, as the reopening of the Indianapolis Motor Speedway.

Meanwhile, as the work at the track began, the 1909 racing season continued. Over the next couple of months, Ray Harroun strung together an impressive list of victories, all in non-stop races over 100 miles. In October, he won the Wheatley Hills trophy race on the Vanderbilt Cup road course at Long Island. He followed in November by winning the New Orleans Prize trophy race on the New Orleans horse track and the Atlanta Automobile Association trophy race on the Atlanta Speedway. The Atlanta Speedway, a two-mile gravel and clay oval opened in 1909, most closely resembled the Indianapolis Motor Speedway.

After taking time to get married in October, Carl Fisher, along with the other Speedway partners, finalized the schedule for the two-day reopening in December. They scheduled events for all classes of stock chassis with time trials ranging from a quarter of a mile to one mile, including one kilometer. Additional trials were also scheduled for five, ten, 50 and 100 miles. The classes were determined by cubic inch piston displacement (CID) and were as follows: class 1 for 450 - 600 CID, class 2 for 301 – 450 CID, class 3 for 231 – 301 CID, class 4 for 161 – 231 CID, and class 5 for less than 161 CID. Carl Fisher hoped that some of the motorcycle riders would also attend, so he arranged time trials for them as well. Once they secured the American Automobile Association sanction, they sent notices of the reopening schedule to all auto manufacturers in hopes of attracting a large number of entrants.

The improvements at the Speedway were completed within 63 days of the start date with W.T. Blackburn of Paris, Illinois, and C.G. Moore of Cleveland, Ohio, both employees of the National Paving Brick Manufacturers' Association, serving as inspectors and advisory engineers. Over 500 loads of brick, approximately 3,200,000 bricks, were required to complete the job along with 80 loads of concrete. Each brick weighed approximately ten pounds and measured nine inches long by four inches wide by four inches deep.

"The Speedway contracted with the Wabash Clay Company in Veedersburg, Indiana, to provide the bricks. The company, in turn, subcontracted with four other brick companies to help fill the massive order. The Wabash Clay Company itself provided the greatest number of bricks which were marked 'W.C. CO., CULVER BLOCK, PAT. MAY 21, 1901'. (The date referred to the patent, not the date of manufacture.) Additionally, the company also provided the 'WABASH' brick and three different versions of the Veedersburg brick, labeled: 'VEEDERSBURG PAVER', 'DUNN PATENT, VEEDERSBURG, DUNN PATENT', and 'DUNN PATENT, THE VEEDERSBURG PAVER CO., DUNN PATENT'. The latter two had the unique characteristic of having the name of the company stamped on the end of the brick instead of the side. One of the subcontractors was the Poston Paving Block Company of Crawfordsville, Indiana. This company provided bricks identified as 'POSTON, CRAWFORDSVILLE, IND.,' 'C. E. POSTON, POSTON PAVER, ATTICA, IND.,' 'W. C. CO., POSTON BLOCK, PAT.' and 'POSTON'S KNOBSTONE BLOCK'. Reportedly, Poston employed 100 men, worked twelve-hour shifts, and produced 60,000 bricks a day. Another company that provided bricks was the Indiana Block Company in Brazil, Indiana, whose bricks were stamped 'BRAZIL' and 'IND. BLOCK, BRAZIL, IND.' Additionally, the Marion Brickworks Company of Montezuma, Indiana, provided the 'MARION PAVER' and the Terre Haute Vitrified Company in Terre Haute, Indiana, supplied the 'TERRE HAUTE BLOCK".[1]

*Scene at the Indianapolis Motor Speedway during the paving of the racing surface with bricks in the fall of 1909. (Photo courtesy of John Darlington)*

The bricks were transported by rail car to the Ben Hur railway station southwest of the Speedway grounds and moved to the track by horse-drawn carts. They were piled around the track in stacks ten bricks wide and placed on a conveyor with clamps that carried them to the bricklayers. The conveyor was mounted on wheels so that it could easily be pulled around the track with the aid of an automobile engine. This method seemed to work well with the biggest day's output reportedly being 140,000 bricks laid in a nine-hour period. Before the bricks were laid, a two-inch sand cushion was spread over the track and leveled by a drag using wooden strips. The bricks were hand-placed in the sand on their side. Then they were rolled with a three-ton steamroller. Later a 12-foot straight edge was used to inspect the surface for any variations exceeding three-eighths of an inch. Once the surface passed this inspection, the filler, composed of equal parts of sand and concrete mixed to the consistency of a thin batter, was applied with shovels. To make sure that the joints between the brick were filled absolutely flush with the surface of the brick, a second coat of filler was applied about an hour after the first coat. The second coat was floated using a squeegee with a rubber edge at a 45-degree angle to the joints in the brick.

New safety features were also put in place to protect the drivers and the spectators. Along each side of the straight stretches and around the inside of each turn, a 5-inch by 24-inch concrete footer was poured, the top being flush with the racing surface. A one-inch expansion joint was placed between the brick and the concrete strip. Additionally, a 9-inch thick reinforced concrete wall that rose 33 inches above the track surface was constructed on the outside of each turn and in front of the main grandstand.

There were other features included as part of the project as well. Warner Autometer Company installed an improved automatic timing device that registered the exact instant at which time a car's tires touched a small wire stretched across the track. C.H. Warner of Beloit, Wisconsin, was in charge of this device for the December events. The timer was equipped with four typing wheels that operated like an odometer. They recorded hours, minutes, seconds, tenths and hundredths of a second. The record was made on a paper tape through a carbon ribbon by small hammers activated by electro magnets located over the typing wheels. Meanwhile, the small wire that stretched across the track a few inches off of the ground connected to a trap that broke the circuit when a car struck the wire. This released the printing hammers, making a record of the exact elapsed time. A small motor which drove the typing wheels was electrically controlled and monitored by a chronometer so that any variations were corrected every second to within one one-thousandth of a second.

*The Warner Electrical Timing System used to score the races at the Indianapolis Motor Speedway during the brick testing sessions and 1910. Pictured above the timer is Charles Warner of Beloit, Wisconsin, inventor of the device. (Photo courtesy of the Indianapolis Motor Speedway)*

A course for aeroplanes 150 feet wide and one and a half-mile in length was graded in the infield. In conjunction, the world's largest aerodrome was built near the bleacher seats at the southeast corner of the grounds. It was 300 feet long, 60 feet wide and 100 feet tall. It had enough space for 10 aeroplanes and two inflated dirigibles. Each end featured large sliding doors. Finally, generators, gasholders, fittings, and reflectors to provide night lighting of the entire track at 20-foot intervals were purchased. Management planned to have them installed after the December events.

Always the opportunist, Carl Fisher did his best to promote the reopening. Knowing the press would take a photo, he arranged to give boxer James J. Jeffries, who was coming out of retirement, a lap around the track. The photo ran in the various newspapers across the country giving the newly bricked Indianapolis Motor Speedway some national exposure. He also arranged for Indiana Governor Thomas Marshall to be on hand for the opening ceremonies to lay the final brick in place, reportedly a gold-plated brick worth about $500. Actually, the brick was coated by the Wheeler-Schebler Company after melting down a brass carburetor. To create more publicity, Carl Fisher even had the brick displayed in a downtown storefront prior to the ceremonies.

*The "gold" brick that was placed in the track by Governor Marshall during the ceremonies prior to the December 1909 brick testing sessions. (Photo courtesy of the Indianapolis Motor Speedway)*

Approximately 11 drivers entered to make trial runs at the reopening as well as a few motorcyclists. The Speedway management was pleased with the response, because Lewis Strang, Walter Christie, and Johnny Aitken were among the drivers. Ray Harroun and Harry Stillman represented the Marmon team. The drivers practiced briefly on Thursday afternoon, sadly between getting used to the track and dealing with the cold weather, the times were not what they could have been. Still, Lewis Strang said that it was the fastest track that he had ever driven on.

The temperature on Friday stayed around the ten-degree mark, but a stiff wind made it feel even colder. Despite the bitter cold, close to 500 spectators showed up to watch the ceremonies and the trials. The drivers, bracing for the effect of the wind at high speeds, covered their heads with cloth made of heavy chamois skin with holes cut out for their eyes. Rubber bands, and goggles placed over it all, ensured that the cloths did not fall off while the men raced around the track. Many drivers mentioned that they did not shave, in order to give their face as much protection as possible. Heavy jackets and gloves completed their winter uniforms.

After the opening ceremonies were complete, Newell Motsinger started the trials by driving an Empire through a mile time trial with a flying start. Incidentally, that particular Empire was the first car produced by the new car manufacturer in which Arthur Newby, James Allison, and Carl Fisher had an ownership interest. Harry Endicott then put his Cole through the same trial. Louis Schwitzer, winner of the first auto race at the Speedway in August, had planned to take his turn in a Fuller, but a broken rear axle pinion prevented him from making an attempt. Motsinger's Empire had an engine with a CID of less than 161 while Endicott's Cole was between 161 – 231 CID. Their times were disappointing and considered slow for their class. The results are listed below.

| Driver | Car | ¼ | ½ | 1 K | 1Mile |
|---|---|---|---|---|---|
| Newell Motsinger | Empire | 18.73 | 38.18 | 48.31 | 1:20.46 |
| Harry Endicott | Cole | 15.69 | 31.70 | 38.88 | 1:05.97 |

Things started to speed up a little when the big blue Nationals of Tom Kincaid and Johnny Aitken took to the track in trials for cars with engines of 301 – 450 CID. Great friends off the track, the duo enjoyed a friendly rivalry when racing. Kincaid covered the mile distance in 50.00 seconds, breaking the old record of 59.10 seconds. Not to be outdone, Aitken blasted through the mile mark in 49.20 seconds, lowering Kincaid's new record. Their breakdown by distance follows.

| Driver | Car | ¼ | ½ | 1K | 1 Mile |
|---|---|---|---|---|---|
| Tom Kincaid | National | 11.80 | 22.60 | 30.20 | 50.00 |
| Johnny Aitken | National | 11.60 | 23.20 | 30.20 | 49.20 |

The Packard of Walter Donnelly followed when the Nationals had completed their trials. Donnelly was driving for car owner D. Busden of Cincinnati, despite never having turned a single practice lap on the track. He completed a half-mile in 27.80 seconds and a mile in 58.60 seconds. The quarter-mile and one-kilometer times were not measured because of a problem with the timing device.

The small crowd then saw Walter Christie take to the track for some trial laps in what people referred to as his "freak" racer. They called it this because it was his hand-built creation, rather than a stock chassis. He promptly treated the crowd to a new American record when he drove a quarter-mile in 8.78 seconds. Only two of his laps were timed and the one-kilometer mark on the second lap was missed due to an error. His speeds by distance follow.

| Driver | Car | ¼ | ½ | 1K | 1 Mile |
|---|---|---|---|---|---|
| Walter Christie | Christie | 8.78 | 18.12 | 23.91 | 47.06 |
| Walter Christie | Christie | 9.02 | 19.17 | | 46.22 |

Christie had a tense moment as he shut down his car while going about 103 mph. When he locked the rear wheels, the car skidded more than 200 feet through the turn. He said later that he was afraid to enter the banked curve at a high rate of speed so he did what he thought was necessary in order to avoid an accident. Since he was not wearing gloves, he reasoned that the cold probably robbed him of the strength in his hands, making it harder for him to turn the car through the corner.

After Christie completed his trials, the crowd cheered when Lewis Strang (Walter Christie's nephew) brought his powerful red Fiat, appropriately nicknamed "the devil", onto the track. Strang made three trial runs. On the first one, he accelerated to a new one-mile record at the Speedway of 40.61 seconds, breaking the record of 43.60 seconds set by Barney Oldfield in his Blitzen Benz during the August events earlier in the year. He was not able to break his own world record of 37.71 seconds for the mile set earlier at Atlanta, but he expressed optimism that he could lower that mark before the events were completed. A summary of his trial runs is listed below.

| Driver | Car | ¼ | ½ | 1K | 1 Mile |
|---|---|---|---|---|---|
| Lewis Strang | Fiat | 9.10 | 18.84 | 23.91 | 40.61 |
| Lewis Strang | Fiat | 11.60 | 21.96 | | 46.18 |
| Lewis Strang | Fiat | 9.21 | 18.83 | | |

Because of a timing error, no times were taken on the last two kilometer marks or the last mile mark. Strang also completed a full lap for time and finished the two and a half miles in 1:43.09.

*Walter Christie's "freak" racer as it appeared during the December 1909 brick testing session. This picture was taken during the auto races held at the Indianapolis Motor Speedway during August 1909. (Stereoscopic photo courtesy of Joe Freeman)*

Johnny Aitken then brought his big blue National back on the track for a couple more tries at the mile mark, improving on his earlier time by completing the second try in 45 seconds even. His times are listed below.

| Driver | Car | ¼ | ½ | 1 K | 1 Mile |
|---|---|---|---|---|---|
| Johnny Aitken | National | 14.99 | 21.04 | 23.13 | 50.53 |
| Johnny Aitken | National | 9.81 | 21.08 | | 45.00 |

The featured event of the day was a 20-mile free-for-all. Although not racing against each other because every car started at different times, the event proved spectacular because it resembled a contest between several ice-covered cars that spat flames and smoke from their exhausts as they went roaring by the main grandstands. This event helped to keep the fans' enthusiasm up – despite the cold temperature. Grandstand spectators jumped up and down throughout the day trying to stay warm. Using his megaphone, Mr. Moross tried to amuse the small but faithful crowd by jokingly directing the ushers to pass the ice cream cones in the grandstand. His orders, greeted with loud cheers and laughter, probably helped to generate a bit of warmth – for a minute or two anyway.

The judges' stand resembled a country store as the men huddled in front of a round coal stove with their caps pulled down over their ears. The drivers themselves had to be even colder than the spectators as they sped around the track with the brisk wind hitting their faces. Many of them would rush to the creek after completing their trials and wash their face and hands in the icy cold water! Some drivers were so frozen that after they pulled their car into the pits they had to be pried from them because they couldn't move.

Howard Marmon (of Nordyke & Marmon) even got into the act when he drove the car that was assigned to Ray Harroun. Despite it being his first experience at track racing, he did a commendable job. Meanwhile, Johnny Aitken set a new American record for 20 miles by completing the distance in 16:18.41, breaking the old record of 16:24.17 set by Louis Chevrolet at Atlanta. Newell Motsinger avenged his slow performance from earlier in the day by setting a new record at 20 miles for cars with engines of less than 161 CID. He covered the distance in 23:50.23. The complete results of the 20-mile trial follow.

| Driver | Car | 5 Miles | 10 Miles | 15 Miles | 20 Miles |
|---|---|---|---|---|---|
| Johnny Aitken | National | 4:06.56 | 8:12.10 | 12:17.01 | 16:18.41 |
| Tom Kincaid | National | 4:04.73 | 8:10.61 | Ran out of fuel | |
| Harry Stillman | Marmon | 4:17.41 | 8:33.11 | 12:47.11 | 17:03.76 |
| Howard Marmon | Marmon | 4:25.86 | 8:50.33 | 13:21.18 | 17:52.87 |
| Walter Donnelly | Packard | 4:42.69 | 9:28.83 | 13:59.81 | 18:43.83 |
| Harry Endicott | Cole | 5:30.61 | 10:41.38 | 16:02.44 | 19:32.11 |
| Newell Motsinger | Empire | 6:28.14 | 12:45.22 | 19:13.24 | 23:50.23 |

The longer trials were cancelled due to the colder than expected temperatures, but a few motorcyclists decided to brave the cold weather to make some short trial runs of their own. Fred Huyck rode an Indian while John Sink and John Merz each rode a Thor. Huyck expected to break 40 seconds for the mile but could only manage 52.60 seconds which was almost ten seconds slower than his record on a third-of-a-mile track. He thought that breaking the record in warm weather would be easy. However, the cold weather, in addition to providing great discomfort, froze his oil and prevented him from completing the mile as fast as he was capable of running. Facing similar problems, the two Thor riders fared no better than Huyck. Their results are listed below.

| Driver | Model | ¼ | ½ | 1K | 1 Mile |
|---|---|---|---|---|---|
| Fred Huyck | Indian | 12.22 | 25.02 | | 54.38 |
| Fred Huyck | Indian | 12.85 | 25.51 | | 52.60 |
| John Sink | Thor | | | | 1:04.28 |
| John Merz | Thor | | | | 54.86 |

There was some thought of canceling Saturday's events, but the drivers talked the organizers into letting them continue. Weather on the second day was a little better because the wind was not as strong; however, the noon temperature of nine degrees only rose to 13 degrees by 2:00 p.m. About 150 people turned out to watch the second day of trials. No admission fee was charged and Walter Christie and Lewis Strang did their best to entertain them.

Both drivers had taken precautions on Friday night to help battle the cold temperatures on Saturday. Walter Christie and his riding mechanic plugged up all of the ventilation holes in the bottom of the car hoping to keep it warmer for both of them. Anthony Scudellary, the riding mechanic for Lewis Strang, placed a sheet of heavy leather in front of the radiator that kept the cold wind from getting back to the carburetor. He also attached a hot air pipe leading from the exhaust pipe to the carburetor to keep it as warm as possible. Strang was known for his love of ice cream, often eating it before, after, and sometimes even during big races. It would have been interesting to note whether or not he indulged in this preference during the cold brick testing sessions!

The two drivers took turns going out on the course and made several attempts at records. Lewis Strang thrilled the crowd when he drove "the devil" for a mile in 39.36 seconds to break his Indianapolis Motor Speedway record from Friday, but he ended up lowering the record to 39.21 seconds a short time later. Not to be outdone, Walter Christie thundered his gray "freak" racer to a new American record for a quarter of a mile in 8.37 seconds. He topped his record of 8.78 seconds set on Friday. Lastly, Newell Motsinger made a trial run in his Empire and was clocked at 1:17.03 for one mile. A summary of the times follows.

| Driver | Car | ¼ | ½ | 1K | 1 Mile |
|---|---|---|---|---|---|
| Walter Christie | Christie | 9.04 | 18.11 | | 50.10 |
| Walter Christie | Christie | 8.92 | 18.22 | 24.50 | 42.58 |
| Walter Chrisite | Christie | 8.37 | 17.53 | 22.86 | 43.03 |
| Walter Christie | Christie | 8.70 | 18.08 | 23.45 | 43.77 |
| Lewis Strang | Fiat | 9.07 | 18.62 | 23.65 | 39.21 |
| Lewis Strang | Fiat | 8.92 | 18.39 | 23.36 | 39.36 |
| Newell Motsinger | Empire | | | | 1:17.03 |

Eventually, Christie broke a spring on his car and put an end to his day. This would be the last appearance at the Speedway for Walter Christie as a driver. Meanwhile, Strang wasn't finished with his assault on the record books. He brought cheers from the crowd as he smashed Barney Oldfield's world record for five miles set at the Speedway in August. Shattering the old record of 4:11.30 by over 53 seconds, he stormed through the five miles in 3:17.70! After that effort, Strang parked his red Fiat and ended the second day of trials. Similar to Christie, this would be Strang's last appearance at the Speedway as a driver except for the 1911 Indianapolis 500. Surely, he would have been in several more 500-mile races had he not been killed in a freak accident in July 1911. Strang's time breakdown for each lap follows.

| Driver | Car | ¼ | ½ | 1K | 1 Mile | 2½ Miles |
|---|---|---|---|---|---|---|
| Lewis Strang | Fiat | 8.05 | 17.82 | 22.70 | 40.02 | 1:38.80 |
| Lewis Strang | Fiat | 9.02 | 18.62 | 23.52 | 39.66 | 1:38.90 |

*Lewis Strang sitting at the wheel of a Buick race car at the Cobe Cup race in Crown Point, Indiana, during June 1909. (Chicago Daily News negatives collection, SDN-055185. Courtesy of the Chicago Historical Society)*

Everyone involved thought that the trials were a huge success, given the weather conditions. Carl Fisher told the press, "While I am exceedingly proud of our high records made in this season, I am more than ever delighted that this mid-winter meet is over. It was my ambition to have the new season open with Indianapolis holding all of the laurels. I am sure that we have a track now that will permit much faster time under better weather conditions. I predict marvelous records on this track for next summer."[2]

*A view of the backstretch during the early years at the Indianapolis Motor Speedway. (Photo courtesy of the Indianapolis Motor Speedway)*

The big question on most people's minds as they were leaving the trials was just how high the speed records could reach. Race starter Fred Wagner was quoted by the local press as saying, "100 mph is as fast as the American public will care for. That is, I mean as fast as they will have any personal interest in. I believe that few stock cars will excel that speed and the average man is most interested in stock cars. That is the kind he buys and not the 'freak' cars like Christie's. These cars may go as fast as 130 miles an hour but the public will not enjoy such racing."[3]

Fred Wagner also had high praise for Indianapolis after the trials. Sharing the sentiments of many, he told the *Indianapolis Star*, "Indianapolis is a wonderful automobile center. This city is much better represented in racing by the cars that it produces than Detroit although Detroit manufactures a few more cars. I believe that the coming year will be a great one and I give a lot of the credit to the Speedway. I also believe that Mr. Fisher can get all of the European cars that raced in the Savannah race to come here for an international meet this coming season. This is a wonderful track and will allow for the speed that any car today has stored away in it. I expect to spend a great deal of my time next summer in Indianapolis."[4]

The trials had accomplished exactly what Carl Fisher had hoped. The manufacturers, drivers, and spectators were impressed with the Speedway and anxious about the future possibilities for speed. With the bricks laid, new safety features in place, and new records already established, the stage was set for a very promising 1910 racing season at the Indianapolis Motor Speedway.

*Chapter 6*

# Indianapolis Cars Dominate May Races

The December trials proved that the Indianapolis Motor Speedway was fast as well as safe. Given that outcome, it was no secret that the car manufacturers involved in racing had worked hard over the winter to bring their best to the Speedway. This further fueled the intense rivalry between the car manufacturers of Indianapolis and Detroit. Indianapolis stood second to Detroit in the number of cars manufactured, but it ranked first in the number of cars entered in races. These two geographic areas had more racing cars and drivers than any other area in the United States. It was also the general feeling among the car manufacturers that auto racing gave them the best publicity to generate sales. The manufacturers believed if their cars could hold up under the strain of a long race that would convince potential buyers they would surely hold up through years of ordinary use.

Many changes would greet the crowds as they arrived at the Speedway for the 1910 racing season. Besides the brick racing surface, the grandstands had been expanded and three large scoreboards were set up to give the spectators full details of every race from start to finish. One was on top of the Wheeler-Schebler Carburetor garage across from the main grandstand while another one was on top of the contestant's garage number one. A third sat in front of the south end stands. Each had a foreman equipped with a telephone head attachment connected to the judges' stand so officials could direct the scoreboard operators on the progress of the races. The operators, three at each scoreboard, displayed numbers according to the drivers' positions after each lap. The size of the scoreboards allowed for up to 30 cars to be scored. The 18-inch tall black numbers on a white metal enamel ensured visibility for at least a quarter of a mile.

The management of the Indianapolis Motor Speedway had planned a full schedule of events for 1910, which included the following.

| | |
|---|---|
| Friday, May 27 | Auto races |
| Saturday, May 28 | Auto races |
| Monday, May 30 | Auto races |
| | |
| Monday, June 13 | Aviation meet (all week) |
| | |
| Friday, July 1 | Auto races |
| Saturday, July 2 | Auto races |
| Monday, July 4 | Auto races |
| | |
| Friday, August 12 | 24-hour auto race |
| Friday, August 12 | Balloon meet |
| | |
| Friday, Sept. 2 | Auto races |
| Saturday, Sept. 3 | Auto races |
| Monday, Sept. 5 | Auto races |
| | |
| Saturday, Sept. 17 | Balloon championships |

*View of one of the scoreboards at the Indianapolis Motor Speedway. Based on the numbers shown, this photograph is likely from the 1911 Indianapolis 500; however, it is a good representation of how the scoreboard would have looked for the 1910 races. (Photo courtesy of the Indianapolis Motor Speedway)*

The May program was highlighted by the 100-mile Prest-O-Lite trophy race, the 50-mile Remy Grand Brassard race, and the 200-mile Wheeler-Schebler trophy race. The July auto events gained prominence when the Chicago Auto Club announced plans to hold its prestigious Cobe trophy race at the Speedway on July 2. It would be a 200-mile race scheduled in addition to the 50-mile G & J trophy race and the 100-mile Remy Grand Brassard race. The September contests would include a 100-mile free-for-all race as well as a 200-mile open race. Additionally, the aviation meet in June would be the first nationally licensed meet in the United States and the balloon meet on August 12 was scheduled to take place prior to the start of the 24-hour auto race.

Before the 1910 racing season started, the Speedway played host to a series of contests for the local car manufacturers. This was held in conjunction with the festivities of the annual Indianapolis auto show. Held on Thursday, March 31, the purpose of the contests was to show everyone what could be done with a car and how easily it could be handled. It also provided many of the 5,000 spectators in attendance a first opportunity to view the Speedway racing surface since being paved with brick.

There were a total of six events, and a contestant had to compete in all six to be eligible for the grand prize. The first contest was called the balloon trick. Ten balloons were anchored to the track at various intervals, half on each side of the track. The object was to pop the balloons on the left side with the left front wheel and the balloons on the right side with the right front wheel. The next was the circus ring stunt. A ring two feet in diameter was suspended on a wire across the track approximately five feet above the heads of the contestants. Caps were provided to each driver and as they passed under the ring they threw them through the ring and tried to catch them on the other side as their car kept moving. The next challenge required smooth driving and concentration. Drivers were required to maneuver their cars through a marked course around obstacles at high speed while a passenger held a rubber ball in a spoon. The goal was to complete the course without the passenger dropping the ball from the spoon. For the fourth event, five tall wooden pins were placed along the edge of the track near the grandstand. The object of the cane rack contest was for the passenger to throw a ring around each of the pins as the car sped past. The potato race, the fifth contest, was one of the most amusing of the day. Ten baskets were set along the track and the passenger of each car was given a bag of ten potatoes. As the car went past the baskets the passenger was supposed to drop a potato in each basket. The crowd roared with laughter as the potatoes had a tendency to bounce out of the baskets. The final test was the teeter balance. A large plank was tilted to one side so the driver could drive his car up on the plank. The driver had two minutes to find the exact center and balance his car on the teeter.

Bert Bronson, driving an Austin, made in Grand Rapids, Michigan, was the overall winner of the event. Harry Endicott was second in a Cole. H.W. Martz drove a Maxwell to third, and C.R. Johnson was fourth in a Buick. There were over 20 contestants including Johnny Aitken and one woman. Katrina Fertig drove a Premier.

In early May, about 50 individuals involved in the auto industry, as well as other auto enthusiasts, formed the Indianapolis Auto and Aero Club. After accepting an invitation from the Speedway to build a $15,000 clubhouse and restaurant on the grounds, the club initiated a membership drive to obtain 1,000 members. Annual dues of $25 would entitle members to use of the clubhouse facilities and a complimentary pass through the $1.00 gate to all events at the Indianapolis Motor Speedway, plus affiliation with the American Automobile Association. Plans called for the two-story clubhouse to be built in the grove at the north end of the track, using brick already on the grounds left over from resurfacing the track. The architectural plans showed a basement with a gymnasium, lockers, and bathing facilities. The first floor was to have a café accompanied by a reception area, while the second floor called for a ballroom surrounded by other reception rooms. The Speedway had also announced that a 100-foot long shed complete with repair facilities would be constructed to accommodate the automobiles of the members. The architects had also designed verandas to be built all around the clubhouse on both the first and second floors to enable members to watch events from the clubhouse.

The public received a preview of just how strong the local racing contingent would be in 1910 when Indianapolis drivers and cars won nine of the ten races on the Atlanta Speedway during the May 5–7 events. They raced to many second and third place finishes as well as a one-two-three sweep in some events. The Marmon, National, American, and Cole teams dominated the races. The results were especially encouraging for Nordyke & Marmon because Ray Harroun won three races. Bill Endicott, in a Cole, won every event that he entered. Tom Kincaid won the 200-mile race in his National on the last day of the meet and his teammate, Johnny Aitken, was also a race winner – despite an accident in the first long race of the meet. While leading a race, Aitken drove off of the track. At Atlanta, that meant about a 30-foot drop off from the racing surface. Witnesses said it was a miracle that he escaped with his life, much less with only a few scratches. Herbert Lytle drove his American to a first place finish in the 50-mile race on the second day despite making a late pit stop to change tires. He chased down Tom Kincaid, caught him on the last lap and beat him by about 25 feet. What made these performances even more impressive was the competition that was beaten. Ralph DePalma was there with his Fiat, joined by Lewis Strang in a foreign-made SPO and Walter Christie in his homemade "freak" racer. The *Indianapolis Star* reported that the three of them could only look on and witness the "Hoosier Holiday" unfold.

"I am only practicing for Indianapolis,"[1] Ray Harroun said after the races. Johnny Aitken was quoted in the *Indianapolis Star* as saying, "this is merely a workout for me, and I have my eye on Indianapolis."[2] Herbert Lytle said that he felt like he was back in his old stride while young Bill Endicott gained a lot of confidence from the Atlanta races. "This is a new game for me," Endicott told the *Indianapolis Star*. "I am the last to enter the racing ranks of the Indiana drivers. Three wins at Atlanta were not so bad. I hope to do as well at Indianapolis."[3] Another young Indiana driver, Joe Dawson, showed a lot of promise at Atlanta and was Harroun's teammate on the Marmon team.

The program for May was an ambitious one with 24 races in addition to a handful of trials scheduled for the three-day event. The schedule was as follows.

Friday, May 27

- Event 1 – Trial runs for the records from one quarter mile to one mile
- Event 2 – Five-mile race open to stock chassis with engines of 160 or less cubic inch piston displacement (CID)
- Event 3 – Five-mile race open to stock chassis with engines of 161 – 230 CID
- Event 4 – Ten-mile race open to stock chassis with engines of 231 – 300 CID
- Event 5 – Five-mile race open to stock chassis with engines of 301 – 450 CID
- Event 6 – Ten-mile race for stock chassis with engines of 451 – 600 CID
- Event 7 – Five-mile free-for-all handicap race
- Event 8 – Five-mile amateur race
- Event 9 – Five-mile free-for-all race
- Event 10 – 100-mile Prest-O-Lite trophy race open to all stock chassis with engines of 301 – 450 CID

Saturday, May 28

- Hazard Race
- Event 1 – Trial runs for the records at one mile
- Event 2 – Ten-mile race open to stock chassis with engines of 301 – 450 CID
- Event 3 – Five-mile race open to stock chassis with engines of 451 – 600 CID
- Event 4 – Ten-mile free-for-all handicap race
- Event 5 – Ten-mile amateur race

- Event 6 – Ten mile free-for-all race
- Event 7 – 200-mile Wheeler-Schebler trophy race open to stock chassis with engines of less than 600 CID

Monday, May 30

- Event 1 – Five-mile race open to stock chassis with engines of less than 161 CID
- Event 2 – Ten-mile race open to stock chassis with engines of 161 – 230 CID
- Event 3 – Five-mile race open to stock chassis with engines of 231 – 300 CID
- Event 4 – Ten-mile race open to stock chassis with engines of 231 – 300 CID
- Trial runs for the one kilometer and one mile records
- Event 5 – Five-mile race open to stock chassis with engines of 301 – 450 CID
- Event 6 – Ten-mile race open to stock chassis with engines of 301 – 450 CID
- Event 7 – Five-mile race open to stock chassis with engines of 451 – 600 CID
- Event 8 – Ten-mile race open to stock chassis with engines of 451 – 600 CID
- Event 9 – None listed
- Event 10 – Five-mile free-for-all race
- Event 11 – Ten-mile free-for-all race
- Event 12 – Five-mile free-for-all handicap race
- Trials runs for the one kilometer and one mile records
- Event 13 – 50-mile race for the Remy Grand Brassard and Grand trophy cup open to stock chassis with engines of 231 – 300 CID
- Event 14 – Touring car trials

*The seven-and-a-half- foot tall silver Wheeler-Schebler trophy. (Photo courtesy of the Indianapolis Motor Speedway)*

The touring car trials scheduled as event 14 on Monday were for the John A. Wilson trophy awarded to the first stock touring car that ran a full mile in one minute or less under regular touring conditions while carrying four passengers. Barney Oldfield and Howard Wilcox were scheduled to take part in these trials.

The three-day meet was one of the richest auto racing events ever scheduled. Trophies and other awards were valued in excess of $22,000. The Wheeler-Schebler trophy, valued at $10,000, carried a $1,000 cash award and topped all of the prizes. The Remy Grand Brassard was valued at $2,500 plus a weekly salary of $75 as long as the Brassard was defended. Three other coveted awards were the Prest-O-Lite trophy valued at $1,400, the Speedway Helmet valued at $100 plus a $100 weekly salary as long as it was defended, and the gold-plated Overland auto valued at $1,200 for the driver achieving the fastest mile time in the trials. Gold and silver medals totaling around $2,700 were offered for the various races in addition to cash prizes of over $3,600.

During this time, many drivers were already practicing at the Speedway. The strong possibility of new records combined with the impressive list of prizes – not to mention the prestige for the auto manufacturers of winning at Indianapolis – brought out the best drivers in the fastest cars. Many of the cars were either newly assembled or freshly overhauled just for the Indianapolis events.

The main grandstand was about half-filled with people during the days just before the races as they watched the drivers make practice runs. Local favorites Johnny Aitken, Tom Kincaid, and Ray Harroun set quick paces in practice as did Barney Oldfield, Cincinnati millionaire Caleb Bragg in his Fiat, and the powerhouse Buick team of Louis Chevrolet and Bob Burman. The only incident in practice occurred on Thursday, May 26 when Roy Beall, driving a Knox roadster, lost a wheel. The car flipped over with Beall still holding on for dear life. Fortunately, he escaped with only a slightly fractured rib, but the injury kept him out of the weekend races.

It was obvious that the Buick team came prepared to give it their all. Besides having more cars than any other team, they also brought along all sorts of trunks, boxes, chests, and cases. Each contained supplies, parts, and wardrobes in addition to various other items that the team thought they would need. They had also transported four large cases that weighed about a half a ton apiece – complete with heavy iron handles and huge ball bearing casters. Once up on end and opened each huge case revealed a complete stock room! They contained everything a car could need from the smallest cotter pin or nut to the steering wheel. The inventory of supplies had been meticulously assembled based on previous racing experiences.

A total of 50 sirens were scattered around the track to assist with the running of the races. The pattern of the siren blasts stood for the following: one long blast with a car number displayed signaled to the driver to stop. Two long blasts would be used to call the cars from the paddock to the line for the next race. Three long blasts before the start of the meet indicated that all gates leading across the track were to be closed after which time the spectators would have to use the bridges to cross the track. Three long blasts after the meet called for all gates to be opened. Also, a series of short blasts during a race warned the drivers that there was an accident on the course at which time the blue flag would be displayed.

# LIST OF REFRESHMENTS

| | | | |
|---|---|---|---|
| Chicken Box Lunch | $1.00 | Jumbo Peanuts, package | ..05 |
| Box Lunch | .50 | Cracker Jack | .05 |
| National Biscuit | .15 | Ice Cream Cone | .05 |
| ½ Spring Chicken, fried | .50 | Lemonade | .05 |
| Hot Roast Beef Sandwich | .25 | Soda | .05 |
| Bread Ham Sandwich | .10 | Buttermilk | .05 |
| Cheese Sandwich | .10 | Hot Coffee | .10 |
| ½-lb. Box Candy | .35 | Cigars | .05 |
| (Chocolate Bon Bons.) | | Cigars, (straight) | .10 |
| Small package Candy | 5 & .10 | Cigars, 2 for | .25 |
| Salted Peanuts | .05 | Imported Cigars, (straight) | .25 |

*The menu at the Indianapolis Motor Speedway concessions as printed in the May 1910 racing programs. (Courtesy of Dave Goss)*

Before the racing even began, the three-day program got off to a disappointing start for the team representing the American Motors Company of Indianapolis. The contest board of the American Automobile Association declared that their cars were ineligible for all but the trials and free-for-all races, because the company had not manufactured the required percentage of cars for the particular models entered. For the same reason, much to the disappointment of the spectators, the Buick team was allowed to only enter raccs for stock cars with engines of between 161 - 230 CID, the trials, the free-for-all races and the Wheeler-Schebler race. Dr. Wadsworth Warren, manager of the Buick racing team, reported that the building of the Buick Model 16 was proceeding, noting that stock had been ordered and that the parts were being produced as fast as possible.

By 1:00 p.m. on Friday, May 27, over 15,000 spectators had filed into the Speedway to witness the start of the three-day program. After the opening fanfare, the events began in a rather unspectacular manner because none of the six drivers in the trials for records from one-quarter mile to one mile were able to establish new records. Caleb Bragg, driving a Fiat, had the fastest mile time of 39.50 seconds; however, that was nearly 2.50 seconds off of the record set by Lewis Strang at the brick testing session in December. The second event, a five-mile contest for cars with engines of 160 or less (CID), was cancelled due to a lack of entrants.

The racing finally got under way with the third event of the day, a five-mile contest for stock chassis with engines of 161 – 230 CID. Although many of the local faithful in attendance were hoping for a victory by one of the Indianapolis-made Cole entries, reality suggested a one-two finish by the Buicks. Louis Chevrolet took the suspense out of the race by the end of the second turn. Despite Bill Endicott's valiant effort, neither he nor the rest of the field could keep pace with Chevrolet. Even Bob Burman got off to a slow start from which he never recovered. Chevrolet drove around the course with clocklike precision. He built up a 14-second lead over Endicott by the end of the first lap. The second lap played out much like the first, and Chevrolet waved to the crowd as he crossed the line to win with ease. His time of 4:41.07 shattered Louis Schwitzer's record of 5:13.40 set in the very first auto race at the Speedway in August of 1909. Endicott hung on for second place and Chevrolet's teammate, Bob Burman, had an uncharacteristically bad race to bring up the rear of the field. The final results of the race follow.

| Place | Car # | Driver | Car | Laps | Led |
|---|---|---|---|---|---|
| 1 | 36 | Louis Chevrolet | Buick | 2 | 2 |
| 2 | 6 | Bill Endicott | Cole | 2 | 0 |
| 3 | 26 | Arthur Miller | Warren-Detroit | 2 | 0 |
| 4 | 4 | Lee Frayer | Firestone-Columbus | 2 | 0 |
| 5 | 5 | Louis Edmunds | Cole | 2 | 0 |
| 6 | 35 | Bob Burman | Buick | 2 | 0 |

*Louis Chevrolet and his riding mechanic in a Buick racer during the auto races at the Indianapolis Motor Speedway in May 1910. (Photo courtesy of the Indianapolis Motor Speedway)*

The Marmons of Harroun and Dawson were the class of the field in the fourth event; a ten-mile race for stock chassis with engines of 231 – 300 CID. Both drivers wasted little time in disposing of the rest of the field as they rocketed into the first turn side-by-side. Harroun was credited with leading the first two laps, but Dawson had hounded him for the lead every inch of the way. The other cars in the race were no match and quickly fell off the pace. The persistent Dawson nosed ahead of his teammate at the judges' stand to lead the third lap by the smallest of margins. As Harroun fought back, the two ran neck-and-neck for the entire final lap with Harroun maintaining an advantage by staying on the inside groove. In what turned out to be the closest finish of the three-day meet, Harroun pulled out the win at the line by a mere 0.04 of a second. He set a new American record of 8:16.80 for ten miles in the 231 – 300 CID class and broke Louis Chevrolet's record of 9:03.18 set in Atlanta. The race results follow.

| Place | Car # | Driver | Car | Laps | Led |
|-------|-------|--------|-----|------|-----|
| 1 | 33 | Ray Harroun | Marmon | 4 | 3 |
| 2 | 34 | Joe Dawson | Marmon | 4 | 1 |
| 3 | 15 | E.F. Scheifler | Jackson | 4 | 0 |
| 4 | 20 | George Clark | Cutting | 4 | 0 |
| 5 | 3 | Frank Fox | Pope-Hartford | 4 | 0 |
| 6 | 25 | Gil Anderson | Marion | 4 | 0 |
| 7 | 24 | Ray Tinkler | Marion | 4 | 0 |

*#33 Ray Harroun edges out Marmon teammate #34 Joe Dawson in a 10-mile race on May 27, 1910. (Photo courtesy of the Indianapolis Motor Speedway)*

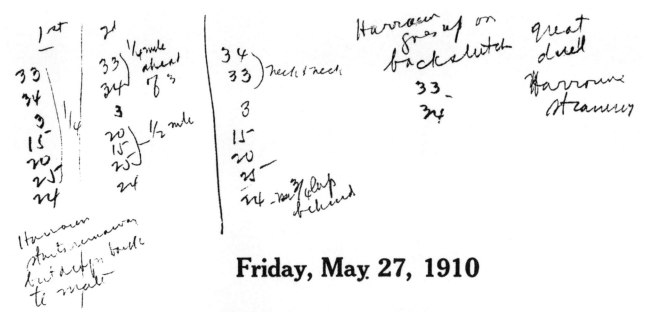

# Friday, May 27, 1910

EVENT No. 4.—Stock chassis cars, Class B, Division 3—231 to 300 cubic inches piston displacement. Minimum weight, 1,700 pounds.

Distance, 10 miles.

First Prize—$100.00 in Gold and Gold Medal.

Second Prize—$50.00 in Silver and Silver Medal.

| No. | Car | Cylinder | Bore of Cylinder | Driver |
|---|---|---|---|---|
| 3 | Pope-Hartford | 4 cylinder | 4 5-16x5⅛ | Fox |
| 15 | Jackson | 4 cylinder | 4½x4½ | Scheifler |
| 20 | Cutting | 4 cylinder | 4¼x5 | Clark |
| 21 | Cutting | 4 cylinder | 4¼x5 | Bisbee |
| 24 | Marion | 4 cylinder | 4¼x4½ | Tinkler |
| 25 | Marion | 4 cylinder | 4¼x4½ | Anderson |
| 33 | Marmon 32 | 4 cylinder | 4½x4½ | Harroun |
| 34 | Marmon 32 | 4 cylinder | 4½x4½ | Dawson |
| 37 | Buick 16A | 4 cylinder | 4 23-64x5 | Burman |
| 38 | Buick 16A | 4 cylinder | 4 23-64x5 | L. Chevrolet |

1st.................... 2d.................... 3d.................... Time........

*A spectator's race notes from a 10-mile race on May 27, 1910. Note the reference at the top to the #33 of Harroun and the #34 of Dawson being neck-and-neck. Also notice in the upper right-hand corner the words "great dual" and Harroun and Dawson written below it. (Courtesy of Dave Goss)*

*E.F. Scheifler and riding mechanic John Casey in a Jackson at Elgin, Illinois in 1910. (Chicago Daily News negatives collection, SDN-056233. Courtesy of the Chicago Historical Society)*

The participation of five Indianapolis drivers in the five-mile race for stock chassis with engines of 301 – 450 CID kept the local fans on their feet after the close finish of the last contest. National driver Tom Kincaid was joined by National teammates Johnny Aitken and Charlie Merz. The Marmon team was represented by Joe Dawson and Ray Harroun. Leigh Lynch was the lone non-Indianapolis entry. The Nationals occupied the first three starting positions; however, Joe Dawson looked more determined than ever after his narrow defeat in the previous event. Out-racing everyone else, he drove his Marmon hard into turn one. Harroun was engaged in a competitive tussle with the three Nationals as Lynch's Jackson brought up the rear. Dawson controlled the lead through the first lap but soon afterward was heavily challenged by Kincaid. Meanwhile, Harroun had his hands full keeping Aitken and Merz behind him. As the leaders zipped down the frontstretch, racing past Dawson in a sudden, calculated burst of speed, Kincaid brought the crowd to a frenzy. He guided the blue National past the yellow Marmon at the finish in 4:05.76, breaking the world record set by the late Wilfred Bourque at the Speedway in August 1909 by 40 seconds. The Indianapolis group claimed the top five positions. The race results follow.

| Place | Car # | Driver | Car | Laps | Led |
|-------|-------|--------|-----|------|-----|
| 1 | 10 | Tom Kincaid | National | 2 | 1 |
| 2 | 31 | Joe Dawson | Marmon | 2 | 1 |
| 3 | 30 | Ray Harroun | Marmon | 2 | 0 |
| 4 | 9 | Johnny Aitken | National | 2 | 0 |
| 5 | 11 | Charlie Merz | National | 2 | 0 |
| 6 | 16 | Leigh Lynch | Jackson | 2 | 0 |

A ten-mile race for stock chassis with engines of 451 – 600 CID followed as the crowd anxiously anticipated the arrival of Barney Oldfield. Although Oldfield was entered in the event, he had to withdraw because of a broken steering knuckle on his Knox racer. That left only three Nationals entered in the contest, Kincaid and Aitken, who had just finished the previous event, along with young Howard Wilcox. This was the first race at the Speedway for the 21-year-old Wilcox. Some wondered if Aitken and Kincaid might lay back and let their inexperienced teammate take the victory. That was answered quickly as Aitken thundered into the lead. Kincaid overcame a sluggish start to catch Aitken and inch ahead of him at the line to lead the first lap. Wilcox never challenged the two. The next three laps featured a see-saw battle between Aitken and Kincaid, each taking turns leading a lap. Aitken finally prevailed, taking the victory in 8:25.94 with Kincaid close behind. The race summary follows.

| Place | Car # | Driver | Car | Laps | Led |
|---|---|---|---|---|---|
| 1 | 9 | Johnny Aitken | National | 4 | 2 |
| 2 | 10 | Tom Kincaid | National | 4 | 2 |
| 3 | 11 | Howard Wilcox | National | 4 | 0 |

The seventh event, a five-mile free-for-all handicap, provided the largest field of the day with 14 starters. The little Hupmobile driven by Frank Gelnaw was the first car to start the race. Twenty seconds later, Newell Motsinger's Empire was given "Pop" Wagner's signal to start, followed 40 seconds later by Arthur Miller in a Warren-Detroit. After Miller, the Cole of Bill Endicott and the Marion of Ray Tinkler started. Some 15 seconds later, the last five cars entered the race in quick succession – just five seconds apart. In order, they were: Gil Anderson in a Marion, Leigh Lynch in a Jackson, Don Herr in a National, and Johnny Aitken in a National. The cars formed a long procession all around the course by the time Aitken started, almost two minutes after the first car. This made for big changes in position during the race, such as Frank Fox in a Pope-Hartford who went from eleventh place on the first lap to sixth place. Arthur Miller dropped from sixth place on the first lap to last at the end of the race. The eventual winner, the National of Arthur Greiner, came from fifth place on the first lap to win in 5:44.90. The complete race results follow.

| Place | Car # | Driver | Car | Laps | Led |
|---|---|---|---|---|---|
| 1 | 48 | Arthur Greiner | National | 2 | 1 |
| 2 | 47 | William Tousey | National | 2 | 0 |
| 3 | 45 | Jack Reed | Stoddard-Dayton | 2 | 0 |
| 4 | 1 | Newell Motsinger | Empire | 2 | 1 |
| 5 | 11 | Don Herr | National | 2 | 0 |
| 6 | 3 | Frank Fox | Pope-Hartford | 2 | 0 |
| 7 | 16 | Leigh Lynch | Jackson | 2 | 0 |
| 8 | 2 | Herbert Lytle | American | 2 | 0 |
| 9 | 8 | Johnny Aitken | National | 2 | 0 |
| 10 | 6 | Bill Endicott | Cole | 2 | 0 |
| 11 | 25 | Gil Anderson | Marion | 2 | 0 |
| 12 | 24 | Ray Tinkler | Marion | 2 | 0 |
| 13 | 27 | Frank Gelnaw | Hupmobile | 2 | 0 |
| 14 | 26 | Arthur Miller | Warren-Detroit | 2 | 0 |

Many in attendance dubbed the eighth event of the day the millionaire race because it was a five-mile contest for amateurs in privately owned cars. The crowd eagerly awaited the appearance of Caleb Bragg of Cincinnati. Bragg had defeated Barney Oldfield not once, but twice – on the boards of Playa del Rey in Los Angeles on the 15th and 16th of April. The quiet Bragg, the son of a wealthy Cincinnati publisher never craved money or prestige. In fact, he had once told starter "Pop" Wagner that he was sorry that he beat Oldfield because it created such a stir. Unfortunately, Bragg was disqualified from the race because he allegedly had a connection with the Fiat Company, which had shipped his car to Indianapolis at the company's expense. The officials determined that this was a violation of amateur rules. After the disqualification, Arthur Greiner of Chicago and William Tousey of Syracuse, both driving Nationals, were left to fight it out for the win. It turned out to be a rather uneventful contest. Greiner snatched up the early lead and gradually built upon it throughout the race. He beat Tousey by 13 seconds to claim the win in 4:09.30. The race summary follows.

| Place | Car # | Driver | Car | Laps | Led |
|---|---|---|---|---|---|
| 1 | 48 | Arthur Greiner | National | 2 | 2 |
| 2 | 47 | William Tousey | National | 2 | 0 |

The coveted Speedway Helmet was up for grabs in the ninth event of the day, a five-mile free-for-all. Even before the start, a murmur circulated throughout the grandstands, and for good reason. The dash for the Helmet featured six outstanding drivers. Included in the lineup were Bob Burman in the Buick, Herbert Lytle in the American, Ray Harroun in the Marmon, Caleb Bragg in the Fiat, and the Nationals of Aitken and Kincaid. Burman and Aitken carried riding mechanics.

Johnny Aitken made a masterful charge for the early lead followed by Burman and Kincaid. Bragg, the prohibitive favorite, did not get a good start but soon began to gain ground on the others. He had captured the lead by the end of the first lap, chased closely by Burman. The cars of Aitken, Lytle, Harroun, and Kincaid followed in that order. Bragg and Burman waged a colossal dual and swapped positions throughout the second lap. In the end, Burman crossed the line first to pull off the upset over Bragg's Fiat in a time of 3:37.24. Harroun made a sensational rush forward on the second lap to move from fifth to third. The final results of the race follow.

| Place | Car # | Driver | Car | Laps | Led |
|---|---|---|---|---|---|
| 1 | 41 | Bob Burman | Buick | 2 | 1 |
| 2 | 14 | Caleb Bragg | Fiat | 2 | 1 |
| 3 | 32 | Ray Harroun | Marmon | 2 | 0 |
| 4 | 2 | Herbert Lytle | American | 2 | 0 |
| 5 | 8 | Johnny Aitken | National | 2 | 0 |
| 6 | 7 | Tom Kincaid | National | 2 | 0 |

The final event of the day was the much anticipated 100-mile Prest-O-Lite trophy race for stock chassis with engines of 301 – 450 CID. Ray Harroun seemed to be the driver who most people thought would win the race, although many believed that he would face stiff competition from his own teammate and the National of Tom Kincaid.

*The Prest-O-Lite trophy awarded at the Indianapolis Motor Speedway during the August 1909 and May 1910 race programs. (Photo taken from a 1909 Buick Motor Company brochure)*

Things certainly started out well for Harroun as he raced to the early advantage over the rest of the field and led the first 12 laps of the race. During that time, Frank Fox suffered steering problems on the seventh lap, requiring him to park his Pope-Hartford. Meanwhile, Harroun established new 20 and 30-mile records along the way with times of 16:24.17 and 24:31.73, respectively. Unfortunately, Harroun's Marmon broke a valve on the thirteenth lap and he lost valuable time as he nursed it back to the pits. The other Marmon of Joe Dawson then took the lead and began pulling away from the field. Flying around the track lap after lap, he set five new records in the process. Dawson set records of: 32:31.82 for 40 miles, 40:32.03 for 50 miles, 49:01.60 for 60 miles, 57:30.53 for 70 miles and 67:49.17 for 80 miles. Everything was looking good for Dawson. He built a lead of over two and one half miles on the second place car of Tom Kincaid with only six laps to go. On lap 35 misfortune struck the Marmon team again as a spark plug went bad in Dawson's machine and forced him to the pits for repairs. This allowed Tom Kincaid to inherit the lead, a position that he kept through the end of the race. Crossing the line in 1:23:43.12, he established a new record for 100 miles at an average speed of 71.670 mph. This was a remarkable feat, considering that he had to stop three times during the race to replace worn out tires! Kincaid almost met with misfortune on one of those occasions when the tread from his rear tire flew off hitting him in the arm. Don Herr, his riding mechanic took control of the car momentarily and brought it to a safe stop until Kincaid could continue on his way. The brick surface took a toll on the big heavy National cars, but the lighter Marmons on the other hand were able to go the entire distance without changing a tire. The final results of the race follow.

| Place | Car # | Driver | Car | Laps | Led |
|-------|-------|--------|-----|------|-----|
| 1 | 10 | Tom Kincaid | National | 40 | 6 |
| 2 | 11 | Charlie Merz | National | 40 | 0 |
| 3 | 16 | Leigh Lynch | Jackson | 40 | 0 |
| 4 | 31 | Joe Dawson | Marmon | 40 | 22 |
| 5 | 30 | Ray Harroun | Marmon | 32 | 12 |
| 6 | 3 | Frank Fox | Pope-Hartford | 6 | 0 |

The Prest-O-Lite race concluded the first day's events, which were deemed a huge success by all in attendance. The Indianapolis drivers did not completely dominate the day like they had in Atlanta, but they did win four of the eight races in addition to making a strong showing in the events they did not win.

All indications pointed to record-breaking attendance for Saturday and Monday's events. The hotels in the city were booked full. Hundreds of people were turned away. Many hotels began to double up people in rooms and put cots in the hallways.

"By tonight, it is expected that the crowd will approach that of a State Fair crowd," said Carl Fisher. "Many people will have to seek resting places for the night in boarding houses or in hotels of the surrounding towns."[4]

Seven events were on the schedule for Saturday's portion of the program. While all of the races had the potential of being good ones, everyone's mind was on the last event of the day, the 200-mile race for the coveted Wheeler-Schebler trophy. There were 19 entries for the contest, and it was certain that all of them would have their best cars ready to go.

A throng of 25,000 fans was lured to the Speedway on Saturday as a result of Friday's successful program. Again, the day's events were kicked off at 1:00 p.m.; however, this time the racing began with the hazard race. The most unusual auto race ever held at the Indianapolis Motor Speedway, its objective was not to be one of speed necessarily but to test the skill of the drivers in various situations. The Overland Automobile Company of Indianapolis, who provided the cars for the event, wanted to show the crowd just what an automobile was capable of when controlled properly.

*Looking down the front straightaway from the first turn during racing action at the Indianapolis Motor Speedway on May 28, 1910. (Photo courtesy of the Detroit Public Library, National Automotive History Collection)*

The entrants started in an area behind the main grandstand before entering the track at the north end of the grandstand. From there they drove down the front straightaway over a portable bridge ten feet high at an incline of about 45 degrees. After negotiating the bridge, the drivers continued on until they came to a mark instructing them to turn toward the infield and into the creek at the southwest corner of the track. The cars continued running through the creek until reaching another mark that instructed them to dash back onto the high banking of the track which they followed until just before the bleachers at the south end. At that point, another marker instructed them to leave the track for the creek bed again, following it under the bridge and out into the parking lot. The cars then reappeared, climbed the automobile bridge over the track east of the bleachers and dropped down inside the aviation grounds before making a short turn that put them back onto the track in the backstretch. From there they encountered another steep portable bridge, after which they raced around the north end of the track and back to the main grandstand. The race ended after the drivers negotiated the initial bridge in front of the main grandstand and raced for the finish line in front of the judges' stand.

Myers won in a time of 3:28.00 followed by McGee and Gregg in 3:38.00 and 4:04.30, respectively. The other participants in the race were Baird, Rickeets and Shessler. Starter "Pop" Wagner summed up everyone's feelings best when he said, "In all of my experience around races from coast to coast I have never witnessed such a perfect exhibition of a car's possibilities. I think that it is marvelous that the winner was able to take the time required to climb those inclines and then make two and a half miles in a few seconds over three minutes."[5]

After the inclines were removed from the track, six drivers took their turn at a one-mile time trial. Newell Motsinger put his Empire on the track first, recording a time of 1:07.10 for one mile. The little car was far off of the track record of 37.10 seconds set by Lewis Strang in a Buick during the December brick testing session. The spectators were somewhat disappointed because none of the drivers approached Strang's record. Caleb Bragg made the quickest time when he went a mile in 41.30 seconds in his Fiat. The other times were as follows: 44.44 seconds for Herbert Lytle in an American, 46.80 seconds for Johnny Aitken in a National, 42.33 seconds for Ray Harroun in a Marmon, and 41.83 seconds for Ben Kirscher in a Darracq. Throughout the weekend's activities, the crowd watched Kirscher's green Darracq closely. The French-made car was the same car that Frenchman Victor Hemery drove to victory in the 1905 Vanderbilt Cup race, a 28.3-mile road race held on Long Island, New York. Despite being five years older than most of its competitors, the car held its own in competition.

The third event of the day was a ten-mile race for stock chassis with engines of 301 – 450 CID. The locals were consumed with anticipation because five of the six starters were Indianapolis drivers with Indianapolis-made cars. Still others were anxious to see what Johnny Aitken would do after setting an American record in this event on Friday.

As the race started, another classic battle between the Nationals and Marmons began to take shape. Tom Kincaid positioned his big blue National at the front of the field to establish the early lead. Joe Dawson drove his yellow Marmon past him in the middle of the backstretch before Kincaid regained the lead on the last turn of the first lap. Dawson nosed ahead of Kincaid at the line; however, he encountered mechanical trouble, which forced him to drop out of the race near the first turn of the second lap. Kincaid regained the lead and held it until Johnny Aitken and Ray Harroun made it three abreast on the backstretch during the third lap. The two roared past Kincaid with a vengeance, leaving him in their wake. Aitken was credited with leading the lap as he nosed ahead of Harroun at the line. Meanwhile, Kincaid continued to slide backward and was eventually passed by Charlie Merz. Lynch remained far behind in the Jackson. Harroun did his best to stay with Aitken, but the National driver again set a record pace in driving to victory with another new American 10-mile record for the class of 8:08.03. The race summary follows.

| Place | Car # | Driver | Car | Laps | Led |
|-------|-------|--------|-----|------|-----|
| 1 | 9 | Johnny Aitken | National | 4 | 2 |
| 2 | 30 | Ray Harroun | Marmon | 4 | 0 |
| 3 | 11 | Charlie Merz | National | 4 | 0 |
| 4 | 10 | Tom Kincaid | National | 4 | 1 |
| 5 | 16 | Leigh Lynch | Jackson | 4 | 0 |
| 6 | 31 | Joe Dawson | Marmon | 1 | 1 |

Barney Oldfield made his official debut at the three-day program in the next event, a five-mile race for stock chassis with engines of 301 – 450 CID. The unflappable Oldfield acknowledged his fans by giving them one of his characteristic grins while holding onto his cigar. There were also cheers for Johnny Aitken who was trying to make it two wins in a row. He lined up his big blue National next to Oldfield's brown Knox. Don Herr, driving another National, was the third competitor in the race.

Oldfield led the two Nationals into turn one and was able to keep them behind him as he motored onto the backstretch. Aitken stayed right on his back wheels while Herr assumed a similar position on Aitken. Despite the tight racing for two complete laps, the order of the three cars remained the same. In winning the race, Oldfield sailed to a new record of 4:03.44. Aitken finished a half a second behind with Herr another half a second back. The race summary follows.

| Place | Car # | Driver | Car | Laps | Led |
|-------|-------|--------|-----|------|-----|
| 1 | 46 | Barney Oldfield | Knox | 2 | 2 |
| 2 | 9 | Johnny Aitken | National | 2 | 0 |
| 3 | 11 | Don Herr | National | 2 | 0 |

The next race, a ten-mile free-for-all handicap, was a real thriller! Nineteen cars started at various times, making for a high-speed circus. The little Hupmobile, driven by Frank Gelnaw, was first off of the line and had completed a lap by the time Aitken, Greiner, Lytle, and Oldfield had even started. The bigger cars were rushing past the smaller ones with breathtaking speed, often times creating frightening changes for position. The Jackson of Leigh Lynch leaped from ninth place on the first lap to third on the second lap to first on the third lap before dropping back to second on the fourth lap. The largest shifts saw Howard Wilcox in his National go from thirteenth place on the first lap to first place by the end of the fourth lap in the winning time of 10:55.33. Louis Edmunds in his Cole faded from fifth place on the first lap to fourteenth at the finish. As with the handicap race from the previous day, the final positions were hard to determine and the local papers did not provide a complete list of the finishing order.

The first accident of the day occurred during the race when Herbert Lytle's American skidded off of the track and overturned on the third lap. He broke his left leg as a result, but his riding mechanic, William Clifton of Philadelphia, escaped with only a sprained right shoulder. This was a reversal of the usual outcome of racing accidents, for it was more often the driver who escaped injury while the riding mechanic was the victim of serious injuries. Lytle's young son was in the grandstand when the accident occurred. The driver sent word to him that he was fine, and under no circumstances should he attempt to cross the track until the Wheeler-Schebler race was completed.

Driver of the American car, Herbert Lytle. (Photo courtesy of the Indianapolis Motor Speedway)

Lytle's accident caused the Indianapolis driver to announce that he was retiring from racing altogether (although he did come back to drive in the 1911 Indianapolis 500). While lying on a cot in the Indianapolis Motor Speedway Hospital he said, "It's all over, I am through with the motor racing game. Never again will I take a seat behind the wheel of a racing car in a contest. The game is alright for those who are lucky, but I seem to be out of luck every season." Lytle had been the victim of other accidents. He recently had suffered serious injuries in the 1909 Vanderbilt Cup race. He also said that he had a premonition that something would happen. "I was restless last night and couldn't sleep. It is seldom that I am caught that way but last night it seemed to me that something was wrong. I told my riding mechanic before the race that I thought I would get into trouble before the end of the day. He laughed but I felt rather sure about it."[6]

Lytle was very complimentary of the hospital at the Speedway. It was so well managed that one could mistake it for one of the greater hospitals in this country, even though it was set up to serve the Speedway exclusively with accommodations for only four to six patients. The staff, quick to react to emergencies, took only a few minutes after an accident occurred to arrive on the scene. To assist with this effort, an Indiana National Guard soldier stationed at a tower near the starter's stand, kept a constant watch over the grounds. Using field glasses, he was able to watch all of the cars entered in the events.

If there was an accident, he blew a bugle and signaled to a second soldier stationed a few feet away. This soldier signaled to a third soldier waiting in an automobile on the inside of the track. The third soldier dispatched the ambulance to the scene of the accident. A group of soldiers followed to help keep order at the scene. A wrecking crew was also sent to the scene to clear any debris. The doctor who accompanied the ambulance attended to the injured before they were rushed back to the hospital located in the infield of the grounds. Dr. H.R. Allen was in charge of the hospital, assisted by a team of nurses and doctors. Once sufficiently stabilized, the patient was transported to one of the local hospitals.

The next two events on the program were not run. The ten-mile amateur race was cancelled due to a lack of entries, and the ten-mile free-for-all race for cars in class D was postponed to the first race on Monday. The cars for the latter event were not ready in time for the start, so the officials decided that the contest could easily be moved to Monday.

Cheers from the mass of spectators filled the grandstands as the time for the big event of the day, the 200-mile Wheeler-Schebler trophy race, had finally arrived. A total of 19 entrants lined up on the frontstretch including Leigh Lynch in his Jackson, the defending champion of the ill-fated Wheeler-Schebler race at the Speedway on August 21, 1909. A clash of the Indianapolis-made Marmons and Nationals against the Flint-made Buicks was expected by all. However, Barney Oldfield had hoped to crash the party as well.

Arthur Chevrolet, younger brother of Louis, led the field of cars into the first turn, but kept his position for only a few laps before Ray Harroun took control of the race. Harroun's game plan was to maintain a steady pace throughout the contest to conserve his tires and he carried out his plan flawlessly. In fact, the whole Marmon team looked good early in the race. Joe Dawson and Bruce Keen ran fifth and seventh, respectively. The car of hard-charging Johnny Aitken suffered from excessive tire wear very early and he blew a tire just after having passed the pits on the fifth lap. This caused him to drive an entire circuit around the Speedway on the bad tire before he could stop to change it. More tire trouble came on lap 16 when Barney Oldfield blew a rear tire entering the first turn. The demountable rim quickly loosened, causing the tire to roll up on the incline against the wall. The big Knox careened wildly for a few seconds before Oldfield could get it under control and continue on to complete the two-and-a-half-mile lap on the rim. The crowd gave him a standing ovation as he rolled into his pits for repairs. This put him out of contention; however, he eventually made up some time lapping many competitors toward the finish of the race.

The second incident of the day came on lap 17. Dawson's car lost a tire in the backstretch, and his car slid into the soft dirt at the side of the track. The car was traveling so fast when it hit the dirt that it did a complete end-over-end flip. With Dawson still hanging on to the wheel, the car careened into the outside fence. The car bounded away from the fence before hitting it again, and eventually broke through it. Miraculously, Dawson remained in the car until it came to a stop. The car was destroyed but Dawson was unhurt. Meanwhile, Harroun continued to dominate the race, although Leigh Lynch had made a steady climb from thirteenth to second by the 40-mile mark. Arthur Chevrolet, who had been running second to Harroun, dropped back to fifth place. Meanwhile, Aitken began to pick up ground after his blown tire as he held the seventh position.

The last half of the race was not as eventful as the first half, but the racing was still very competitive. Throughout the race, thousands in the grandstands stood to see the full round of each lap. Favorite drivers were greeted with shouts of encouragement. As the number of completed laps increased, motors snapped more vigorously. Occasionally, a car would send a thrill through the crowd when flames would shoot out the sides of the hood due to the burn-off of excessive oil. At times, smoke clouds concealed the moving caravan as it rushed past the grandstands.

Louis Chevrolet, Bob Burman, and Tom Kincaid, three of the drivers expected to figure in the final result, suffered engine problems and were never contenders. The eventual top five finishers changed positions only slightly during the final 40 miles. All five remained in the top positions until the

*The Wheeler-Schebler trophy before the race on May 28, 1910. (Photo courtesy of the Indianapolis Motor Speedway)*

*Ray Harroun admiring the Wheeler-Schebler trophy on May 27, 1910, the day before he would win the trophy. (Photo courtesy of the Indianapolis Motor Speedway)*

*The wreck of Joe Dawson's Marmon sits along the fence in the backstretch during the 200-mile Wheeler-Schebler race on May 28, 1910. (Photo courtesy of the Indianapolis Motor Speedway)*

finish. Harroun went on to dominate the race in a record time for 200 miles of 2:46:31.00. He stuck to his plan the whole race – stopping one time only for fuel. Howard and Walter Marmon, along with the rest in the Marmon pits, were the first to congratulate him after the race. Leigh Lynch also drove a brilliant race. He made a masterful charge from thirteenth in the early going and never fell out of the top five after the 20-mile mark. Aitken, showing consummate skill behind the wheel, finished third despite making three stops for tires and spark plugs. Since he was driving a four cylinder National compared to the more powerful six cylinder cars of some of the other competitors, it was also a tremendous accomplishment just to finish third. The race summary follows.

| Place | Car # | Driver | Car | Laps | Led |
|---|---|---|---|---|---|
| 1 | 32 | Ray Harroun | Marmon | 80 | 75 |
| 2 | 16 | Leigh Lynch | Jackson | 80 | 0 |
| 3 | 7 | Johnny Aitken | National | 80 | 0 |
| 4 | 44 | Arthur Chevrolet | Buick | 80 | 5 |
| 5 | 3 | Frank Fox | Pope-Hartford | 78 | 0 |
| 6 | 47 | William Tousey | National | 77 | 0 |
| 7 | 46 | Barney Oldfield | Knox | 77 | 0 |
| 8 | 22 | George Clark | Cutting | 76 | 0 |
| 9 | 11 | Charlie Merz | National | 76 | 0 |
| 10 | 18 | Fred Ellis | Jackson | 75 | 0 |
| 11 | 20 | D. Bisbee | Cutting | 68 | 0 |
| 12 | 31 | Bruce Keen | Marmon | 60 | 0 |
| 13 | 41 | Bob Burman | Buick | 52 | 0 |
| 14 | 17 | Louis Schwitzer | Jackson | 52 | 0 |
| 15 | 21 | Frank Gelnaw | Cutting | 50 | 0 |
| 16 | 42 | Louis Chevrolet | Buick | 32 | 0 |
| 17 | 12 | Bill Endicott | Westcott | 24 | 0 |
| 18 | 10 | Tom Kincaid | National | 20 | 0 |
| 19 | 30 | Joe Dawson | Marmon | 16 | 0 |

By virtue of his win, Ray Harroun set two new American records. He set a new record of 2:02:16.00 for 150 miles, breaking George Robertson's 2:05:63.00 set in a Fiat at Atlanta. Likewise, he set a new record for 200 miles, breaking Louis Chevrolet's old mark of 2:46:47.47, also set at Atlanta. During the two days of racing, 18 records had been set – all but two of the records established by a Marmon or National. By this time, the press had begun to call the Marmon cars "Wasps,"[7] supposedly because the term fit better in the newspapers than "yellow jacket."

The first two days of racing proved an enormous success and the Wheeler-Schebler race confirmed that the Speedway was now the best race course in America. The most recent Wheeler-Schebler race was over an hour faster than the previous year's competition and much safer as well. Walter Hempel, manager of the Los Angeles Motordrome, was at the Speedway for the weekend's program and was quoted as saying, "It is a great place. I could hardly believe it was as big and as great as it is until I laid eyes on it yesterday. The track is wonderful and best of all the fans are enthusiastic. They cheer the drivers and really get excited over the races. It is different in the west. The fans are quiet and fail to get excited even when the racing is at its best. We have pulled off some good race meetings there but I never have seen a California crowd make the racket the crowd did at the Speedway today. I think that I will get some good pointers from the Indianapolis way of doing things and carry them back to the west with me."[8]

The drivers and their teams had a day of rest on Sunday courtesy of the blue laws in effect at the time, so the track was cleaned in preparation for Monday's big events. The Speedway workers used gasoline to clean the bricks, covered with oil the cars had spilled over the first two days of racing. After the gasoline was applied, the bricks were washed with water to guarantee a good clean surface for Monday's races. Meanwhile, trains from all directions swept into Indianapolis throughout the day on Sunday. They came from Louisville, Cincinnati, St. Louis, Chicago, and Detroit to name a few. The smaller cities in Indiana poured great caravans of automobiles into the city for Monday's races.

By early Monday morning the roads were overwhelmed with vehicles, horses, and pedestrians headed to the Speedway. The trains, filled with masses of humanity, shuttled spectators to the grounds every 20 minutes. They began to reach the Speedway by as early as 9:00 a.m. A steady stream of people clogged the gates right up until the start of the first event. An unbelievable crowd of over 60,000 had jammed into the Speedway by the 1:00 p.m. start – the largest crowd in history to ever witness a racing program! There were 13 races and three trials scheduled. The 50-mile race for the Remy Grand Brassard constituted the only long-distance event of the day. With the exception of the Remy Grand Brassard contest, the free-for-all events, a handicap race, and the trials, races were for championships of the various classes. The winners held the championship for a year, regardless of any other races held during that time period. The hazard race, a big hit with the crowd on Saturday, was not run again. It took too much time to position the obstacles on the track and remove them after the event. The Speedway officials had also rearranged the events from the original schedule in order to give the drivers longer rest periods between races.

The first contest of the afternoon was the ten-mile free-for-all race that had been postponed from Saturday. This event featured an interesting mix of entrants. Caleb Bragg in his Italian-made Fiat and Ben Kirscher in his French Darracq lined up against the Nationals of Aitken, Kincaid, and Greiner. Bragg, ruled ineligible as an amateur on Saturday, had been reinstated to amateur status as Mr. Moross explained that confusion on the registration of his car had been cleared up.

The Fiat of Bragg surged forward from the standing start so quickly that it looked as if the other starters were caught by surprise. He continued on to complete the first lap in a remarkable time of 1:54.89! Kirscher, victim of an agonizingly slow start, steadily gained on the field. Meanwhile, Bragg was simply untouchable for over two laps. The powerful green Darracq gradually gained ground on the Fiat until Kirscher suddenly found himself right on Braggs's rear wheels. Between turns three and four of the third lap, Kirscher made a slingshot move past Bragg that appeared to take him by surprise. With Bragg in hot pursuit, Kirscher led the third lap and looked well on his way to victory. Then fate dealt the Darracq a cruel misfortune when one of its tires blew on the last lap. Bragg was close enough to take advantage of the situation and went on to win in a time of 7:21.93. Despite his bad luck, Kirscher held on and finished third. Many in the crowd believed that he would have won the race if it hadn't been for his blown tire. Kincaid was also able to overtake Kirscher to capture second place, but his National teammate, Johnny Aitken, was forced to retire from the race early in the fourth lap and finished in fifth place. The complete race results follow.

| Place | Car # | Driver | Car | Laps | Led |
|-------|-------|--------|-----|------|-----|
| 1 | 14 | Caleb Bragg | Fiat | 4 | 3 |
| 2 | 7 | Tom Kincaid | National | 4 | 0 |
| 3 | 54 | Ben Kirscher | Darracq | 4 | 1 |
| 4 | 48 | Arthur Greiner | National | 4 | 0 |
| 5 | 8 | Johnny Aitken | National | 3 | 0 |

*Cincinnati millionaire and Fiat driver Caleb Bragg and his riding mechanic Anthony Scudellary. (Photo courtesy of the Indianapolis Motor Speedway)*

Originally scheduled as the last event of the day, the trials for the John A. Wilson trophy were run next. Barney Oldfield, driving a Knox, made two attempts at capturing the trophy by trying to drive a mile in a minute or less while carrying four passengers. Neither attempt succeeded. His first try was in 1:13.60 followed by a second try in 1:10.45. Howard Wilcox, the only other entrant, was not able to complete his attempt.

The five-mile race for stock chassis with engines of 160 or less CID, the first event on the original schedule for the day, was not run due to a lack of entries.

Buick drivers Louis Chevrolet and Bob Burman were the headliners for the ten-mile championship for stock chassis with engines of 161 - 230 CID. Lee Frayer in a Firestone-Columbus and Arthur Miller in a Warren-Detroit hoped to play the role of spoilers. However, the race turned out to be a rather uneventful one. Frayer and Miller were simply no match for the Buicks, finishing third and fourth, respectively. At the front, Chevrolet led Burman from the start and never relinquished the lead. His time of 9:03.60 lowered the old mark of 9:49.46 made by Matson in a Chalmers at Atlanta. The race results follow.

| Place | Car # | Driver | Car | Laps | Led |
|---|---|---|---|---|---|
| 1 | 36 | Louis Chevrolet | Buick | 4 | 4 |
| 2 | 35 | Bob Burman | Buick | 4 | 0 |
| 3 | 4 | Lee Frayer | Firestone-Columbus | 4 | 0 |
| 4 | 26 | Arthur Miller | Warren-Detroit | 4 | 0 |

The next race was the five-mile championship for stock chassis with engines of 231 - 300 CID. Ray Harroun and Joe Dawson, representing the Marmon team, were joined by the red Marion of Gil Anderson and the red Cuttings of George Clark and D. Bisbee.

Gil Anderson made an aggressive move from the outside to challenge the two Marmons at the start and secured the lead as he drifted through turn one. The Marion's speed continued to escalate but the Marmons were able to keep the pace while the Cuttings lagged far behind. On the second lap, Harroun tagged on to the back of Dawson's machine as the teammates drafted past Anderson down the backstretch. The two Marmons held their position as Dawson crossed the line in 4:41.34 to set a new world record for ten miles in this class. The old record was 4:48.00, set in Atlanta by Lewis Strang's Buick in 1909. The final results of the race follow.

| Place | Car # | Driver | Car | Laps | Led |
|---|---|---|---|---|---|
| 1 | 34 | Joe Dawson | Marmon | 2 | 1 |
| 2 | 33 | Ray Harroun | Marmon | 2 | 0 |
| 3 | 25 | Gil Anderson | Marion | 2 | 1 |
| 4 | 20 | George Clark | Cutting | 2 | 0 |
| 5 | 21 | D. Bisbee | Cutting | 2 | 0 |

*Marmon driver Ray Harroun. (Photo courtesy of the Indianapolis Motor Speedway)*

Before the next race, Barney Oldfield brought his big Benz onto the track for trial runs at the one kilometer and one mile records. The press called Oldfield's Benz the fastest and most expensive car in the world, placing the value at around $22,000. Due to a defect in the electrical timing, his first attempt was not timed. On his second attempt he drew cheers from the crowd as he breezed through the one-kilometer mark in 21.45 seconds to set a new American record, breaking his old mark of 23.51 seconds set in the same car at Los Angeles. His mile time was 37.11 seconds, short of his 36.22 second record that he previously set in Los Angeles.

The five-mile free-for-all race had the promise to be a great battle. The Nationals of Aitken, Kincaid, and Greiner were up against Burman's Buick, Bragg's Fiat, and Kirscher's Darracq. Burman had the misfortune of breaking a gear at the start and never even made it to the first turn. Pieces from his Buick were thrown onto the track, forcing his crew to scramble from the pits to clean up the mess. Meanwhile, Caleb Bragg made another one of his patented quick starts to jump into the lead. Bragg executed a different strategy than had been seen in previous races by running way up towards the concrete wall on the high side of the track. This departure from the usual racing groove caused the fans to look on in bewilderment. Kirscher, Aitken, Kincaid, and Greiner, in that order, stayed behind the Fiat but on the inside of the track. The four drivers strained onward trying desperately to close the agonizing interval made by Bragg's Fiat but to no avail. Bragg was never challenged as he led both laps to claim the victory in 3:34.70. The four remaining drivers never shifted positions, finishing in the same order that they had started. The final results of the race follow.

| Place | Car # | Driver | Car | Laps | Led |
|---|---|---|---|---|---|
| 1 | 14 | Caleb Bragg | Fiat | 2 | 2 |
| 2 | 54 | Ben Kirscher | Darracq | 2 | 0 |
| 3 | 8 | Johnny Aitken | National | 2 | 0 |
| 4 | 7 | Tom Kincaid | National | 2 | 0 |
| 5 | 48 | Arthur Greiner | National | 2 | 0 |
| 6 | 41 | Bob Burman | Buick | 2 | 0 |

The next race was the ten-mile championship for stock chassis with engines of 231 - 300 CID. This event was a rematch of the same five cars which had battled for the five-mile championship in this class earlier in the day. As in that contest, Gil Anderson thundered into the first turn establishing a lead on the rest of the field. After fading to third in the previous match, he looked more determined than ever to bring home the victory for the Marion team. He drove through the first five miles in 4:47.10 closely followed by Dawson and Harroun. It looked as if Anderson would win this one because he had command of the race going into the fourth and final lap; but, in one heartbreaking instant, his red machine began to falter. That allowed the Marmons and the Cutting of George Clark to get around him. Harroun was able to overtake his teammate on the final corner to win the race in a time of 9:25.31. Dawson finished second to complete the Marmon sweep while Clark took third, pushing Anderson back to fourth. The results of the race follow.

| Place | Car # | Driver | Car | Laps | Led |
|---|---|---|---|---|---|
| 1 | 33 | Ray Harroun | Marmon | 4 | 1 |
| 2 | 34 | Joe Dawson | Marmon | 4 | 0 |
| 3 | 20 | George Clark | Cutting | 4 | 0 |
| 4 | 25 | Gil Anderson | Marion | 4 | 3 |
| 5 | 21 | D. Bisbee | Cutting | 4 | 0 |

Surprisingly, Barney Oldfield dominated the next race, the five-mile championship for stock chassis with engines of 451 - 600 CID. Everyone expected the three Nationals of Aitken, Kincaid, and Merz to give Oldfield a stiff challenge but that never materialized. Oldfield's big Knox ran away from the Nationals, easily winning in 4:01.36 and breaking his record that he had set on Saturday by 2.08 seconds! The final results of the race follow.

| Place | Car # | Driver | Car | Laps | Led |
|---|---|---|---|---|---|
| 1 | 46 | Barney Oldfield | Knox | 2 | 2 |
| 2 | 9 | Johnny Aitken | National | 2 | 0 |
| 3 | 10 | Tom Kincaid | National | 2 | 0 |
| 4 | 11 | Charlie Merz | National | 2 | 0 |

Aitken and Kincaid were immediately pressed back into action for the five-mile championship for stock chassis with engines of 301 - 450 CID. National teammate Charlie Merz joined them along with Joe Dawson in a Marmon and Fred Ellis in a Jackson. Aitken looked like a streak of blue lightning as he shot from the standing start with a fury. The lead didn't last long; however, because Kincaid eventually caught him before the first lap was over, and positioned his car in front as the first lap ended. The cars resembled a long, swift blue train as the Nationals of Aitken and Merz followed close behind. Dawson and Ellis remained further back in fourth and fifth, respectively. Aitken was able to swoop alongside of his good friend Kincaid as the two raced out of the final turn on the last lap. He surged forward to cross the finish line ahead of him with a time of 4:06.70. Merz, Dawson, and Ellis completed the race in that order. The final results of the race follow.

| Place | Car # | Driver | Car | Laps | Led |
|---|---|---|---|---|---|
| 1 | 9 | Johnny Aitken | National | 2 | 1 |
| 2 | 10 | Tom Kincaid | National | 2 | 1 |
| 3 | 11 | Charlie Merz | National | 2 | 0 |
| 4 | 31 | Joe Dawson | Marmon | 2 | 0 |
| 5 | 18 | Fred Ellis | Jackson | 2 | 0 |

There were 15 starters in the five-mile free-for-all handicap event. Consistent with the previous handicap races, cars started at different times creating a long, drawn out procession of racing machines around the two-and-a-half-mile oval. This resulted in the usual shifts for position. Arthur Miller suffered one of the biggest changes in position when he finished in eleventh place after leading the first lap. Newell Motsinger fared no better. The Empire driver was the first to start and the last to finish. The real story of the race was Jack Reed, who surprised everyone by driving a Stoddard-Dayton to victory. Reed, employed by the Fisher Automobile Company, was a newcomer to racing and drove a car that was owned by James Allison. He won the race in a time of 4:55.65. Johnny Aitken, starting his third race in a row, gave it a valiant effort, charging from fourteenth place on the first lap to finish in third place just behind William Tousey's National. Again, the local papers did not publish a complete list of the results the following day.

*Indianapolis native and driver for the National team Johnny Aitken. (Photo courtesy of the Indianapolis Motor Speedway)*

The Indianapolis-made Nationals were on the track again after the handicap race to battle the brown Knox of Barney Oldfield for the championship in the ten-mile race for stock chassis with engines of 451 - 600 CID. Oldfield led all four laps, winning in 7:50.75, but it wasn't an easy win. The three National drivers bunched together, drafting off of each other throughout the race in an effort to charge past the big Knox in one long line. While they almost succeeded on several occasions, Oldfield was ablc to fight off every serious challenge. This was his second win of the day and third for the three-day program. The race summary follows.

| Place | Car # | Driver | Car | Laps | Led |
|---|---|---|---|---|---|
| 1 | 46 | Barney Oldfield | Knox | 4 | 4 |
| 2 | 11 | Howard Wilcox | National | 4 | 0 |
| 3 | 10 | Tom Kincaid | National | 4 | 0 |
| 4 | 9 | Johnny Aitken | National | 4 | 0 |

Before the next race, the announcers called forth Blanche Scott, who was driving from New York to San Francisco in an attempt to become the first woman to cross the continent alone in an automobile without any assistance from male mechanics. She drove her pure white Overland car onto the track to the thunderous applause of the huge Speedway crowd.

Johnny Aitken started his fifth race in a row as he lined up for the start of the ten-mile championship for stock chassis with engines of 301 - 450 CID. He was joined by National teammates Tom Kincaid and Charlie Merz, the Marmon of Dawson, and the Jackson driven by Fred Ellis – essentially a rematch of the five-mile championship for this class run earlier in the day.

Aitken led the charge into turn one and Merz tucked in behind him for second place. Kincaid ran third followed by Dawson and Ellis. Merz zipped past Aitken heading down the frontstretch to end the second lap but could only hold on to the lead for a brief moment. Aitken seemed to put his machine into overdrive as he swung around Merz and drove it hard into turn one before slamming the door on his teammate. This caused Merz to lose some momentum and allowed Kincaid to get past him as well. Aitken's lead was not threatened over the final two laps. He won in a time of 7:57.10. To the approval of the crowd, this lowered his own mark of 8:08.03 set Saturday, which had bettered the mark that he set on Friday. This was the second win of the day for Aitken, both on his second try of back-to-back races. Kincaid and Merz made it the second one-two-three sweep of the day for the National team. Ironically, the finishing order was exactly the same as that in the five-mile race for the championship in this class. The results follow.

| Place | Car # | Driver | Car | Laps | Led |
|---|---|---|---|---|---|
| 1 | 9 | Johnny Aitken | National | 4 | 3 |
| 2 | 10 | Tom Kincaid | National | 4 | 0 |
| 3 | 11 | Charlie Merz | National | 4 | 1 |
| 4 | 31 | Joe Dawson | Marmon | 4 | 0 |
| 5 | 18 | Fred Ellis | Jackson | 4 | 0 |

A ten-mile free-for-all race brought the Fiat of Caleb Bragg and the ageless Darracq of Ben Kirscher back on the track to race against a pair of Nationals driven by Johnny Aitken and Arthur Greiner. Incredibly, Aitken was participating in his sixth consecutive race of the day! The crowd really pulled for the hometown driver to get his third win of the day but it was not meant to be. Instead, there was another great story made during the race.

Caleb Bragg, with the advantage of another fine start, flashed his Fiat into the lead ahead of Kirscher's Darracq. These two cars began to put some distance between themselves and the Nationals of Aitken and Greiner with each lap. Swerving back and forth trying to create an opening that wasn't there, Kirscher was all over the back of Bragg's Fiat. Bragg continued to forge ahead, knowing that the slightest mistake would send the Darracq to the front. He drove a great race to hold off Kirscher. The quiet Cincinnati driver earned his third win of the day. Bragg's time was 7:20.60, just a little faster than the green Darracq of Ben Kirscher.

This would be Bragg's final win at the Speedway and his last race at Indianapolis until the 1911, 1912, and 1913 500s. Equally as impressive was the job done by Ben Kirscher during the three-day program with a five-year-old car. He never won a race but was right there at the finish for several of them. The race results follow.

| Place | Car # | Driver | Car | Laps | Led |
|-------|-------|--------|-----|------|-----|
| 1 | 14 | Caleb Bragg | Fiat | 4 | 4 |
| 2 | 54 | Ben Kirscher | Darracq | 4 | 0 |
| 3 | 8 | Johnny Aitken | National | 4 | 0 |
| 4 | 48 | Arthur Greiner | National | 4 | 0 |

Before the last event of the day, Barney Oldfield was given another chance to break the American record for the mile in his Benz. Oldfield did not disappoint his fans. He raced the big Benz to a new American one-mile record of 35.63 seconds for an average of 101.1 mph. This broke his own record of 36.22 seconds set in the same car at Los Angeles.

The crowd had enjoyed every minute of racing but it had been a long day and everyone was more than ready for the finale, the 50-mile race for the Remy Grand Brassard and trophy cup. The Brassard, an arm shield made of silver, carried a $50 weekly salary, $75 weekly if the winning car was equipped with a Remy magneto. This lasted until the Remy Grand Brassard race was run again. The Remy Grand trophy, a magnificent silver vase-shaped cup with a value of $2,500, was awarded to the company that owned the winning car. The Remy brothers, who owned the largest plant in the world devoted exclusively to the manufacture of automobile ignition systems, had been enthusiastic supporters of the Indianapolis Motor Speedway from the very beginning. The Anderson, Indiana, plant's 1,000 workers produced magnetos that were shipped out in carloads all over the country.

The first half of the race was a real thriller between the Marmon of Ray Harroun and the Pope-Hartford driven by Frank Fox of Terre Haute, Indiana. Harroun led the first two laps, but Frank Fox stayed right with him to take the lead and hold it for the third and fourth laps. The next four laps were hotly contested between the two drivers as the lead changed hands on every lap. Joe Dawson was able to hold off the rest of the field to maintain third place.

The Pope-Hartford began to suffer from excessive tire wear after leading the ninth lap, allowing Harroun to gain permanent control of the lead with Dawson slipping by Fox for second place. Meanwhile, the two Cuttings driven by Clark and Bisbee dropped out of the race, followed by the Jackson of Scheifler. Harroun was never challenged for the lead again, and raced to the win in 42:31.33, followed by his teammate Dawson just under 12 seconds back.

*The silver Remy Grand Brassard arm shield awarded at all of the race programs held at the Indianapolis Motor Speedway during 1909 and 1910. The Brassard is on display at the Speedway Museum. (Photo taken by Ron McQueeney of the Indianapolis Motor Speedway)*

Harroun's winning time was a new record for 50 miles, but he managed to set new records for 20, 30, and 40 miles as well. He broke Lewis Strang's record for 20 miles of 23:20.10 set in Atlanta by completing the eight laps in 21:48.90. Harroun's other records, 30 miles in 26:06.11 and 40 miles in 34:25.40, broke his own records that he had set in Atlanta. It was truly a remarkable performance for Ray Harroun, considering that earlier in the day he crashed one of the Marmon "Wasps" during a practice run. When a front tire blew out, it had sent the Marmon hurling down the backstretch where it straddled the cement retaining wall for about 110 feet before it plunged through the wall and tore out a four-foot section. It was quite a testament to Harroun's courage that he could continue to race unnerved after such an accident. Ironically, the accident happened *exactly* one year to the day before Harroun would drive another Marmon "Wasp" to victory in the inaugural Indianapolis 500. The final results of the race follow.

| Place | Car # | Driver | Car | Laps | Led |
|-------|-------|--------|-----|------|-----|
| 1 | 33 | Ray Harroun | Marmon | 20 | 15 |
| 2 | 34 | Joe Dawson | Marmon | 20 | 0 |
| 3 | 3 | Frank Fox | Pope-Hartford | 20 | 5 |
| 4 | 29 | Tom Kincaid | Great Western | 20 | 0 |
| 5 | 25 | Gil Anderson | Marion | 20 | 0 |
| 6 | 26 | Arthur Miller | Warren-Detroit | 17 | 0 |
| 7 | 15 | E. F. Scheifler | Jackson | 13 | 0 |
| 8 | 20 | George Clark | Cutting | 12 | 0 |
| 9 | 21 | D. Bisbee | Cutting | 0 | 0 |

*Ray Harroun's crashed Marmon Wasp. Harroun crashed earlier in the day prior to winning the Remy Grand Brassard and trophy race on May 30, 1910, exactly one year to the day before his win in the inaugural Indianapolis 500. (Photo courtesy of the Indianapolis Motor Speedway)*

Following the end of the final race of the day, the Speedway was a scene of hurrying workers pulling up stakes and moving out of the garages. Supplies were frantically packed and carted to the freight house while the cars were driven to town and put on trains for their return trip to the factories. The huge throng of spectators began to file from the Speedway grounds as quickly as possible to begin the journey to their respective homes. Within a few hours after the Remy Grand Brassard race, peace reigned at the Speedway once again.

The Indianapolis cars dominated the three-day program by winning 12 of the 24 races. Ray Harroun and Johnny Aitken led the contingent with four wins apiece during the three-day meet. There were plenty of other stories from the three days of racing as well: Caleb Bragg's three wins in one day, Barney Oldfield's three wins plus new records for one kilometer and one mile, Johnny Aitken's incredible run of starting in six consecutive races, and the impressive performance of Ben Kirscher in his five-year-old Darracq. It will never be known how the Buicks might have fared had they been allowed to enter cars in every class. The fans had to wait until the next three-day program in July to get that answer. One thing was certain though; everyone in attendance – drivers, manufacturers and fans – agreed that the three-day program was a huge success and put Indianapolis on the map as having the finest racing facility in America, if not the world.

*Chapter 7*

# The Wright Brothers and the Brickyard

The busy pace at the Indianapolis Motor Speedway during 1910 continued when the aviation meet began just two weeks after the May auto races. A few of the aviators had already completed practice flights at the Speedway in mid-May to become acquainted with the Speedway's layout, but the majority of them began arriving in Indianapolis the week before the meet.

Many people were looking forward to the aviation meet. It had only been a little over six years since the Wright brothers had made their first flight at Kitty Hawk, North Carolina, and the majority of the people in and around Indianapolis had never seen an aeroplane in flight. With the interest displayed in the 1909 balloon races, the success of the Wright brothers, and the appearance of Halley's Comet just before May's auto races, everyone was anxious to witness the wonder of flight firsthand. It was this curiosity, plus the promise that the Wright brothers themselves were coming to the Speedway, that drove the brisk sale of advance tickets for the meet.

The Indianapolis meet was unique. It was open to all aviators regardless of whether or not they had a license from the Wright Company. The Wright brothers were in the middle of a patent battle on their invention, which led to an intense rivalry with the other aeroplane manufacturers. Consequently, the Wright brothers normally did not permit aviators from rival companies to fly with them.

The Speedway did not want to confine its meet to any one make of aeroplane. The goal was to open it up to all manufacturers with the world's greatest pilots at the controls. On the other hand, the Wright brothers thought that it would weaken their patent case if they let other aeroplanes fly along with them. In the end, it took the generosity of the Speedway management and the desire of the Wright brothers to promote the sport and the industry, to agree to permit any and all aeroplanes and pilots to fly at the Speedway without even payment of a license fee. At the time, this was the only meet at which other than Wright aeroplanes or pilots would be allowed to participate without paying a license fee. Pilots who flew without a license were required to provide an advance deposit of a large bond to cover later fines in case the courts ruled in favor of the Wright brothers on the patent issue. In other words, those who put on meets without the direct permission from the Wright brothers did so at the risk of prosecution. Naturally, the Speedway wanted to avoid such a possibility. Therefore, at what Carl Fisher estimated to be a cost of $95,000, the

*Frank Coffyn, Ralph Johnstone, Wilbur Wright, Orville Wright, and Walter Brookins seated on the ground near a Wright Flyer in the infield at the Indianapolis Motor Speedway in 1910. (Photo courtesy of Special Collections and Archives, Wright State University)*

Speedway management had removed all obstacles to ensure the success of what many were predicting would be the greatest aviation meet in history.

Activity in and around the big aerodrome at the Speedway really began to pick up the week before the meet. The papers covered the story of the Wright Company unloading two biplanes on Tuesday, June 7 that had been shipped to the Speedway by train with more on the way from Dayton, Ohio. The Wright pilots arrived in Indianapolis the next day to begin trial flights on Friday, but Mother Nature did not cooperate with the pilots. The trials were a rainout and rescheduled for 9:00 a.m. Saturday morning.

There were a total of 11 entries for the meet, six of which represented the Wright brothers. Roy Knabenshue, manager for the Wright brothers, was disappointed that there were not more entries. "I regret that more rivals of the Wrights have not entered," Mr. Knabenshue said. "Many of them have been clamoring for a chance to meet us in competition. We have given them every opportunity to line up against us."[1]

The Wright pilots were graduates of the Wright "School for Skylarks" at Simms Station near Dayton, Ohio. The Wright brothers ran this school, consisting of an open field, to teach aviators how to handle their aeroplanes. The Wrights trained many good pilots including Captain Charles Rolls who, on June 2, 1910, completed the first flight across the English Channel and back. Incidentally, Charles Rolls, who had joined with F.H. Royce to form the Rolls-Royce automobile company, was killed in an aeroplane crash less than a month after the Indianapolis aviation meet.

Those pilots flying the Wright brothers' biplanes were Al Welsh, Walter Brookins, Frank Coffyn, Arch Hoxsey, Ralph Johnstone, and Duval La Chappelle. Four other biplane pilots were from Indianapolis: Joseph Curzon in a Farman, Mel Marquette (who went on to drive in the first two Indianapolis 500-mile races) with his own Marquette, Russell Shaw in his own Shaw, and George Bumbaugh in a Fisher-Indianapolis biplane. Lincoln Beachey of Toledo, Ohio, was the only pilot entered with a monoplane, which was of his own creation.

Joseph Curzon was noted as making the first aeroplane flight at the Speedway. On March 5, Curzon had made several successful ascensions in his Farman biplane in preparation for the aviation meet before placing it in the aerodrome. However, as the wind died down, he decided to make another flight. Unfortunately, his engine stalled shortly after takeoff sending the pilot crashing to the ground. Curzon was not injured but his biplane suffered about $300 in damages, most notably the propeller.

Before the rain on Friday, the Overland wind wagon managed to make an appearance in the morning. It provided a big surprise when Carl Baumhofer, head tester at the Overland factory, attained a speed of 53 mph. The wind wagon was the first to be seen in the Midwest and the first, it was said, to prove such a success. It was a regular stock Overland automobile aided by a wooden propeller with added controls exactly the same as an aeroplane. George Bumbaugh, who had considerable experience in making propellers for aeroplanes, made the propeller, which was eight feet in diameter. Superintendent Fred Rinker and the foreman of the machine department, George Mead, built the wind wagon in secret at the Overland factory. It weighed 1,800 pounds and looked similar to an ordinary Overland test car. However, the drive shaft was run back straight almost to the rear axle instead of being run back and down to the rear axle as in an ordinary automobile. The gear on the end of it had a chain that ran over a similar gear about two feet higher up on another drive shaft. At the end of the top driveshaft was the wooden propeller. There was a six-inch clearance between the propeller and the ground. The car was driven by the power of the revolving propeller, which made about 750 revolutions a minute, producing a tremendous current of air. The 53 mph speed obtained on Friday was considered remarkable, because Mr. Baumhofer had hoped to obtain at least 30 mph.

The wind wagon was considered the twelfth entrant in the meet and was used to give demonstrations in addition to racing against the aeroplanes. It received a special paint job at the Overland factory before the meet with the number 12 painted on the front.

The pilots were finally able to make trial flights on Saturday, but it was late afternoon before the winds had subsided enough to allow them to fly. Walter Brookins took his Wright biplane out at about 5:30 p.m. for the first attempt of the day. After a run of about 100 feet on the monorail located near the aerodrome, the biplane rose gracefully into the air at an altitude of about 250 feet. Unlike other planes, the Wright biplanes were not typically equipped with wheels so a monorail system was used. The aeroplanes were brought from the aerodrome on temporary wheels, which were removed as the aeroplanes were placed on the monorail. After the propeller was turned, the engines started and the pilot was in his seat, someone ran alongside the aeroplane to guide the wing. When the aeroplane reached the end of the monorail, it lifted off to begin its flight. Brookins flew the biplane around one lap of the course with what seemed like little effort. He rose to an altitude of 400 feet for the second lap of the course, dipping the wings of his biplane as he passed over the heads of the small crowd on hand to witness the trials. He went up to 500 feet in making a third and fourth lap of the course at speeds of approximately 40 mph. In landing, the biplane slid along the ground for about 25 feet before coming to a gentle halt within a few feet of the original starting point.

After the first flight by Brookins, other Wright pilots took to the air for trials. Arch Hoxsey went through several successful maneuvers before making a gentle landing in the same biplane that Brookins had used for his flight. Later in the evening, Brookins achieved an altitude of 1,560 feet as measured by the other pilots with the aid of instruments. Wilbur Wright, the older of the Wright brothers, was on hand to

*The Overland wind wagon during the June 1910 aviation meet at the Indianapolis Motor Speedway. (Photo courtesy of the Indianapolis Motor Speedway)*

watch the trials which lasted until about 7:30 p.m. that evening. Carl Fisher gave him a ride around the two-and-a-half-mile brick track in his Stoddard-Dayton after which Mr. Wright paid the Speedway a great compliment by calling it one of the greatest, if not the greatest, place of its kind in the world. It surprised some that Mr. Wright rode around the track as it had been reported that he cared very little for the automobile. Among other reasons he said that the automobile was somewhat objectionable because the rider was soon covered with dust and dirt.

Upon completion of the trial flights, the stage was set for the opening of the aviation meet on Monday, June 13. The Speedway management had prepared for crowds larger than any ever seen at an aviation meet and expected spectators from all parts of Indiana, Dayton, Ohio, and many parts of the Midwest.

The inside of the Speedway grounds had been transformed into an almost perfect aviation field. The aeroplane course, 150-feet wide and a mile and a half in distance, was situated at the southern end of the two-and-a-half-mile brick track. It was laid out so that the pilots took off from the monorail by the aerodrome at the south end of the track. They circled inside the track passing in front of the grandstands, providing the spectators with a complete view of the aeroplanes in flight. The circuit was marked with American flags and a white line wide enough that it could be seen from the grandstands as well as the air. Director of Contests at the Speedway, Ernst Moross, had devised a system of triangular flags by which the spectators scattered around the grounds could determine the status of the events. A white flag meant that the conditions were such that the pilots would

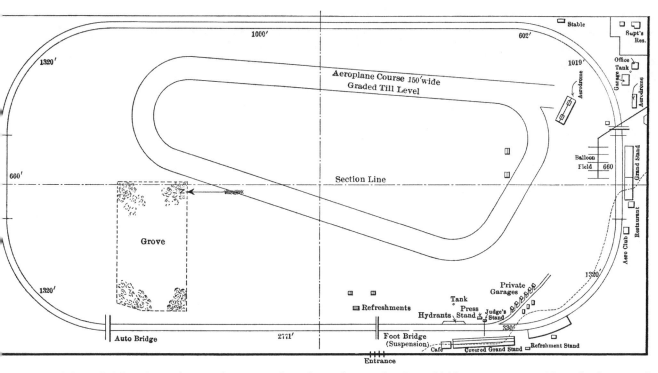

*Diagram of the infield at the Indianapolis Motor Speedway during the June 1910 aviation meet. Note the layout of the aeroplane course and the location of the large aerodrome in the upper right-hand corner (southeast corner of the track).*

flying. If they would not be flying, a black flag was displayed. A white flag with a heavy black stripe through the middle meant that flights were possible later in the day.

The first day's activities were scheduled to begin at 2:00 p.m. with the following events on the schedule.

1. 5-lap exhibition by Walter Brookins
2. 5-lap exhibition by Al Welsh
3. 5-lap pursuit race between Walter Brookins and Frank Coffyn
4. 5-lap pursuit race between Al Welsh and Ralph Johnstone
5. 5 to 10-lap pursuit race between Al Welsh and Walter Brookins
6. 5 to 10-lap pursuit race between Ralph Johnstone / Al Welsh vs. Frank Coffyn / Walter Brookins
7. Attempts to establish an Indianapolis Motor Speedway record for altitude
8. Match race between two or more aeroplanes with entries to be announced

Orville Wright preceded the activities on Monday by making a short flight just before noon. His biplane left the monorail at the entrance of the aerodrome and glided gradually into the air rising to an altitude of about 75 feet. He flew in a northerly direction until reaching the end of the Speedway grounds where he followed the turn of the brick racing surface as he headed back toward the south end. He increased his altitude to about 125 feet before making two laps of the course. After completing the second lap, he flew to the center of the Speedway and performed two complete circles in the air before making an approach toward the aerodrome, safely landing close to his original starting point.

The attendance on Monday presented a far different scene than those from the recent auto races. At 1:30 p.m., a half an hour before the start of the events, fewer than 500 people were in the main grandstand while the bleachers were relatively empty. Carl Fisher did not look for many spectators until the middle of the week, at which time he expected the crowds to approach those seen at the recent auto races. The grandstands did not fill up much more by the 2:00 p.m. start time, approaching just short of 2,000 in total.

The events of the day did not follow along exactly as the program had outlined, but the crowd was kept informed of the happenings. A man with a megaphone stood close to the starting point of the aeroplanes and announced to another man with a megaphone the heights attained, speed, names of the pilots, and other interesting information. This second man then made the announcements to the spectators, such as informing them of the delay in getting the program started. The day's events were late getting started due to the great care the Wrights and their assistants took in preparing the biplanes for flight. At 2:00 p.m. the biplanes were still in the aerodrome receiving final preparations. In the meantime, the Indianapolis Military Band entertained the spectators in the main grandstand and the City Band played music in the south bleachers. Not long after aeroplane number 1 was set onto the monorail, two assistants counting "one, two, three," revolved the propellers and started the engine. Finally, at 2:48 p.m. Walter Brookins, wearing his cap backwards, took a seat in the biplane and grasped the control lever as the biplane gained momentum while rolling down the monorail. The biplane began to ascend, and the first national licensed aviation meet was under way. Brookins flew east and over the aerodrome before soaring gracefully around the track. At the end of his fifth lap, he lowered the biplane to the grass and slid along the ground for a few yards before coming to a stop. Brookins' total flight time was 6 minutes and 45 seconds.

While pulleys were being placed under the biplane to be hauled back toward the monorail for a later flight, Al Welsh ascended in another Wright biplane at approximately 3:04 p.m. He was only in the air for a little over two minutes before landing. It was determined that he left the monorail before the biplane had reached the end of the track. This was due to the uneven condition of the ground, so various workers helped in moving the monorail a few feet to level ground. It was moved in sections and positioned running north to south when assembled.

*The Wright brothers and others working on a launch rail similar to the one used at the Speedway during the June 1910 aviation meet. (Photo courtesy of Special Collections and Archives, Wright State University)*

Walter Brookins, tossing cigarette aside, climbed into another Wright biplane and ascended skyward at 3:36 p.m. to start the third event of the day. He was scheduled to complete five laps along with Frank Coffyn in another biplane; however, Coffyn did not join him for this flight. Brookins ascended to about 200 feet before displaying some expert maneuvering on his second lap – making sharp turns and shooting suddenly downward at times. After remaining in the air for almost nine minutes, he swooped down over the heads of the spectators like a big hawk before bringing the biplane to an easy, graceful escent. Many of the Wright assistants clapped as he landed. The Wright brothers themselves grinned because Brookins had just given Indianapolis its most picturesque flight to date.

Two Wright biplanes were sent into the sky for the next event. Al Welsh and Ralph Johnstone controlled one while Walter Brookins and Frank Coffyn occupied the other. Welsh and Johnstone negotiated the first lap of the course in 1 minute and 45 seconds, the best time to date. They stayed in the air a total of 12 minutes and 40 seconds. Brookins and Coffyn had descended a few minutes earlier.

In the fifth event, Brookins was successful in his attempt to break his Speedway record for altitude that he had established during Saturday's trials. Obeying Orville Wright's order to "show 'em something," Brookins soared to 284.5 feet on his first lap of the course. On his second lap he ascended to 1,124.5 feet. Then shortening his circles, he began to fly in the center of the field where he reached a height of 2,093 feet. Immediately, the pilot began lowering himself, dropping to a height of 306 feet, before making a quick landing after 18 minutes and 30 seconds of flying. The 2,093 feet attained by Brookins was not only the highest altitude obtained to date at the Speedway but also the highest altitude obtained by an American aeroplane. Wilbur Wright commented, "The air is boiling. Conditions are not just right for an altitude flight but they will improve later in the afternoon".[2] The events later in the day would prove just how accurate he was with his prediction.

*Frank Coffyn in a Wright Flyer. (Photo courtesy of Special Collections and Archives, Wright State University)*

Next, Al Welsh and Ralph Johnstone teamed together in a Wright biplane. The pair flew around the course for five laps for a total flight time of 9 minutes and 45 seconds. Arch Hoxsey and Walter Brookins versus Ralph Johnstone and Al Welsh in a match race was the next event of the day and featured one of the most unique maneuvers ever seen. After traveling the course on different sides, the two biplanes met up at the north end of the Speedway, flying side-by-side toward the southern end of the Speedway where Hoxsey and Brookins turned their biplane to the right, returning in a northerly direction. At the same time, Johnstone and Welsh steered to the left, also heading back in a northerly direction. According to the Wrights, this pattern had never been attempted before because they feared the rush of air would hamper both biplanes as they simultaneously made their turns back to the north. The move was successfully repeated several times. As they raced, Hoxsey and Brookins usually led at the end of each lap. They landed after about 12 minutes of flight time. Welsh and Johnstone landed about a minute later.

That evening, Walter Brookins took off in a Wright biplane for another attempt at increasing the altitude record. The biplane was equipped with a recording device to measure altitude while the Wright brothers and A.B. Lambert of the St. Louis Aero Club took measurements from the ground with the Wright altitude device. Wilbur Wright estimated that Brookins had reached about 350 feet after little more than a minute in the air. Brookins was circling the entire aeroplane course, gracefully rounding the curves, rising to about 1,875 feet, as measured on the ground, after about seven and a half minutes. As he flew far to the south, still heading upward, Wilbur Wright gazed up at the aeroplane and said, "He is knocking all records silly. He's going 40 mph!"[3] As he continued to go higher, the buzz of the little motor became fainter and fainter until it could barely be heard. Brookins had been in the air for almost 18 minutes when he passed over their heads again. Cheers greeted Mr. Lambert's announcement that the altitude device had taken a measurement of 3,476 feet. Brookins continued to climb higher as Wilbur Wright declared, "The machine looks like it is standing still."[4] Confirmation that the aeroplane was not standing still came shortly after that as Mr. Lambert read another measurement, 4,187 feet! This news was greeted by shouts of "Paulhan's beaten!"[5] This referred to Frenchman Louis Paulhan who had set the previous altitude record of 4,165 feet at the Los Angeles aviation meet on January 12, 1910. Still, the 21-year-old pilot from Dayton, Ohio, continued upward as he appeared to be carried by the breeze. After passing over spectator's heads, he again flew off to the south, circled around to the east, then north, before heading back in a southerly direction over the crowd for what would be one last measurement. The Wright contingent roared with approval as the height was announced at 4,384.5 feet!

Having made history, Brookins appeared content with his triumph making a long trip around the course. He had passed higher than the altitude instruments could measure! The "man-bird", as the excited crowd began to call him, soared around for five or six minutes before dipping the front of his aeroplane towards the earth to begin his long descent. The history-making aeroplane glided grace-

*Arthur Welsh in a Wright Flyer. (Photo courtesy of Special Collections and Archives, Wright State University)*

fully to within a few feet of the ground when the motor gradually hushed and the runners struck the grass. Shortly after the aeroplane came to a stop, Brookins sprang from his seat with a slight smile across his face. Orville Wright was the first to rush up and say, "Congratulations," as he shook his hand enthusiastically. Then Wilbur Wright, Coffyn, Welsh and the rest of the Wright team arrived to welcome him back to earth.

Altogether Brookins was in the air for a little over 30 minutes, longer than he had ever been on any other trip. The feat was quite amazing, considering that Brookins only started flying in March of 1910 and had less than 15 hours in the air to his credit. "The air's pretty cold up there," Brookins said quietly after receiving handshakes from his fellow team members. "My right hand became numb shortly after I had been up and I had to rub it against the control lever time and again. The left was almost as bad but I did not permit it to get cramped."[6]

"Could you have gone higher?" someone asked.

"Sure," he answered in a modest tone. "But I didn't feel that it was necessary. I knew that I was going mighty high right at the start and then I kept the machine pointed upward after that. When I was in the south, I got lost. I saw things below me that I had never seen before."[7]

It was a day of triumph for the Wright flyers. The weather was ideal, and the crowd was astonished at the ease and accuracy with which the aeroplanes flew through the air. Additionally, the spectators were kept entertained as the events of the day were run with only a few intermissions. However, two accidents marred the program. A Fisher-Indianapolis biplane, flown by George Bumbaugh, was demolished in a fiery crash shortly after beginning a trial flight. Bumbaugh was badly shaken up and bruised but not seriously injured. After the scheduled events of the afternoon, while preparing for a flight to carry James

*A Wright Flyer in flight. (Photo courtesy of Special Collections and Archives, Wright State University)*

Allison, a Wright biplane caught fire from a gasoline explosion; however, the flames were extinguished before significant damage was done. Nevertheless, Mr. Allison decided to remain on the ground.

Around 7:30 p.m., Carl Fisher accepted Orville Wright's invitation for a flight around the Speedway. Since the sun had started to set about 7:15 p.m., the aviator took Mr. Fisher on a flight that lasted only about ten minutes but included some maneuvers such as dips, curves, and turns. "I've had a lot of respect for the Wright brothers for a long time, but I never had half as much respect as I have now," Mr. Fisher said as he climbed out of the aeroplane. He was happy to have had the chance to fly but also relieved to be on solid ground again. "I've had enough," he announced. "Believe me to be honest when I say I never will be a successful aviator. The way we hit things up there was a caution and if there are no dents in the framework where I had it gripped it is because I couldn't squeeze hard enough. I think we hit a bump in the air up there somewhere. I don't know exactly what it was, but it made an impression on me. Mr. Wright says it was a small whirlwind, but I am not so sure about the 'small' part of it."[8]

The scheduled events for the second day were as follows.

1. 5-lap exhibition by Ralph Johnstone
2. 5-lap exhibition by Duval La Chappelle
3. Quick start by Walter Brookins and Al Welsh
4. Short circle flight for record
5. Pursuit race between Walter Brookins, Al Welsh and Duval La Chappelle
6. Match race between Walter Brookins and Al Welsh
7. Trials to break the newly established altitude record

Thunderstorms shortly before noon threatened to cancel the second day's events. Despite the high winds and constant threat of additional storms, it was decided to continue with the program as much as possible with only Wright machines taking to the air. In spite of the weather, a crowd of 5,000 people made the trip to the Speedway – perhaps attracted by the record altitude obtained by Walter Brookins on Monday.

*A Wright Flyer leaving the launch rail during the June 1910 aviation meet at the Indianapolis Motor Speedway. The huge aerodrome can be seen in the background at the far left of the picture. (Photo courtesy of the Indianapolis Motor Speedway)*

The weather delayed the start of the program slightly, but Ralph Johnstone started things off a little after 2:30 p.m. with a 5-lap exhibition in a Wright biplane. Immediately after his flight, Al Welsh ascended for a 5-lap exhibition but encountered trouble with his motor, preventing him from rising more than ten feet off the ground. Welsh managed to keep the plane level, and gently glided it to the ground soon after take off.

"There can be no quick start as the program calls for," Orville Wright told Mr. Moross. "The wind is against us. We'll have to wait. We'll let Brookins go five laps for time."[9] With that, Walter Brookins climbed into one of the Wright biplanes and started down the monorail. He seemed to pick his route carefully and ascended no higher than 100 feet while circling the course six times in 15 minutes and seconds.

After finishing a cigarette, Brookins was ready to return to the skies in a race against the Overland wind wagon driven by Carl Baumhofer. Brookins flew north and circled around to get an even start with the wind wagon which was speeding to the south past the judges' stand. The wind wagon had the lead but the race got interesting on the turn at the north end of the track when Brookins began to overtake the wind wagon. As they made the turn at the northwest corner, both sped south toward the main grandstand with the crowd on its feet. Brookins went across the finish line first in 4 minutes and 58 seconds, winning by a very small margin.

The next event was to be a match race between Brookins and Welsh, but the propeller on Welsh aeroplane quit while he was in flight. This forced him to use all of his skill to make a safe landing. Meanwhile, Brookins continued his flight by making short circles, dips, and other impressive moves before bringing the aeroplane back to earth after a little over eight minutes in the air.

At 4:20 p.m., when the breeze was blowing the strongest it had all day, Brookins ascended to make one of the most thrilling flights of the week. Orville Wright, using the Wright altitude-measuring device, concluded that Brookins had soared to 395 feet at the end of the first lap of the course. As Brookins finished his second lap, Orville Wright pointed out that the presence of low-hanging clouds would prevent the pilot from achieving new record for altitude. Mr. Wright then called attention to the fact that the sun was behind the clouds. "Brookin can see it anyhow," said the Dayton inventor. "I flew in Dayton late one evening and saw the sun behind the clouds when it was not visible to those on earth. It was a beautiful sight."[10]

By the end of Brookins' third lap, he had obtained an altitude of 2,083 feet in a little over 12 minutes time. Shortly thereafter, he shut off the motor to begin his descent. At the end of the fourth lap, he was less than 100 feet above the ground, making one more lap before skillfully guiding his aeroplane to another safe landing.

The events of the second day came to a conclusion after Brookins' flight. However, the crowd got a chance to view one of the Wright biplanes up close as it was rolled out in front of the main grandstand. Spectators came running from their respective seats, anxious to inspect the aeroplane for themselves. After much persuasion, Walter Brookins hopped over the curbing to the track to join the crowd where he received an ovation. The spectators crowded around him shouting question after question. In describing the sensation in altitude flights, Brookins said, "I find very little difference between high flying and the ascents which do not carry the machine far from the ground. The only difference appears to be in the temperature. It is fearfully cold as you rise higher and I believe that an altitude will be reached eventually which will hamper the aviator to such an extent that he will not be able to handle his machine unless he wears special clothing to protect him from the cold. You see, an aeroplane is moving so rapidly that the wind causes the temperature to appear much lower than it would to a man in a balloon which is moving slowly upward."[11]

*Spectators at the June 1910 aviation meet rush to inspect a Wright Flyer that had been rolled out in front of the main grandstand at the Indianapolis Motor Speedway. (Photo courtesy of the Indianapolis Motor Speedway)*

As news of the aviators' exploits spread, the attendance began to pick up. Wednesday's crowd was estimated at around 19,000, perhaps helped slightly by thousands of visitors who were guests of the Indianapolis Trade Association. The program included eight events, highlighted by a quadruple flight with four Wright flyers in the air at the same time. The program of events included the following.

1. Exhibition flight by Walter Brookins
2. Exhibition flight by Ralph Johnstone
3. Quadruple flight by Arch Hoxsey, Frank Coffyn, Al Welsh and Walter Brookins
4. Short circle competition
5. Novelty race consisting of two aeroplanes circling in opposite directions
6. Match race between Walter Brookins and the Overland wind wagon
7. Pursuit race between Walter Brookins and Al Welsh
8. Trials to break the newly established altitude record

*An automobile and a Wright Flyer sit beside the huge aerodrome in the infield of the Indianapolis Motor Speedway during the June 1910 aviation meet. (Photo courtesy of Special Collections and Archives, Wright State University)*

Again, the weather interrupted the day's activities, so the events were rearranged from what had been scheduled in the program. However, Walter Brookins was still the first pilot to take to the skies. Although the breeze was very strong, Brookins ascended to circle the course at about 2:30 p.m. He performed many dips and quick ascensions while maintaining an altitude of 150 to 200 feet. After flying in a figure-eight formation a few times, he flew by the grandstand and bleachers, made one more lap of the course, and glided the aeroplane safely back to the ground.

"The wind is more severe than on Tuesday, making flying very difficult,"[12] Orville Wright said as Brookins landed. This prompted several of the Wright assistants to emphatically state that many of the other pilots would not even attempt to fly as Brookins did unless the wind subsided.

*Duval La Chapelle sitting in a Wright Flyer. (Photo courtesy of Special Collections and Archives, Wright State University)*

From a monorail laid in the middle of the field parallel to the one behind the judges' stand, Al Welsh took off shortly after his teammate had landed. Welsh ascended no more than 100 feet, making three and a half laps of the course before landing safely near his original take off point.

At about 3:15 p.m., the rain started to fall in large drops while the wind grew more powerful. Roy Knabenshue instructed his men to take the planes back to the aerodrome while the "may fly later" flags were displayed. Meanwhile, the soaked crowd divided its time between watching the Overland wind wagon perform on the track and listening to the bands play. By 4:00 p.m. the rain had stopped and the sun reappeared; but just when an aeroplane was being wheeled to the monorail, it started to rain again. This quickly caused a mad scramble among the spectators. Some ran to the main grandstand for protection while others left for their homes. In an effort to help entertain the remaining crowd during the delay, 16 Hoosier Zouaves gave an exhibition on the track. The original Zouaves were a French infantry unit composed of Algerians. Clad in red turbans with yellow tassels, green shirts with blue sashes, maroon pantaloons, white leggings and white shoes, the squad made an attractive appearance. The men even fired a salute before they marched off the track.

Finally, at 5:10 p.m. Brookins and Welsh started the third event of the day, a pursuit race between the two pilots. With their aeroplanes mounted on parallel monorails, Welsh secured a 20-second head start, flying north over the brick racing surface before turning southward. He was only 100 feet in the air and made the turn at the southeast end of the track first. Brookins had climbed to about 200 feet. Welsh had lapped Brookins by the end of the third lap, because Brookins sailed far to the north and outside of the Speedway boundaries while Welsh continued to make short laps. In the meantime, Arch Hoxsey joined the duo and kept his aeroplane less than 100 feet off of the ground. Shortly thereafter, Welsh and Hoxsey landed safely and were joined by Brookins – but not before the latter had obtained an altitude of 1,402 feet after 18 minutes of flying.

Attempting his first flight alone, Duval La Chappelle made a flight that lasted a little over seven and a half minutes. Ralph Johnstone followed up Chappelle's performance with a quick five-minute flight of his own.

By this time, it was after 7:00 p.m. and all but a few dozen spectators had departed for the day. However, Orville Wright was about ready to go for a flight of his own. Both he and Walter Brookins ascended in Wright biplanes and stayed in the air until after sundown. The small gathering that remained could only stand in wide-eyed wonder as the daring pilots maneuvered their aeroplanes in the dark. After the flight, Orville Wright commented that it was one of the most thrilling and awe-inspiring that he had ever taken. "After reaching an altitude of about 2,000 feet, a light appeared far below the western horizon," the aviator said. "Going up still farther I could see the sun."[13]

The threatening clouds in the west, along with the strong winds, kept many away from the Speedway on Thursday. Nevertheless, it turned out to be a brilliant day of flying for the Wright pilots. The scheduled events for the day were as follows.

1. Exhibition by members of the Wright team
2. Short circle event
3. Lap race
4. Match race with the Overland wind wagon
5. Novelty race
6. Trials to break the newly established altitude record

There were only three days remaining in the aviation meet. While the Wright Company pilots had all made flights, none of the amateur pilots had made it off the ground. Some of this was due to the unfavorable weather conditions. Others had tried but failed. Lincoln Beachey made an attempt to fly his monoplane Wednesday afternoon, but he broke his rudder when it smashed against the ground. Melvin Marquette, a young Indianapolis aviator, was busy installing a new motor with hopes of flying before the end of the meet. Joseph Curzon chose not to fly his Farman biplane because he thought that the aviation course had too many bumps. Russell Shaw, another Indianapolis aviator, had ambitions of ascending in his own plane as soon as he thought the winds were calm enough. Finally, George Bumbaugh did not expect to fly the rest of the week because he was still recovering from his accident on Monday. Despite injuries, he had been in attendance each day of the meet.

As scheduled all week, Walter Brookins opened the events of the day shortly after 2:00 p.m. with a 20-minute flight at an altitude of just under 1,000 feet. During the flight, Orville Wright told the spectators around him that Brookins was flying the same plane used by Wilbur Wright earlier in the year to fly over the Hudson River and circle the Statue of Liberty. Al Welsh and Ralph Johnstone made exhibition flights as well.

The crowd delighted in the next event, a rematch between Brookins and the Overland wind wagon. Carl Baumhofer, driver of the wind wagon, completed a lap of the two-and-one-half-mile track in a little over two minutes while Brookins flew the one-and-a-half-mile aeroplane course. After winning the first lap, Brookins was joined by Welsh as the two Wright biplanes flew side-by-side at an altitude of a little over 800 feet. At times, Brookins flying just above Welsh, provided the spectators with a formation that they had not witnessed all week.

After Welsh and Brookins descended from their flights, the pilots took a break in hopes that the wind would subside. Then, shortly before 4:30 p.m., Walter Brookins performed the most remarkable exhibition of the week. He flew his biplane to the south end of the course where, little more than 100 feet in the air, the daring young pilot nearly stood the plane on end before performing a series of death-defying spirals, shattering all known marks for a complete aeroplane revolution by completing a full circle in 6.4 seconds! "I was going 60 mph," exclaimed Brookins after the flight. "I was at an angle of 82 degrees, thus lacking only eight degrees of being at a right angle or straight up and down. Had I tried to turn at 90 degrees, the plane would have been useless and gravity would have sent the machine flopping to the ground. I think that no one will attempt the revolution any nearer a right angle than I. I believe it next to impossible to beat the time I made, therefore it seems the record will stand for many a day."[14]

The crowd could only stand in awe. Even his fellow aviators held their breaths. As Brookins sprang from the biplane after landing safely, he was greeted with enthusiastic applause. Even the reserved Wilbur Wright shouted, "I must shake that young man by the hand!" "One watch timed the complete circle in 6.2 seconds," said Orville Wright, "while another registered a little under 6.4 seconds so we will just call it 6.4 seconds. This beats the old record of a little over 11.0 seconds!"[15]

Wilbur Wright's response as someone asked him if Brookins would try to beat the record was "Never again with my consent," said the inventor, "I don't think he or anybody else could do it again and get away with it. It's once in a lifetime that the wind is as kind to Brookins as it was then. One little gust of wind hitting that machine at the moment he was at his deepest angle would have sent him over and heaven only knows what the result might have been. Those who saw Brookins make that turn have something to remember in the way of miracles, I don't want to see him try it again. I felt myself gasp when he did it."[16]

Soon after the spectators had settled down from Brookins' remarkable feat, Wright pilots Hoxsey, Welsh, and Johnstone took to the air for additional flights of varying length. Johnstone stayed in the air the longest with a flight of 44 minutes. Arch Hoxsey provided some anxious moments when his engine stalled while circling the aeroplane course. He passed outside the Speedway and out of site on his way down to earth. Everyone had pictures of a young pilot being hurled to his death running through their minds as the hysterical rush of press cars, along with the ambulance, rushed from the Speedway to the probable landing site. Hoxsey had been able to guide his aeroplane to a safe landing in a field about a mile southeast of the Speedway. It startled several cows and a horse at the sight but both pilot and aeroplane came away without injury or damage. When Hoxsey returned to the aerodrome he told the other aviators that he knew Johnstone was ascending, and fearing a midair crash, he decided to take himself far out of danger.

*Arch Hoxsey filling the radiator of a Wright Flyer with water. (Photo courtesy of Special Collections and Archives, Wright State University)*

Sometime after 6:30 p.m., Brookins put on his green sweater and climbed into one of the Wright biplanes. The sweater meant only one thing; Brookins was going for the altitude record. Upward he went until he was merely a dot as the sun was sinking. In fact, he was at such an altitude that the sun's rays shone on the bottom of the aeroplane. He didn't break his altitude record, only obtaining an altitude of 3,876 feet, but he did set a record for duration, having stayed in the air for 54 minutes and 20 seconds.

Friday's events were again hampered by the strong winds, which did not allow for any flights until 4:47 p.m. The crowd was larger than those of the previous days; however, many left before the flights concluded. A special train arrived in the morning, bringing close to 1,000 people from Dayton, Ohio, to see the Wright flyers. The original program called for the following events.

1. Trials to break the duration record
2. A novelty race
3. Trials to break the altitude record
4. A match race with the Overland wind wagon
5. Lap races
6. Short circle trials

The Overland wind wagon entertained those in the stands before the flights started by completing two laps around the brick track in 5 minutes and 30 seconds. As soon as the wind wagon finished, Walter Brookins ascended from the monorail in a Wright biplane for a flight lasting 13 minutes and 28 seconds. It's doubtful that the average spectator was as appreciative of this otherwise unspectacular flight as they should have been. The aviators told Orville Wright that they had measured the wind speed at about 35 mph during his flight. It was quite remarkable that Brookins could fly at all in winds that strong! However, the daring pilot did not seem to be afraid of it, ascending for another flight of just over 23 minutes shortly after he landed from the first one.

Governor Marshall made a brief appearance at the Speedway just after Brookins' second flight. He stayed long enough to inspect a few of the aeroplanes before shaking the Wright brothers' hands while remarking that he was fond of the flying game. "We're all proud of the Wright boys for their wonderful achievements,"[17] he said. As he was leaving, Arch Hoxsey began a flight that lasted about 15 minutes, during which he never climbed higher than about 500 feet. Soon afterwards, Lincoln Beachey rose several feet above the ground in his monoplane. Unfortunately, as Beachey was descending, one of the pins that held a wheel to the chassis broke, allowing the wheel to fly off. This caused the propeller to strike the ground as he landed, shattering it into several pieces. Beachey immediately began the task of replacing the propeller in hopes of making additional flights.

*Wilbur and Orville Wright talking to Walter Brookins (right) during the June 1910 aviation meet at the Indianapolis Motor Speedway. (Photo courtesy of the Smithsonian National Air and Space Museum, SI 2004-55418)*

Shortly after 6:30 p.m., Ralph Johnstone left the monorail in his Wright biplane followed by Brookins and Hoxsey. For several minutes the small crowd had the thrill of watching three Wright biplanes in the air at the same time. Hoxsey performed several low altitude feats before landing after about 27 minutes in the air. Johnstone rose to a height of 2,000 feet while staying in the air for over 55 minutes to break Brookins' duration record for the Speedway. But it was Brookins who provided some tense moments for the remaining spectators. It was clear to everyone that he was attempting to set a new altitude record as he began climbing immediately after taking off from the monorail. Soon afterward, Brookins was a mere dot in the sky while sailing in a broad circle. He had been seen as far away as Riverside Park, two miles east of the Speedway, where hundreds of people were also watching him. City Engineer Harry Klaus measured Brookins' altitude as 4,938 feet before he started descending, breaking his altitude record from Monday by 554 feet! It was almost dark as his aeroplane reversed its course and headed for the Speedway. Suddenly, the aeroplane vanished from sight, causing alarm from the small crowd, which included Brookins' parents and sister from Dayton, Ohio. Several people, including the Wright brothers, quickly alighted from the Speedway to look for the lost aviator. Everyone was concerned that he had been seriously injured, perhaps lying dead beneath the shattered biplane. Spotted almost by chance in a wheat field next to the County Poor Farm east of the Speedway, Brookins was found perched up on his machine calmly puffing on a cigarette. Upon learning of his official altitude reading he felt cheated because he was sure that he had exceeded a mile. "The instrument on the aeroplane registered 5,300 feet," said Brookins, "so firmly believing that I had climbed higher than a mile I started to descend but when I was 4,000 feet in the air I discovered that the motor was missing out so I shut it off and headed for the Speedway. But, tossed by the wind, I saw that I would be unable to reach that place so I picked out a spot in a nearby field and glided to earth."[18]

As some left to find out the fate of Brookins, Frank Coffyn ascended in a Wright biplane for a short flight around the aeroplane course. This was the last flight of the day. The Wright brothers viewed it as a successful day even though the wind prevented many of the scheduled flights.

Factory closings, coupled with the Wright brothers' amazing antics during the preceding week, fueled high expectations for larger crowds on the last day of the meet. However, the crowd was less than expected, possibly because of the high winds. The temperature climbed to 90 degrees on Saturday and the gusty conditions continued to cause problems for the pilots. The monorail added to their troubles. It began to come apart and required constant repairs. The original program for the day was as follows.

1. Trials to beat the short circle record
2. Novelty race
3. Exhibitions by the Wright pilots
4. Trials to break the flight duration record
5. Match race with the Overland wind wagon
6. Lap races

Walter Brookins opened the program shortly after 3:00 p.m. by making a grand entrance into the Speedway. He appeared in the eastern sky flying towards the Speedway. A monorail was moved to his landing site the previous night so that he could start the day's program by flying the aeroplane back into the Speedway. His surprise entrance was impressive and the spectators on hand cheered his arrival.

Shortly after Brookins landed, Carl Bumhofer entertained the crowd by driving the Overland wind wagon two laps around the brick racing surface to the applause of an appreciative crowd. The announcement was made that his time of 5 minutes and 25 seconds for five miles set a new world's record for a wind wagon.

While the wind wagon was completing its five-mile trip, Arch Hoxsey and Ralph Johnstone made a combined five unsuccessful attempts to ascend. The strong winds coupled with the problems experienced with the monorail prevented a successful ascension. Wilbur Wright tried to explain the failures to one of the local newspaper reporters standing a few feet away. "There is a strong side wind," said the

*Walter Brookins and Arch Hoxsey in a Wright Flyer. (Photo courtesy of Special Collections and Archives, Wright State University)*

Dayton aviator, "which the boys are not accustomed to. Also, they have done a great deal of flying this week, which has been unusual for them. It seems the strain has been a little too much. Besides, the monorail is not working properly."[19]

The Wright's star pupil, Walter Brookins, did manage to make a successful ascension about 4:15 p.m., followed about 20 minutes later by Hoxsey. The duo remained in the air together performing various stunts for about 15 minutes before landing almost simultaneously, seemingly putting an end to the week-long aviation meet.

Around 6:00 p.m., the aides to the Wright brothers started putting the aeroplanes back in the aerodrome for disassembly. When moving the aeroplanes for long distances, they were disassembled and shipped by rail car. The remaining crowd of about 150, sensing the end of the flights for the meet, began to make their way to the aerodrome. Suddenly, an aeroplane left the monorail. Who was the pilot? No one seemed to know. The small crowd was astonished by the skill of the "mystery" pilot as they witnessed him floating above in the clouds then quickly skimming low over the Speedway. "It must be Brookins," someone cried while others agreed. The pilot flew over the course at an unusually fast pace. Swooping downward, he circled the field several times, missing the earth by only a few feet at times. As the crowd marveled in awe, he thrilled everyone by completing a series of dazzling revolutions. After revolving the aeroplane for a few minutes, the pilot made a beeline for the northeast corner of the Speedway where he turned back and glided to a perfect landing just outside of the aerodrome. The pilot was only in the air for about ten minutes, but in that short time he executed some daring maneuvers making the short flight one of the most memorable of the entire meet.

As the pilot stepped from the machine, everyone was provided with a good laugh at the expense of a young woman in the crowd. "Why it's Orville Wright!" she exclaimed. "What do you think of that? He's almost as clever as Brookins!"[20]

It was a fitting end to a successful aviation meet. Orville Wright opened the meet with the first flight and closed it with one of the most sensational exhibitions of the week. Both Orville and Wilbur Wright expressed their pleasure with the outcome of the meet. They agreed that the one flight when Walter Brookins broke the world's altitude record served as ample reward for their efforts to build aeroplanes and train new aviators. From Indianapolis the Wright team headed to Montreal, Canada, for exhibition flights on the 4th of July.

Through the years, many of the pilots on the Wright team performed in other exhibitions. However, little did anyone know at the time that Ralph Johnstone and Arch Hoxsey, the "Star Dust Twins" as the press referred to the pair, were giving one of their last performances. Both were killed in crashes a few months later, Ralph Johnstone on November 17 in Denver and Arch Hoxsey on December 31 in Los Angeles.

*Chapter 8*

# Buick Controversy at July Races

The Speedway barely had a chance to quiet down from the aviation meet before the race teams started their practice for the July auto races. The local National team of Johnny Aitken and Tom Kincaid began practice just a few days after the aeroplanes departed. The Marmon racing team appeared at the Speedway on Monday, June 27 to begin Ray Harroun and Joe Dawson's practice runs. On that same day, the Buick team arrived from Flint, Michigan, with Bob Burman and the Chevrolet brothers, Louis and Arthur. By mid-week, practice was in full swing as virtually all of the entrants were at the Speedway. For the most part, the Marmons, Nationals and Buicks displayed the fastest times. The only incident of any consequence occurred during practice on Wednesday when Louis Chevrolet flipped one of the Buick Specials. He suffered a sprained knee, but both driver and car were back in action on Friday.

The Buick team was out to prove something after losing the Wheeler-Schebler trophy in May. In addition, since their Model 16 was ruled ineligible for the May races, they had been stopped from defending the Prest-O-Lite trophy and racing for the Remy Grand Brassard and trophy. The team traveled to Indianapolis with ten cars, including some of their Model 16's and two Buick Specials, affectionately referred to as Buick "Bugs", to be used in the time trials. The contest board of the American Automobile Association had inspected the Buick factory at Saginaw, Michigan, only days before the team's arrival at the Speedway. The board determined that the Company had made enough of the Model 16 to qualify it as a stock car model, thus making it eligible for all races at Indianapolis. Since the car was manufactured by Buick's Marquette Motor Company in Saginaw, William Durant, the head of the Buick Motor Company, had decided to call the Model 16 a Marquette-Buick. Actually, many who followed the sport didn't believe that was the reason for the name at all. Most people suspected that the name was just a way to prevent the Model 16 from being held to the same specifications as the other Buicks. Regardless, with the Buick team at full strength, the usual strong contingent of local teams and many new entries coming to Indianapolis, including Black Crow, ALCO and Maytag, the July races promised to be spectacular.

*The wreck of Louis Chevrolet's Buick Special (referred to as a Buick "Bug") during practice for the July 1910 automobile races at the Indianapolis Motor Speedway. Arthur Chevrolet is standing just to the right side of the driver's seat. (Photo courtesy of the Detroit Public Library, National Automotive History Collection)*

Some of the other race promoters had trouble attracting entries for the 1910 season, but the Speedway had no such trouble. First of all, the Speedway had always been a good place to win an event. The races had always been so skillfully advertised that excellent attendance was assured – more so than anywhere else in the world. Performing before enormous crowds was exactly what the car manufacturers coveted, and the Indianapolis Motor Speedway gave them that opportunity. Additionally, the Speedway had a practice of charging nominal entry fees. The entrance fees to the 1909 Cobe trophy race held in Crown Point, Indiana, were very high in comparison with the entry fees for the 1910 Cobe trophy race at the Speedway, which were only $5 per car. Despite the low entry fees, the Speedway paid out a tremendous amount in prize money. An estimated $9,000 in cash and prizes were awarded at the July races. These included the Cobe Cup, G & J trophy, Speedway Helmet, and the Remy Grand Brassard and trophy. All of this not only helped to promote the sport of auto racing but also placed the Indianapolis Motor Speedway at the forefront of the sport.

A couple of changes greeted the spectators and participants at the Speedway for the July races. First, the seating capacity was expanded from 35,000 to 50,000, plus a special fenced paddock area was added – capable of holding another 10,000 spectators if needed. The other change was procedural. During the May races, there were accusations that pieric acid and ether were placed in the gasoline tanks of some of the cars to attain higher fuel efficiency. The week before the races the Speedway management notified the race teams that they had purchased a medical case containing several empty six-ounce bottles to be used to test the gasoline in the cars before the start of each race. Any traces of pieric acid or ether would result in a disqualification.

The races for the program were evenly distributed across all three days with a featured race scheduled as the last event on each day. The schedule for the three-day program was as follows.

## Friday, July 1

- Event 1 – Trial runs for the records from one-quarter mile to one mile
- Event 2 – Five-mile race open to stock chassis with engines of 160 or less cubic inch piston displacement (CID)
- Event 3 – Five-mile race open to stock chassis with engines of 161 - 230 CID
- Event 4 – Ten-mile race open to stock chassis with engines of 231 - 300 CID
- Event 5 – 15-mile race open to stock chassis with engines of 301 – 450 CID
- Event 6 – Ten-mile race open to stock chassis with engines of 451 – 600 CID
- Event 7 – Ten-mile free-for-all handicap race
- Event 8 – Five-mile amateur race
- Event 9 – Ten-mile free-for-all race for the Speedway Helmet
- Event 10 – 50-mile G & J trophy race open to stock chassis with engines of 231 – 300 CID

## Saturday, July 2

- Event 1 – Trial runs for the one-mile record
- Event 2 – Ten-mile race open to stock chassis with engines of 160 or less CID
- Event 3 – Ten-mile race open to stock chassis with engines of 161 – 230 CID
- Event 4 – Five-mile race open to stock chassis with engines of 231 - 300 CID
- Event 5 – Ten-mile race open to stock chassis with engines of 301 – 450 CID
- Event 6 – 20-mile race open to stock chassis with engines of 451 – 600 CID
- Event 7 – Ten-mile free-for-all handicap race
- Event 8 – Ten-mile amateur race
- Event 9 – Five-mile free-for-all race
- Event 10 – 100-mile Remy Grand Brassard and trophy race open to stock chassis with engines of 301 – 450 CID

## Monday, July 4

- Event 1 – Five-mile race open to stock chassis with engines of 160 or less CID
- Event 2 – Ten-mile race open to stock chassis with engines of 161 - 230 CID
- Event 3 – Five-mile race open to stock chassis with engines of 231 - 300 CID
- Event 4 – Ten-mile race open to stock chassis with engines of 301 – 450 CID
- Event 5 – Five-mile amateur race
- Event 6 – 20-mile free-for-all race
- Event 7 – Ten-mile free-for-all handicap
- Event 8 – 200-mile race for the Cobe trophy

Friday saw a continuation of the heat wave that Indianapolis, as well as the rest of the country, had been enduring for the last week. It was a hot and humid day with the temperature climbing close to a sultry 94 degrees by 4:00 p.m. Perhaps this was one reason that the crowd was surprisingly small. The spectators who began trickling in about noon accounted for only about 2,000 people by the 1:00 p.m. start. They continued to arrive throughout the day until about 5,000 had gathered midway through the day's events. The small crowd was entertained with music performed by the Indianapolis Military Band in the main grandstand, which alternated playing time with the Overland Band stationed in the south bleachers. The Overland band was provided by the Overland Automobile Company in Indianapolis who transported the

*The 1910 Buick racing team and Buick executives. Buick drivers Bob Burman and Louis Chevrolet are seated behind the steering wheel. (Photo courtesy of the Detroit Public Library, National Automotive History Collection)*

band to the Speedway by three big auto trucks.

Emmett Meddock started off the first event of the day, time trials for distances from a quarter-mile to one mile. The National of Johnny Aitken and the Benz of Eddie Hearne followed. Others making trial runs included Louis Chevrolet and Bob Burman in Buick Specials, Len Zengel in a Chadwick, and William Tousey in a Simplex. Burman, driving the black, low-built Buick Special with the glaring figure of a buck's head painted on the hood, set a record for a quarter-mile run when he was clocked in 8.51 seconds. This was an average speed of 105.87 mph. Both Burman and Chevrolet had quick kilometer times of 22.60 seconds and 22.43 seconds respectively, but neither broke Barney Oldfield's record of 21.45 seconds from the May trials. Hearne, Zengel, Burman, and Aitken made second attempts, but only Aitken slightly improved his times from his first attempt.

The first race of the day was a five-mile contest open to stock chassis with engines of 160 or less CID. The race featured a pair of Detroit-made Herreshoffs against the Indianapolis-made Empire. Detroit's Mortimer Roberts held the early advantage when his Herreshoff beat the other two cars into turn one. The Empire of Emmett Meddock tucked in right behind Roberts, but E. R. McCormick in the other Herreshoff lost considerable ground from the start. Meddock was content to stay a close second until the little cars approached the judges' stand where he inched his red and white Empire past the Herreshoff to lead the first lap by a fraction of a second. The two cars waged a nip and tuck battle all around the big track. McCormick continued to fall back. The two leaders, wheel-to-wheel, zoomed down the stretch when Roberts gained a half a car length on Meddock to claim the victory in 5:30.61 for an average of 55.44 mph. This established a new record for the class at five miles, because there was not an existing record. The race summary follows.

| Place | Car # | Driver | Car | Laps | Led |
|---|---|---|---|---|---|
| 1 | 19 | Mortimer Roberts | Herreshoff | 2 | 1 |
| 2 | 4 | Emmett Meddock | Empire | 2 | 1 |
| 3 | 20 | E. R. McCormick | Herreshoff | 2 | 0 |

Five starters lined up for the next event, a five-mile race for stock chassis with engines of 161 – 230 CID. This contest featured the Speedway debut of two car manufacturers, Maytag and E-M-F. The Maytag-Mason Motor Company of Waterloo, Iowa, manufactured the Maytag racer referred to as "The Goat" because of its hill climbing ability. The principal owner was Fred L. Maytag whose primary business was manufacturing farm equipment and washers. The engineers for the auto were a couple of brothers who had worked at the Mason Motor Car Company in Des Moines, Iowa – Fred and August Duesenberg. Years later, the brothers moved to Indianapolis to start the Duesenberg Automobile and Motors Corporation where they built the Duesenberg, often referred to as one of the greatest achievements in automobile history. The Everitt-Metzger-Flanders Company of Detroit produced the E-M-F, which was the result of a merger between the Wayne Automobile Company and the Northern Motor Car Company. The name was comprised of the initials of the three principle owners: Barney Everitt, William Metzger, and Walter Flanders. A clever idea but unfortunately for the owners many people referred to the cars as "Every Mechanical Failure". That didn't matter to the hometown crowd however because local driver Harry Endicott was behind the wheel. The younger brother of Bill Endicott, Harry was good-natured, known for his witty jokes, and well liked by everyone. Actually, Bill Endicott had been entered in this race in a Cole, in addition to the Cole of Louis Edmunds. They were ruled ineligible because changes had been made to their engines since the May races. This was not allowed under the rules at the time.

Chevrolet and Burman quickly made the race a Buick affair as they outdistanced the rest of the field soon after "Pop" Wagner waved the starter's flag. Swapping the lead continuously throughout the race, the two put on a splendid show for five miles. Either Buick could have won; however, Chevrolet just happened to be in the lead when the pair crossed the finish line. The time of 4:41.77, an average speed of 64.1 mph, broke his own record set during the May 1910 races at the Speedway. Arthur Miller was able to urge his Warren-Detroit ahead of Endicott's E-M-F down the frontstretch to finish third and N. J. Sutcliffe barely lost fourth position to Endicott. The complete race results follow.

| Place | Car # | Driver | Car | Laps | Led |
|---|---|---|---|---|---|
| 1 | 35 | Louis Chevrolet | Buick | 2 | 2 |
| 2 | 36 | Bob Burman | Buick | 2 | 0 |
| 3 | 24 | Arthur Miller | Warren-Detroit | 2 | 0 |
| 4 | 26 | Harry Endicott | E-M-F | 2 | 0 |
| 5 | 2 | N. J. Sutcliffe | Maytag | 2 | 0 |

After the race, the crowd immediately focused on the starters in the ten-mile event for stock chassis with engines of 231 – 300 CID. This would be most people's first glimpse of racing action at the new Marquette-Buick – the very car that was ruled ineligible for the May races. This had been the most talked about and controversial car of the 1910 season. A buzz filled the grandstands as the spectators engaged in lively conversations as to whether the car was actually a stock car. Although somewhat overshadowed, two more car manufacturers made their Speedway debut in this race. The Crow Motor Car Company of Elkhart,

*Looking south down Georgetown Road during the early days of the Indianapolis Motor Speedway. (Photo courtesy of the Indianapolis Motor Speedway)*

Indiana, produced the Black Crow and the FAL Motor Company of Chicago produced the FAL car.

Bob Burman helped the Marquette-Buick make an immediate impact by rocketing to the lead as the cars headed for the first turn. The Marmon of Joe Dawson was second and teammate Ray Harroun fell in behind the pair. Louis Chevrolet, in the other Marquette-Buick, suffered a terrible start and found himself behind everyone except the Great Western driven by Glenn Davis of Winchester, Indiana. Burman continued to lead at the end of the first lap, but Dawson and Harroun seemed content to sit behind Burman and wait for their chance to overtake him. There were long stretches of daylight between the remainder of the cars with the two FAL cars holding down fourth and fifth. The Great Western of Moore and the Black Crow of Cook were a distant sixth and seventh. Chevrolet and Davis brought up the rear.

As Burman continued to lead, he caught a break when the two Marmons began to battle each other for second place. With the two of them racing each other, Burman was able to lengthen his lead. On the third lap, Glenn Davis suffered engine problems forcing him to leave the race. Burman won in a time of 8:14.40, breaking Ray Harroun's record of 8:16.80 from the May races. Joe Dawson nipped Harroun at the wire with a time of 8:25.01 to Harroun's 8:25.35. Meanwhile, Louis Chevrolet made a tremendous comeback to gain three positions in the last three laps and rallied for a fifth place finish. The complete race results follow.

| Place | Car # | Driver | Car | Laps | Led |
|---|---|---|---|---|---|
| 1 | 38 | Bob Burman | Marquette-Buick | 4 | 4 |
| 2 | 33 | Joe Dawson | Marmon | 4 | 0 |
| 3 | 34 | Ray Harroun | Marmon | 4 | 0 |
| 4 | 45 | Billy Pearce | FAL | 4 | 0 |
| 5 | 37 | Louis Chevrolet | Marquette-Buick | 4 | 0 |
| 6 | 44 | Louis Heineman | FAL | 4 | 0 |
| 7 | 14 | C. F. Moore | Great Western | 4 | 0 |
| 8 | 16 | David Cook | Black Crow | 4 | 0 |
| 9 | 15 | Glenn Davis | Great Western | 4 | 0 |

Judging from the results of the race, it looked as if Buick had a superior car in its Marquette-Buick. The FAL car also showed signs of being competitive while the officials of the Crow Motor Car Company were enthusiastic about their involvement in racing. Between races, an *Indianapolis Star* reporter interviewed Mr. Darnell, the General Sales Manager for the Crow Motor Car Company. "We have just decided to maintain and support the racing team," Mr. Darnell said. "This decision has been reached, not from a publicity standpoint alone, but because we believe the experiences will make it possible for us to maintain a higher standard of excellence in the manufacture of our product, and in consequence the buyers of Black Crow cars will receive material benefits. The possibilities for gaining these benefits and utilizing them quickly in producing results are far greater at the present time because of the advances which have been made in developing and perfecting the racing features."[1]

Some of the same drivers were in action in the next race, a 15-mile race for stock chassis with engines of 301 – 450 CID. Burman and Chevrolet were right back in action for the third race in a row, joined by Ray Harroun and the National trio of Johnny Aitken, Tom Kincaid, and Howard Wilcox. The spectators had witnessed what Burman could do with the Marquette-Buick against the Marmons of Harroun and Dawson in the previous race. Now the big question on everyone's mind was how the Marquette-Buick would stack up against the Nationals and their drivers.

The National of Kincaid jumped out to an early lead followed closely by Chevrolet. Meanwhile, Aitken and Burman struggled at the back. Kincaid held the lead for another lap before his engine started to sputter – leaving the door open for Chevrolet to push his Marquette-Buick to the front. During that time, Burman had passed Aitken at the back of the field. Kincaid eventually dropped out on the third lap due to engine trouble. Incredibly, by the time Kincaid had dropped out, Burman was in position to grab the lead with Aitken right behind him. Many could see it coming. After Burman had passed him, Aitken very wisely decided to tow along in his draft, allowing the two to hook up and run right up through the pack. The duo caught Chevrolet as the three cars roared down the frontstretch. Burman was credited with leading the third lap, but you could have thrown a blanket over the three of them. Wilcox followed in fourth and Harroun was far behind in fifth.

The top three cars were locked in a relentless tussle for three solid laps. The air was filled with the smell of burning gasoline and hot scorching rubber tires as drivers continually swapped positions. They were three-wide, yet, at other times, one could be seen swerving behind the others trying to find that illusive opening. It was truly a battle of epic proportions! Burman roared past the ten-mile mark in a new American record of 7:56.45, lowering Aitken's 7:57.10 that he had set in Atlanta. The three were so close the record could easily have belonged to any one of them. In the end Burman held on to beat Aitken to the line by 2.36 seconds, 11:46.42 vs. 11:48.78. Chevrolet finished only 0.19 of a second behind Aitken.

Burman's winning time set a new American record for the class at 15 miles by virtue of the fact that no previous record existed. Everyone agreed unanimously that this was one of the best races witnessed to date at the Indianapolis track. The final race summary follows.

| Place | Car # | Driver | Car | Laps | Led |
|---|---|---|---|---|---|
| 1 | 40 | Bob Burman | Marquette-Buick | 6 | 4 |
| 2 | 7 | Johnny Aitken | National | 6 | 0 |
| 3 | 39 | Louis Chevrolet | Marquette-Buick | 6 | 0 |
| 4 | 1 | Howard Wilcox | National | 6 | 0 |
| 5 | 31 | Ray Harroun | Marmon | 6 | 0 |
| 6 | 6 | Tom Kincaid | National | 2 | 2 |

The ten-mile race for stock cars with engines of 451 – 600 CID, with three starters, featured the Nationals of Howard Wilcox and Arthur Greiner against Harry Grant in another new car to the Speedway, the ALCO. The American Locomotive Company (ALCO) of Providence, Rhode Island, was better known for its steam locomotives but had also started producing automobiles in 1909. Although the car was untested at the Speedway, Harry Grant had won the 1909 Vanderbilt Cup road race (and would later win the 1910 race as well), so everyone knew that the driver was capable of being very competitive. Well proportioned at 5'11" and 230 pounds, Grant lacked emotion even during the midst of a race. Perhaps this was because he felt he was well prepared. He was known for establishing a race plan and sticking to it no matter what.

*Harry Grant and riding mechanic George Babcock in an ALCO at Elgin, Illinois. (Chicago Daily News negatives collection, SDN-057211. Courtesy of the Chicago Historical Society)*

The ALCO displayed explosive speed as Grant piloted it into the lead followed by Greiner and then Wilcox. The group never strayed from that order as Grant maintained control of the race throughout. Wilcox was able to pass Greiner for second place on the final lap, but neither could approach Grant. The ALCO carried Grant to victory in 8:03.09, giving the manufacturer and driver a victory at Indianapolis in their first try. Wilcox held on to second place with Greiner not far behind. The race summary follows.

| Place | Car # | Driver | Car | Laps | Led |
|-------|-------|--------|-----|------|-----|
| 1 | 27 | Harry Grant | ALCO | 4 | 4 |
| 2 | 1 | Howard Wilcox | National | 4 | 0 |
| 3 | 12 | Arthur Greiner | National | 4 | 0 |

The next contest may have been one of the most confusing races ever witnessed at the Indianapolis Motor Speedway. It was a ten-mile free-for-all handicap, meaning that the 21 entrants started at various times. The first 14 cars had passed the judges' stand to begin their second lap before the final seven entrants had started. This resulted in such chaos as the bigger cars rushed by the smaller ones at a frantic pace and created a treacherous situation all around the track. The race was run without an incident, though. The Maytag of Sutcliffe, benefiting from a handicap of 3:50, led all four laps en route to the victory with an actual running time of 10:01.78. Second and third place went to the Great Western driven by Glenn Davis and the E-M-F driven by Harry Endicott, respectively. Eddie Hearne, usually in a Benz, drove a Diamond T to a seventh place finish after starting well back in the field. The Diamond T, built by C.A. Tilt, founder of the Diamond T Motor Car Company of Chicago, Illinois, represented yet another car manufacturer that was new to the Speedway. Throughout the race, the crowd cheered wildly for hometown favorite Johnny Aitken, who made up several positions in the first three laps before fading back to a ninth place finish. Only 10 of the starters were scored because the other 11 did not finish the race. The race summary for those running at the end follows.

*The start of a 10-mile free-for-all handicap race at the July 1910 automobile races. (Photo courtesy of the Indianapolis Motor Speedway)*

| Place | Car # | Driver | Car | Laps | Led |
|-------|-------|--------|-----|------|-----|
| 1 | 2 | N. J. Sutcliffe | Maytag | 4 | 4 |
| 2 | 15 | Glenn Davis | Great Western | 4 | 0 |
| 3 | 26 | Harry Endicott | E-M-F | 4 | 0 |
| 4 | 10 | Bill Endicott | Cole | 4 | 0 |
| 5 | 24 | Arthur Miller | Warren-Detroit | 4 | 0 |
| 6 | 16 | David Cook | Black Crow | 4 | 0 |
| 7 | 16 | Eddie Hearne | Diamond T | 4 | 0 |
| 8 | 4 | Charlie Merz | Empire | 4 | 0 |
| 9 | 8 | Johnny Aitken | National | 4 | 0 |
| 10 | 45 | Billy Pearce | FAL | 4 | 0 |

The next event included only two starters, Arthur Greiner and William Tousey. This was a five-mile race open only to registered amateurs as defined by the AAA. The short contest with only two starters served as a breather for everyone after the hectic pace of the big handicap race that had just concluded. In an uneventful race, Greiner's National led both laps enroute to a victory in 4:14.95. The race summary follows.

| Place | Car # | Driver | Car | Laps | Led |
|-------|-------|--------|-----|------|-----|
| 1 | 12 | Arthur Greiner | National | 2 | 2 |
| 2 | 1 | William Tousey | National | 2 | 0 |

*Amateur driver Arthur Greiner. He would drive for the National team in the September 1910 auto races at the Speedway. (Photo courtesy of the Indianapolis Motor Speedway)*

The ten-mile free-for-all for the Speedway Helmet was next on the schedule. Everyone was anxiously waiting for this event in addition to the G & J trophy race, the last contest of the day. Bob Burman was the defending champion of the helmet and – as was the custom – as the defending champion, he wore it during the race. Many expected him to face stiff competition from his teammate, Louis Chevrolet, the Marmon of Harroun, and Johnny Aitken's National. The Benz of Eddie Hearne, which was the same car that Barney Oldfield drove at the Speedway in August 1909, was also expected to provide a strong challenge.

Things did not start off well for Burman and Aitken. They were nowhere to be seen as the field attempted a flying start. However, as the cars roared past the judges' stand, the crowd breathed a big sigh of relief as the two drivers rushed in behind the rest of the field to begin the race. Luckily, starter "Pop" Wagner waved off the start because some of the cars had jumped ahead and elected to begin the race from a standing start. This played into Aitken's favor as he grabbed the lead on the restart – winning a close battle with Hearne to lead the first lap. Chevrolet, Zengel, and Harroun completed the top five; however, the crowd was interested in where defending champion Bob Burman was running. Unfortunately, clutch trouble forced him to retire from the race before the first lap was completed. Meanwhile, the battle between Aitken and Hearne continued as they raced side-by-side throughout the entire second lap. It was so close, that not until Hearne passed Aitken in front of the judges' stand was the leader of the second lap decided. The hopes of the Buick team were dashed on the second lap when Chevrolet encountered engine trouble and joined Burman on the sidelines in what was truly a disappointing race for the Buick Specials. Hearne received additional help when, much to the disappointment of the local fans, Aitken was forced to retire from the race as well with engine problems. With Hearne's main competition gone, he led the last two laps with ease to cross the line in 7:13.00, averaging 83.14 mph. He seized possession of the Speedway Helmet from Burman and would defend it in the September races at the Speedway. Although Ray Harroun made a valiant effort to try and catch the Benz, Hearne still maintained a big lead. Harroun had just as much of a lead over the rest of the field who stayed bunched together. Despite the disappointment of not seeing an Indianapolis driver win, it was still a popular victory. Chicago's Eddie Hearne, besides being very wealthy, was well respected by the fans and his fellow drivers. The race summary follows.

| Place | Car # | Driver | Car | Laps | Led |
|-------|-------|--------|-----|------|-----|
| 1 | 22 | Eddie Hearne | Benz | 4 | 3 |
| 2 | 32 | Ray Harroun | Marmon | 4 | 0 |
| 3 | 18 | Len Zengel | Chadwick | 4 | 0 |
| 4 | 29 | Ralph Ireland | Stoddard-Dayton | 4 | 0 |
| 5 | 8 | Johnny Aitken | National | 2 | 1 |
| 6 | 46 | Howard Wilcox | Simplex | 2 | 0 |
| 7 | 42 | Louis Chevrolet | Buick Special | 1 | 0 |
| 8 | 43 | Bob Burman | Buick Special | 0 | 0 |

The feature event of the day was the G & J trophy race scheduled for 50 miles. Since the contest was for stock chassis with engines of 231 – 300 CID, this excluded the Nationals, leaving the two Marmons of Harroun and Dawson along with Burman and Chevrolet in their Marquette-Buicks. Seven other entries were hopeful to compete for the win against the four prohibitive favorites.

From the beginning, Burman and Chevrolet left little doubt that this was going to be a Marquette-Buick event. The two teammates outclassed the other cars at the start and swapped leads throughout the race while leaving the rest of the field far behind. Both the Marmon of Ray Harroun and the Great Western of David Cook quit the race after the third lap due to engine problems. Louis Chevrolet was the leader at the ten-mile mark, completing the distance in 8:17.81. This was about three seconds slower than Burman's winning time for this class in the ten-mile race earlier in the day. Dawson made a good run and held down third position until he was forced to make engine repairs shortly after the 30-mile mark. He eventually rejoined the race, but ran two laps down.

Although Chevrolet and Burman continued to share the lead, it was Burman who managed to hold the lead at each of the remaining ten-mile intervals. Thus, he set new records for each distance. He blazed through the 20-mile mark at an average of 73.36 mph for a time of 16:21.50, breaking the 20-mile record set in Atlanta by Louis Chevrolet. He increased his speed to just over 74 mph to set new 30 and 40-mile records in 24:17.10 and 32:06.50, respectively. While the rest of the field was far back, Chevrolet did no stray from Burman's side. He gave it everything he had before falling short at the finish by less than fou seconds. Burman averaged 74.89 mph for the 50 miles, winning in a record-setting time of 40:03.10 Pearce and Heineman made impressive showings as they piloted their FAL cars to third and fifth plac finishes. Frank Fox split the pair by placing fourth in a Pope-Hartford. The complete race results follow.

| Place | Car # | Driver | Car | Laps | Led |
|-------|-------|--------|-----|------|-----|
| 1 | 38 | Bob Burman | Marquette-Buick | 20 | 12 |
| 2 | 37 | Louis Chevrolet | Marquette-Buick | 20 | 8 |
| 3 | 45 | Billy Pearce | FAL | 20 | 0 |
| 4 | 3 | Frank Fox | Pope-Hartford | 20 | 0 |
| 5 | 44 | Louis Heineman | FAL | 20 | 0 |
| 6 | 14 | C. F. Moore | Great Western | 20 | 0 |
| 7 | 15 | Glenn Davis | Great Western | 20 | 0 |
| 8 | 34 | Joe Dawson | Marmon | 18 | 0 |
| 9 | 24 | Arthur Miller | Warren-Detroit | 10 | 0 |
| 10 | 33 | Ray Harroun | Marmon | 3 | 0 |
| 11 | 16 | David Cook | Black Crow | 3 | 0 |

*The G & J Tire Company trophy awarded at the Indianapolis Motor Speedway during the August 1909 and July 1910 automobile races. The trophy was a shield approximately two to three feet wide and three to four feet tall. (Photo courtesy of the Indianapolis Motor Speedway)*

The first day of racing proved to be spectacular! Ten new records were set, many car manufacturers ebuted at the Speedway, and there were no accidents. The entire day was filled with exceptionally close icing and many thrilling finishes. Bob Burman clearly dominated the competition by setting eight of the n new records.

Saturday continued to be just as hot as Friday's 94-degree temperature. It had rained in the city uring the afternoon; but, despite low-hanging clouds around the Speedway, the rains never came to the ack. Perhaps the threat of rain kept some spectators away. A half an hour before the first event, fewer than ,000 people dotted the stands; however, within a couple of hours incoming trains and trolleys increased e crowd to about the size of Friday's.

Similar to Friday, there were nine races and one trial on the schedule capped off by the 100-mile emy Grand Brassard and trophy race. Indianapolis' Charlie Merz started the day's events when he drove is Empire onto the track for a one-mile trial. The small car was timed in 1:03.38 for the distance. The ollowing drivers also made trial runs: Eddie Hearne in a Benz (40.83 seconds), Howard Wilcox in a implex (45.94 seconds), Johnny Aitken in a National (40.54 seconds), George Robertson in a Simplex 1.48 seconds), and Bob Burman in a Buick Special (38.36 seconds). Louis Chevrolet was scheduled to ake a trial in the other Buick Special but cancelled because of a broken crankshaft. The trials offered the peedway crowd its first glimpse of George Robertson. Winner of the 1908 Vanderbilt Cup road race, obertson was well known on the east coast. He was entered in the five and ten-mile free-for-all races later the day with the label as one of the heavy favorites in his big Simplex machine.

The first race of the day was a ten-mile contest for stock chassis with engines of 160 CID or less. lortimer Roberts, winner of the previous day's five-mile race for the same class, was joined by teammates harles Herreshoff, and E.R. McCormick. Charles, founder of the Herreshoff Motor Company of Detroit, lichigan, in 1909, was not a serious racer but – no doubt – couldn't resist the chance to drive his own eation around the Indianapolis Motor Speedway. The Herreshoff family was better known for building oats than autos, which explains why their early cars featured engines originally designed for marine use. he fourth entrant, clearly the crowd favorite, was Indianapolis driver Charlie Merz in an Empire.

As the cars were sent on their way, the Herreshoff of Roberts took the early lead followed by Merz, 1cCormick, and Herreshoff. By the time the first lap was completed, there were considerable gaps be-veen all of the cars. To the delight of the local fans, Merz started to gain momentum and make up time on oberts over the next two laps. Further back, Charles Herreshoff had passed McCormick for third place ist as McCormick encountered engine trouble, forcing him to drop out of the race. The cheering intensi-ed as Merz kept closing on Roberts until the little red and white Empire was right up behind him coming own the frontstretch on the fourth and final lap. Merz drifted up the track slightly and forced Roberts to unter move with a block as he held on to win by a narrow margin in a time of 10:37.60 for an average of 6.35 mph. This was a new record for ten miles in this class by virtue of the fact that there was no previous cord. Roberts had established five and ten-mile records for stock chassis with engines of 160 CID or less uring the two days of racing. The final race summary follows.

| Place | Car # | Driver | Car | Laps | Led |
|---|---|---|---|---|---|
| 1 | 19 | Mortimer Roberts | Herreshoff | 4 | 4 |
| 2 | 4 | Charlie Merz | Empire | 4 | 0 |
| 3 | 21 | Charles Herreshoff | Herreshoff | 4 | 0 |
| 4 | 20 | E. R. McCormick | Herreshoff | 1 | 0 |

True to his reputation, Starter "Pop" Wagner had the cars for the next race at the line without losing ny time. The races at Indianapolis were usually run like clockwork, primarily due to Wagner's ability to ke control of the situation. Acting as the American Automobile Association's (AAA) representative for e races, he was much more than the starter. He put in long hours working with the track officials, coordi-

*Louis Chevrolet (left) and Bob Burman (right) posing in their Buick "Bugs" inside the first turn at the Indianapolis Motor Speedway in July 1910. Note the construction of grandstands behind them. (Photo courtesy of the Alfred P. Sloan Museum, Flint, Michigan)*

nating everything from safety to prize money. The race, a ten-mile contest for stock chassis with engines o 161 – 230 CID, featured the Buicks of Burman and Chevrolet. They were competing against Harry Endico in an E-M-F, Arthur Miller in a Warren-Detroit, and Sutcliffe in a Maytag.

No one really expected the other cars to give the Buicks much of a fight in this race and that exactly the way it played out. Although Harry Endicott did get a big lead at the start, the two Buicks passe him before the end of the first lap with Chevrolet in first place. The Warren-Detroit of Miller dropped ou in the first lap while the Maytag of Sutcliffe was still in the race but very far back. At the end of the first tw laps, Louis Chevrolet had increased his lead over Burman as he sped to a new five-mile record for the clas of 4:35.47, breaking his record of 4:40.80 set the previous day. The outcome was never in doubt as Chevrol won easily, crossing the line in 8:55.40 with Bob Burman second and Harry Endicott third. Sutcliffe was s far behind that he was not allowed to finish the race. The final results follow.

*Bob Burman in the seat of a Buick racer in 1910. (Photo courtesy of the Indianapolis Motor Speedway)*

*Louis Chevrolet in the seat of a Buick racer in 1910. (Photo courtesy of the Indianapolis Motor Speedway)*

| Place | Car # | Driver | Car | Laps | Led |
|---|---|---|---|---|---|
| 1 | 35 | Louis Chevrolet | Buick | 4 | 4 |
| 2 | 36 | Bob Burman | Buick | 4 | 0 |
| 3 | 26 | Harry Endicott | E-M-F | 4 | 0 |
| 4 | 2 | N. J. Sutcliffe | Maytag | 3 | 0 |
| 5 | 24 | Arthur Miller | Warren-Detroit | 0 | 0 |

The Marquette-Buick made its first appearance of the day in the next race, a five-mile race for stock chassis with engines of 231 - 300 CID. Joe Dawson was Marmon's lone entrant and hoped to fare better against the Buicks than Friday's result. Given the list of entries, most in attendance reasoned that Dawson was probably the only one standing in the way of a Buick sweep.

From the start, it looked as if the powerful Marquette-Buicks were too much for the Marmon. Chevrolet and Burman easily sprinted to the lead. Dawson stayed close to them, but the rest of the field, far back in a pack, had little hope of ever catching the leaders. The only mystery about the outcome of this race was which Buick driver would win. The two teammates diced for the lead over the full five miles of the race. Chevrolet would surge forward, then Burman would swing to the outside and pass him. Despite this repeated pattern of jockeying for the lead, Dawson was never able to take advantage of it. Chevrolet got the win by a small margin over Burman in a record winning time of 4:08.30. Dawson finished about eight seconds behind the pair in third place. The rest of the field was far back as only six of the nine entrants completed the race to be scored. The race summary follows.

| Place | Car # | Driver | Car | Laps | Led |
|-------|-------|--------|-----|------|-----|
| 1 | 37 | Louis Chevrolet | Marquette-Buick | 2 | 2 |
| 2 | 38 | Bob Burman | Marquette-Buick | 2 | 0 |
| 3 | 34 | Joe Dawson | Marmon | 2 | 0 |
| 4 | 45 | C. F. Moore | Great Western | 2 | 0 |
| 5 | 17 | Ed Stinson | Black Crow | 2 | 0 |
| 6 | 15 | Glenn Davis | Great Western | 2 | 0 |

*Start of a 5-mile race on July 2, 1910 at the Indianapolis Motor Speedway. Joe Dawson can be seen in the middle in the #34 Marmon. (Photo courtesy of the Indianapolis Motor Speedway)*

Burman and Chevrolet quickly switched cars, bringing two more Marquette-Buicks to the startin line for the next event, a ten-mile race for stock chassis with engines of 301 – 450 CID. The Marmons o Joe Dawson and Ray Harroun and the Nationals of Johnny Aitken and Tom Kincaid joined the two Buic drivers. Due to the dominance of the new Buick cars, the hometown crowd had become vocal in the wishes for the Marmon and National cars to beat the powerful Marquette-Buick.

The local drivers provided the fans some hope when Kincaid lead the first lap followed by other local drivers Dawson, Harroun, and Aitken. The Marquette-Buicks were fifth and sixth. They continued to run in that order through the five-mile mark. However, spectators grew concerned when Chevrolet started to make his move. One-by-one he passed his competitors. Just before the end of the third lap, he overtook Kincaid with alarming ease to leave him behind. Sighs of disappointment hung over the grandstands as the big blue National of Kincaid faded all the way to last place after being overtaken. Meanwhile, Johnny Aitken had made a run of his own. Seemingly without notice, he had slipped in behind Chevrolet to drive his own way up through the field. Chevrolet was not going to be denied a second straight victory. He kept on the inside groove and held off Aitken by 0.32 of a second to average 75.82 mph for the win. This broke Bob Burman's record of 7:56.45 for ten miles set on Friday. The Marmons had to settle for third and fourth; but they did beat out the Marquette-Buick of Burman, who never really was a factor in the race. The race summary follows.

| Place | Car # | Driver | Car | Laps | Led |
|-------|-------|--------|-----|------|-----|
| 1 | 37 | Louis Chevrolet | Marquette-Buick | 4 | 2 |
| 2 | 7 | Johnny Aitken | National | 4 | 0 |
| 3 | 31 | Joe Dawson | Marmon | 4 | 0 |
| 4 | 30 | Ray Harroun | Marmon | 4 | 0 |
| 5 | 40 | Bob Burman | Marquette-Buick | 4 | 0 |
| 6 | 6 | Tom Kincaid | National | 4 | 2 |

The stock chassis with engines of 451 – 600 CID took to the track next in a 20-mile race that featured three entrants. Harry Grant was trying to make it two for two with the ALCO in a rematch of Friday's ten-mile race when he scored the first Speedway victory for the ALCO in its first attempt. Grant's habits were a testament to the durability of the ALCO. Unlike other competitors, he did not spend time tearing down his car between race meetings. When he was ready to race he simply pulled the car out and went racing.

There was no suspense in this race as the Nationals of Howard Wilcox and Arthur Greiner provided no match at all for the ALCO. Grant had this race to himself, flying through the first four laps in 8:15.65 before lapping Wilcox on the fifth circuit and Greiner on the sixth. Grant won in a time of 16:27.13, far off of Ralph DePalma's record of 15:57.41 set at Atlanta in May, but good enough for an easy victory here. The race summary follows.

| Place | Car # | Driver | Car | Laps | Led |
|-------|-------|--------|-----|------|-----|
| 1 | 27 | Harry Grant | ALCO | 8 | 8 |
| 2 | 12 | Arthur Greiner | National | 8 | 0 |
| 3 | 1 | Howard Wilcox | National | 8 | 0 |

Next, the timers braced themselves for the ten-mile free-for-all handicap. After Friday's handicap event, the fans were not surprised by the confusion created after all 21 entrants had started at different times. Emmett Meddock was the first off of the line in his little red and white Empire followed by Roberts in the Herreshoff. These two drivers had already completed one lap by the time the Simplex of George Robertson and the National of Johnny Aitken started. Robertson put on quite a display of skillful driving. He was eighteenth at the end of the first lap, but made a steady climb toward the top each lap – going from fourteenth to fourth to the victory on the last lap with a time of 6:53.88. The charge through the field personified Robertson's character behind the wheel of a race car. Fierce, he demanded everything from his car – no matter what. Many said that he either won a race or broke trying to win it. Robertson averaged a sensational 87.08 mph to break Caleb Bragg's track record for ten miles established at the May races. W.K. Smith in a National and Ralph Ireland in a Midland rounded out the top three finishers. For good reason, the rest of the finishing positions were not published.

It was somewhat of a Speedway debut for Robertson's Simplex, which was built by the Simplex Automobile Company in New York City. William Tousey of Syracuse, New York, drove his privately-owned Simplex in the trials on Friday. Later on Friday, Howard Wilcox drove the same car in the Speedway Helmet race, but Robertson's was the first entry officially backed by Simplex. This company was easily confused with the Simplex Motor Car Company of Mishawaka, Indiana, which built a car called the Amplex. Ralph Ireland, driving a Midland, also had an impressive showing in the handicap races with yet another car manufacturer new to the Speedway. The Midland was manufactured by The Midland Motor Car Company in Moline, Illinois. The Company came into existence after the Deere-Clark Motor Company reorganized when the John Deere Company split off to focus exclusively on farm machinery.

*George Robertson sitting in a Simplex with his riding mechanic at Elgin, Illinois in 1910. (Chicago Daily News negatives collection, SDN-056228. Courtesy of the Chicago Historical Society)*

After the handicap event, the timers breathed a sigh of relief as the racing resumed under "normal" circumstances. However, there was controversy surrounding the next contest, a ten-mile race for registered amateurs. The problem was not with the amateur status of the drivers, as one might expect; but, rather, with one of the cars. A.L. McMurtry, a representative of the AAA and an official at the Speedway events in July, had ruled the Mercedes of Spencer Wishart ineligible to race at the Speedway. This ruling was made because the manufacturers had not filed a certificate with the AAA in New York. However, Referee A.R. Pardington overruled McMurtry's decision and allowed Wishart to enter the Mercedes.

This was the first appearance at the Speedway for Spencer Wishart of Portchester, New York. Perhaps because he was racing off of his father's money, he never seemed to get too emotional while racing. He was known for changing tires or examining his engine at a leisurely pace, even calmly sipping water during a pit stop!

Wishart made a promising showing in his first race. He held down second place behind Arthur Greiner until he had trouble with the Mercedes on the last lap, forcing him from the race. Wishart looked strong enough to win before his trouble, leaving many to wonder what the outcome might have been otherwise. The National of Greiner won in a time of 8:16.66 with William Tousey finishing second in another National. The race summary follows.

| Place | Car # | Driver | Car | Laps | Led |
|-------|-------|--------|-----|------|-----|
| 1 | 12 | Arthur Greiner | National | 4 | 4 |
| 2 | 1 | William Tousey | National | 4 | 0 |
| 3 | 48 | Spencer Wishart | Mercedes | 3 | 0 |

Speculation was rampant as to who would win the next race. The five-mile free-for-all featured some of the most famous drivers of the time. The field of six starters included Bob Burman in a Buick Special, George Robertson in a Simplex, Johnny Aitken in a National, Eddie Hearne in a Benz, Len Zengel in a Chadwick, and Howard Wilcox in a National. Many felt that four or five drivers could win, but others, after witnessing his amazing performance in the ten-mile handicap event, were certain that Robertson would win.

At the drop of the flag, Aitken jumped out to a quick start, but Robertson soon flew by him as if he was going to leave the rest of the field behind. The big Benz of Eddie Hearne whipped around Aitken on the backstretch and never lost sight of Robertson, catching him down the frontstretch and making the pass just after the end of the first lap. Early in the second lap, Robertson was relegated to third place when Aitken passed him going into turn two. Just when it looked as if Hearne was on his way to a victory, Aitken caught him and roared past the Benz down the backstretch. Hearne was right there to join them as the three raced wheel-to-wheel for the last half a lap. Amid the cheers from the crowd, which was now on its feet, the three raced down the frontstretch where Aitken crossed the line in first place with a time of 3:39.74 to pull off the upset over Robertson. Following in second and third place were Robertson and Hearne, respectively. The Buick Special of Bob Burman was never a factor in the race. He dropped out before the completion of the first lap. The final race summary follows.

| Place | Car # | Driver | Car | Laps | Led |
|-------|-------|--------|-----|------|-----|
| 1 | 8 | Johnny Aitken | National | 2 | 1 |
| 2 | 90 | George Robertson | Simplex | 2 | 1 |
| 3 | 22 | Eddie Hearne | Benz | 2 | 0 |
| 4 | 46 | Howard Wilcox | Simplex | 2 | 0 |
| 5 | 18 | Len Zengel | Chadwick | 2 | 0 |
| 6 | 43 | Bob Burman | Buick Special | 0 | 0 |

There was a lengthy delay before the last race, because George Robertson's Simplex broke a flywheel as he finished the previous event, scattering parts all over the track. The work crews took several minutes in cleaning up all of the pieces and inspecting the track before everyone was satisfied that it was safe to continue racing.

During the break, the crowd along the pits was kept entertained by the Buick team's new mascot. One of the crew members had bought a goat for $1.50 while in Indianapolis. They named her Lizzie Burman Chevrolet Buick and perched her atop one of the Buick Specials while several cameramen took her picture. The team announced that they planned to take their new mascot with them when they left Indianapolis. "We got Indianapolis's goat!"[2] one of them shouted as laughter broke out all around.

Several minutes after 4:00 p.m., hometown hero Johnny Aitken was given a hearty welcome as he drove on to the track to line up for the 100-mile Remy Grand Brassard and trophy race. This event was for stock chassis with engines of 301 – 450 CID. A total of 13 cars were ready for the start of what looked like a battle between the Marquette-Buicks, Marmons, and Nationals.

*The Remy trophy which was awarded along with the Remy Grand Brassard at all of the automobile race programs at the Indianapolis Motor Speedway during 1910. (Photo courtesy of the Indianapolis Motor Speedway)*

Ray Harroun jumped out to an early lead but was passed by several cars before the first lap was completed. Louis Chevrolet had his Marquette-Buick in first place as they crossed the line for the first time, closely pursued by Tom Kincaid and Johnny Aitken. Arthur Chevrolet and Joe Dawson rounded out the top five. There didn't appear to be anything wrong with Harroun's Marmon, but he had dropped back to sixth place for some reason. The top five stayed bunched together throughout the second lap as positions changed rapidly. At the end of the second lap, Aitken had grabbed the lead, followed by Kincaid. Louis Chevrolet faded back to fourth place. Dawson moved up to third and Harroun was still in sixth. The two National teammates battled for the next couple of laps until Kincaid had the lead at the end of ten miles. Aitken, Arthur Chevrolet, and Dawson followed in that order.

Aitken would never be a threat again after he stopped to change spark plugs on lap four. Despite returning to the race, the problem continued to plague him. Another race favorite, Louis Chevrolet, had troubles as well. He stopped to change tires on the eighth and ninth laps, a problem that he would not be able to remedy. Meanwhile, Arthur Chevrolet and Joe Dawson had worked their way to first and second at the end of lap six or 15 miles.

Tom Kincaid, fifth after six laps, surged ahead of the field to set a record at the 20-mile mark. His time of 15:57.63 broke the record set by Ray Harroun in Atlanta earlier in the year. By this time, Joe Dawson and Bob Burman had settled into second and third place, respectively. The next 50 miles of the race saw a continuous battle up front between Kincaid, Burman, and Dawson. Kincaid continued to lead through the 30-mile mark, setting a record for the distance of 23:43.30, breaking Ray Harroun's record of 24:18.15 from Atlanta. Bob Burman grabbed the lead on lap 13 and held it for eight laps. During this time, he set new 40 and 50-mile records of 31:47.80 and 39:47.86. Ray Harroun and Joe Dawson had set the old records in Atlanta.

Attrition started to set in just after the 50-mile mark. Howard Wilcox, in what would be the only accident of the day, lost a wheel in turn three after breaking a steering gear. His car left the track but remained upright, allowing him to escape unhurt. The Great Western driven by Glenn Davis also was out of the race for unknown reasons. Additionally, much to the disappointment of the crowd, Johnny Aitken pulled his big blue National in the pits after continually suffering from spark plug problems.

Finally, Joe Dawson put his Marmon in the lead on lap 21. He held the lead for ten laps and set three records of his own. He set a record for 60 miles of 48:15.20, 70 miles of 56:05.65, and 75 miles of 1:08:00.00. He had set the previous records for 60 and 70 miles in Atlanta, but the record for 75 miles had belonged to Louis Chevrolet, also set in Atlanta. Unfortunately, Dawson had to come in to the pits to change tires after lap 30, allowing Bob Burman to take the lead. Dawson was able to get back out quickly to battle his way up to second place, but the late pit stop cost him the race.

Once Burman had his Marquette-Buick in the lead, he took control of the race. He set new records for 90 and 100 miles of 1:12:27.8 and 1:20:35.60, respectively. Tom Kincaid had set both previous records in the Prest-O-Lite trophy race at Indianapolis in May. Joe Dawson, Ray Harroun, and Arthur Chevrolet finished second, third and fourth, less than a quarter of a mile behind Burman. Tom Kincaid was destined for a top two or three finish until tire trouble on lap 37 pushed him back to fifth place, allowing both Harroun and Arthur Chevrolet to pass him inside of the last ten miles. The rest of the remaining cars were flagged because there were no other cars on the lead lap when the checkered flag fell for Burman. The final race summary follows.

| Place | Car # | Driver | Car | Laps | Led |
|---|---|---|---|---|---|
| 1 | 43 | Bob Burman | Marquette-Buick | 40 | 18 |
| 2 | 31 | Joe Dawson | Marmon | 40 | 10 |
| 3 | 30 | Ray Harroun | Marmon | 40 | 0 |
| 4 | 41 | Arthur Chevrolet | Marquette-Buick | 40 | 2 |
| 5 | 6 | Tom Kincaid | National | 40 | 8 |
| 6 | 45 | Billy Pearce | FAL | 36 | 0 |
| 7 | 16 | David Cook | Black Crow | 32 | 0 |
| 8 | 14 | C. F. Moore | Marmon | 28 | 0 |
| 9 | 39 | Louis Chevrolet | Marquette-Buick | 24 | 1 |
| 10 | 17 | Ed Stinson | Black Crow | 20 | 0 |
| 11 | 7 | Johnny Aitken | National | 18 | 1 |
| 12 | 15 | Glenn Davis | Great Western | 16 | 0 |
| 13 | 1 | Howard Wilcox | National | 15 | 0 |

Both Harroun and Burman benefited from the fact that neither was forced to make a stop during the race. Burman took a gamble in not stopping. His tires after the race had some of the tread torn from the casing. He told one of his crew members that they had been that way for about the last 50 miles of the race. Harroun's tires were worn but still in better condition than Burman's. Ray Harroun had the patience to run a consistent pace throughout a race, lessening wear on the car and tires. It was this discipline that would help him win the inaugural Indianapolis 500 less than a year later.

The second day of racing saw continued success at the Indianapolis Motor Speedway. Several new records were established, two more car manufacturers debuted, and two former Vanderbilt Cup winners won races. Most important of all, there was only one minor accident. Clearly, the Marquette-Buick continued to be the class of the program, but this didn't come without controversy. There was constant talk that the Marquette-Buick was so dominating because it was not a stock car as defined by the rules. This speculation was further fueled by the fact that it seemed to have the upper hand over the majority of the other cars. As their victories added up, the talk intensified. Would this be the last of the story?

There was a morning shower on Monday, July 4 prior to the start of the races before the skies finally cleared. A slight breeze even provided some relief from the heat of the past couple of days. Given that it was a holiday, combined with the successes of the past two days, a large crowd was anticipated. Many were calling it "Cobe Day" because of the 200-mile Cobe trophy race that was scheduled to close out the three-day program. Ira M. Cobe, president of the Chicago Automobile Club and donor of the cup, had arrived in Indianapolis on Sunday to witness the race from the private box of the Speedway officials. Automotive enthusiasts from Chicago began arriving Sunday afternoon. Additionally, several hundred more spectators arrived from Chicago around noon on Monday by a special train.

The Cobe race, referred to as the "Western Vanderbilt," was first run

*The Cobe trophy. (Photo from a 1909 Buick Motor Company brochure)*

in 1909 on a road course between Crown Point and Lowell in northern Indiana. Louis Chevrolet won the event, despite one of his four cylinders going bad during the race. The 1910 edition, hosted at the Speedway, was rich in rewards. The Indianapolis Motor Speedway awarded $500 to the winner, $300 for second, $200 for third and $100 for fourth. On top of that, the Bosch Magneto Company awarded $300 to the winner, $200 to second, and $100 to third – provided that the winning cars were equipped with Bosch magnetos. The Michelin Tire Company agreed to pay the winner $400 if the car was equipped with Michelin tires. The winner also received the beautiful Cobe trophy valued at $3,000.

Despite all of the positives that warranted a huge turnout, only 20,000 people showed up at the Speedway grounds. It was a good-sized crowd, one that any other venue would have appreciated. However, it didn't meet the Speedway's expectations. Nevertheless, anticipation mounted as the spectators remained very enthusiastic about being treated to one of the greatest days of auto racing to date.

The schedule of events was changed due to the wet conditions. The ten-mile race for stock chassis with engines of 161 – 230 CID was run first in hopes that it would assist in drying the track better than the shorter five-mile race originally scheduled as the first event. This race featured the Buicks of Chevrolet and Burman against virtually the same field of cars that they had dominated in two earlier races during the three-day program. The other entrants were Harry Endicott in an E-M-F, Louis Schwitzer in a Fuller, Arthur Miller in a Warren-Detroit, and Sutcliffe in a Maytag. The Fuller, making its Speedway debut, was produced in Jackson, Michigan, by George Matthews, one of the directors of the Jackson Automobile Company. The name was misleading. Mr. Matthews used the name from his Fuller Buggy Company; however, the car was often mistaken for one of the same name manufactured in Angus, Nebraska, by the Fuller Brothers' Angus Automobile Company.

Sutcliffe, Burman, and Miller got the early jump on the rest of the field, but by the end of the backstretch, Chevrolet had caught the trio, pulling to the outside to pass all three. Chevrolet's Buick thundered down the stretch in front of the grandstands to lead the first lap. Burman was about 50 yards back in second place and the rest of the field was strung out about 100 yards behind him. Early in the second lap, Arthur Miller dropped out with engine problems. Chevrolet continued to lead Burman by a comfortable ten seconds. Over 30 seconds behind Burman, Endicott and Sutcliffe waged their own battle for third place. Louis Chevrolet drove the rest of the way uncontested to win the race in a time of 9:12.23, beating his teammate by a little over nine seconds. Endicott and Sutcliffe had a close race for third with Endicott edging out the Maytag by only a third of a second. The race summary follows.

| Place | Car # | Driver | Car | Laps | Led |
|-------|-------|--------|-----|------|-----|
| 1 | 35 | Louis Chevrolet | Buick | 2 | 2 |
| 2 | 36 | Bob Burman | Buick | 2 | 0 |
| 3 | 26 | Harry Endicott | E-M-F | 2 | 0 |
| 4 | 2 | N. J. Sutcliffe | Maytag | 2 | 0 |
| 5 | 5 | Louis Schwitzer | Fuller | 2 | 0 |
| 6 | 24 | Arthur Miller | Warren-Detroit | 1 | 0 |

The second event was a five-mile contest for stock chassis with engines of 160 or less CID. Three Herreshoffs were in this race, called the patriotic race on the 4th of July, because the cars carried a red, white, and blue paint scheme. Although colorful, the race itself was anything but dramatic. Mortimer Roberts grabbed the lead at the start, building up a 200-yard lead by the end of the first lap. He continued to stretch the lead until he was 300 yards ahead by the time he crossed the finish line in 5:22.88. This was his third victory during the three-day program. Charles Herreshoff was second followed by E. R. McCormick who placed a distant third. The race summary follows.

*Mortimer Roberts and riding mechanic at Elgin, Illinois. Roberts is sitting in an Abbott-Detroit rather than the smaller Herreshoff car that he raced at Indianapolis. (Chicago Daily News negatives collection, SDN-057196. Courtesy of the Chicago Historical Society)*

| Place | Car # | Driver | Car | Laps | Led |
|-------|-------|--------|-----|------|-----|
| 1 | 19 | Mortimer Roberts | Herreshoff | 2 | 2 |
| 2 | 21 | Charles Herreshoff | Herreshoff | 2 | 0 |
| 3 | 20 | E. R. McCormick | Herreshoff | 2 | 0 |

As the cars lined up for the following race, the Remy trophy and Remy Grand Brassard were presented to Bob Burman, winner of the 100-mile Remy Grand race on Saturday. Ernst Moross reminded the crowd during the presentation that the Brassard, a silver arm shield, entitled the winner to a weekly salary of $75 as long as he successfully defended the title.

When the racing resumed, it was time for the five-mile race for stock chassis with engines of 231 - 300 CID. The unique thing about this event was that it did not include the Buicks or Marmons that previous races for this class had featured. Perhaps the Buick drivers were no different than Harroun or Dawson; they were saving themselves for the Cobe trophy race. That left two each of the FAL cars, Black Crows, and Great Westerns plus the Pope-Hartford of Frank Fox to battle for the win. By default, one of these car manufacturers was about to get its first win at the Indianapolis Motor Speedway.

The FAL car of Billy Pearce charged into turn one and enjoyed a brief lead down the backstretch before Louis Heineman passed him going into turn three. Meanwhile, back at the line, C.F. Moore stalled the engine on his Great Western, which caused him to drop out of the race. The two FAL cars continued unchallenged throughout the first lap, oblivious to the hard charging Black Crow of Ed Stinson. However, before the Black Crow caught the duo, Heineman looked as if he had found another gear. He began to pull away, leaving Pearce and Stinson locked in a skirmish for second. Heineman built up an 11-second cushion enroute to the victory with a time of 4:44.31, giving FAL their first win at Indianapolis. Stinson continued to battle Pearce for second, but time ran out on him when Pearce beat him to the line but only by one and half seconds, giving FAL the sweep. The race summary follows.

*Louis Heineman at Elgin, Illinois in August 1910. Heineman drove a Marmon in the Elgin races in 1910. (Chicago Daily News negatives collection, SDN-056227. Courtesy of the Chicago Historical Society)*

| Place | Car # | Driver | Car | Laps | Led |
|-------|-------|--------|-----|------|-----|
| 1 | 44 | Louis Heineman | FAL | 2 | 2 |
| 2 | 45 | Billy Pearce | FAL | 2 | 0 |
| 3 | 17 | Ed Stinson | Black Crow | 2 | 0 |
| 4 | 3 | Frank Fox | Pope-Hartford | 2 | 0 |
| 5 | 15 | Glenn Davis | Great Western | 2 | 0 |
| 6 | 16 | David Cook | Black Crow | 2 | 0 |
| 7 | 14 | C. F. Moore | Great Western | 0 | 0 |

By this time, it was about 3:00 p.m. and the officials had decided that the track was dry enough start the Cobe trophy race. Starter "Pop" Wagner announced that the race would be run at the full distanc of 200 miles. A total of 14 cars came onto the track to line up for the big race. The crowd greeted them wi enthusiastic cheers. The race was open to all stock chassis with engines of less than 600 CID, creating a impressive field. Included were three Marquette-Buicks, three Nationals, two Marmons, the big Mercede of Spencer Wishart, and the ALCO of Harry Grant. Two Black Crows, a FAL, and a Pope-Hartford con pleted the field.

The roar of the engines shook the grandstands as 14 starters thundered for the first turn. The Na tional of Tom Kincaid forged to the front, pursued by the Mercedes of Spencer Wishart. The two ca stayed in that order as they crossed the line to complete the first lap. Arthur Chevrolet and Johnny Aitke were not far behind them. Arthur Chevrolet then took control of the race, a position that he would hold fo several laps. Johnny Aitken fell in behind him for second place. Aitken's luck was short-lived as he deve oped problems with his spark plugs on the third lap, forcing him to make a lengthy pit stop. By the time h returned on the fourth lap, he was shown in last place. Incredibly, Aitken fell victim to the same problen that plagued him during the Remy Grand Brassard race on Saturday. As a result, he made numerous p stops throughout the race that caused him to lose several laps, taking him out of contention. The new wasn't much better for Aitken's teammate, Tom Kincaid. Although he had led the first lap, he soon droppe back to ninth and was never a factor in the race again.

By the 25-mile mark, Arthur Chevrolet had built up about a half-a-mile lead over the field. Burmai Harroun, and Louis Chevrolet were chasing him while the other Marmon of Dawson was shown in sixtl

*...ooking from behind pit road during the early days of the Indianapolis Motor Speedway. (Photo courtesy of the ...dianapolis Motor Speedway)*

...oon afterward, things were shuffled up a bit when Arthur Chevrolet was forced to pit for tires on lap 15. ...arroun came in for the same reason on the next lap.

At the 50-mile mark, Burman was the leader followed by Dawson, Arthur Chevrolet, Wishart, and ...arry Grant. All 14 starters still ran; however, the Pope-Hartford of Frank Fox had taken a lengthy pit stop ...ecause of engine trouble after only ten laps. The National of Wilcox was also in the pits.

Arthur Chevrolet regained the lead from Burman on lap 27. Burman stayed in second position ...ollowed by Dawson. The three drivers stayed in that order until lap 46, or 115 miles, when Burman passed ...is teammate for the lead. Right about this time, Grant treated the crowd to a spectacular feat. His ALCO ...lew a tire in front of the main grandstand, spreading bits of rubber all over the track. He had been carrying ...spare tire, the only car to have one, so he quickly jumped from his car and changed the tire right on the ...ack! The crowd looked on in amazement and cheered wildly as he hopped back in to continue on his way.

On lap 61, the FAL car of Billy Pearce dropped out of the race. On the very next lap Louis Chevrolet ...ad a broken steering knuckle that forced him from the race. Chevrolet's tire problems throughout the race ...revented him from running any higher than fifth since the early laps.

Burman remained in control for the next 70 miles with Dawson about a minute behind. Harroun ...ayed in third, another minute behind Dawson. On lap 67, Burman made a 40-second stop for tires, return-...ng to the track only about 19 seconds ahead of Dawson. With fresh tires and a 19-second lead, Burman

seemed destined for victory. Suddenly, on lap 75, less than 15 miles from the finish, Burman surprise
everyone by coming in the pits for more tires. The Marquette-Buick's tire problems were just what Dawso
needed to gain the advantage and shoot into the lead. Burman was able to get back out in front of Harrou
but could never catch Dawson, who sailed on to victory in a record time of 2:43:26.14. Louis Disbrow
a Rainier had set the old record of 2:53:48.31 at Atlanta. Burman was able to close the gap in the last te
miles, cutting about 30 seconds off of Dawson's lead to finish only three seconds behind him. Harroun wa
a couple of minutes behind Burman and the ALCO of Grant was another ten minutes behind Harroun. Th
Marquette-Buick of Arthur Chevrolet, plagued in the later stages of the race by engine problems and
leaking radiator, finished a full ten minutes behind Grant. The final race summary follows.

| Place | Car # | Driver | Car | Laps | Led |
|-------|-------|--------|-----|------|-----|
| 1 | 31 | Joe Dawson | Marmon | 80 | 6 |
| 2 | 40 | Bob Burman | Marquette-Buick | 80 | 40 |
| 3 | 30 | Ray Harroun | Marmon | 80 | 0 |
| 4 | 27 | Harry Grant | ALCO | 80 | 0 |
| 5 | 39 | Arthur Chevrolet | Marquette-Buick | 80 | 33 |
| 6 | 17 | Ed Stinson | Black Crow | 76 | 0 |
| 7 | 16 | David Cook | Black Crow | 76 | 0 |
| 8 | 41 | Louis Chevrolet | Marquette-Buick | 62 | 0 |
| 9 | 45 | Billy Pearce | FAL | 61 | 0 |
| 10 | 7 | Johnny Aitken | National | 55 | 0 |
| 11 | 6 | Tom Kincaid | National | 55 | 1 |
| 12 | 48 | Spencer Wishart | Mercedes | 20 | 0 |
| 13 | 1 | Howard Wilcox | National | 16 | 0 |
| 14 | 3 | Frank Fox | Pope-Hartford | 10 | 0 |

*Ed Stinson and riding mechanic J. Taylor sitting in a Black Crow at Elgin, Illinois in 1910. (Chicago Daily News negatives collection, SDN-056317. Courtesy of the Chicago Historical Society)*

*Marmon driver Joe Dawson. (Photo courtesy of the Indianapolis Motor Speedway)*

Joe Dawson, who was mobbed as he climbed from his car, received $1,200 for his victory. The beautiful silver Cobe trophy cup was presented to Howard Marmon during a ceremony after the race.

The Cobe race was a big success, but the officials had a little bit of a problem. It was 6:15 p.m. and there were still four events left on the schedule. After a brief discussion, it was decided that the last two contests of the day would be the five-mile amateur race and the 20-mile free-for-all. The ten-mile event for stock chassis with engines of 301 – 450 CID and the ten-mile handicap race were cancelled.

The five-mile amateur race was a rematch of the same contest held on Saturday. Arthur Greiner had won. The big Mercedes of Spencer Wishart failed to complete the event because of engine trouble. Most people felt that Wishart could have won had he not fallen victim to problems.

This race, although short, was exciting all of the way. Wishart and Greiner were side-by-side for the entire five miles. Tousey was about 30 seconds off the pace. The two leaders were helpless to shake each other. If Wishart surged, Greiner surged, and vice versa. Mirroring the first lap, the two were dead even at the finish line. After a short discussion, the judges gave Wishart the victory in a time of 4:21.34. Greiner was scored a mere 0.01 of a second behind in second place! The race summary follows.

| Place | Car # | Driver | Car | Laps | Led |
|---|---|---|---|---|---|
| 1 | 48 | Spencer Wishart | Mercedes | 2 | 2 |
| 2 | 12 | Arthur Greiner | National | 2 | 0 |
| 3 | 1 | William Tousey | National | 2 | 0 |

The final race of the day was a 20-mile free-for-all featuring seven entrants. The event offered an intriguing match up. Bob Burman, fresh from his disappointing second place finish in the Cobe trophy race, brought out his Buick Special for this race. He was matched up against Eddie Hearne in his big Benz, the National of Johnny Aitken, and Ray Harroun in a Marmon. Tripp in a Stoddard-Dayton, Wilcox in William Tousey's big Simplex, and the Chadwick of Len Zengel completed the starting field.

The crowd in the main grandstand let out a collective groan just as the race started when Howard Wilcox ran into the Chadwick of Zengel, forcing Wilcox out of the race. He said later that the excessive smoke blinded him, causing the miscue with Zengel. Despite the mishap, all of the other starters, including

*Ray Harroun during racing action at the Indianapolis Motor Speedway in July 1910. (Photo courtesy of the Indianapolis Motor Speedway)*

Zengel, continued on their way. Hearne owned the early lead, followed by Aitken and Burman. He opened up a five-second lead as Burman and Aitken battled fiercely for second place. Burman had captured second by the five-mile mark, but the struggle between the two continued until

Aitken had a two-and-a-half-second advantage at the ten-mile mark. Meanwhile, Harroun and Tripp were about 45 seconds back with Zengel another ten seconds behind them.

Hearne continued to maintain a ten-second lead over the field, stretching it to 12 seconds by the time he took the win in 14:06.72. This shattered the previous mark of 15:31.80 set by Robertson's Fiat in Atlanta. Aitken finally prevailed against Burman by stretching a 16-second lead at the 15-mile mark into a minute and a half at the finish. Harroun never could get higher than fourth, and Zengel was far back in fifth. The race summary follows.

| Place | Car # | Driver | Car | Laps | Led |
|---|---|---|---|---|---|
| 1 | 22 | Eddie Hearne | Benz | 8 | 8 |
| 2 | 8 | Johnny Aitken | National | 8 | 0 |
| 3 | 43 | Bob Burman | Buick Special | 8 | 0 |
| 4 | 32 | Ray Harroun | Marmon | 8 | 0 |
| 5 | 18 | Len Zengel | Chadwick | 7 | 0 |
| 6 | 29 | Tripp | Stoddard-Dayton | 5 | 0 |
| 7 | 46 | Howard Wilcox | Simplex | 0 | 0 |

*The Marmon racing team in a 1910 Model 32 truck with Ray Harroun at the wheel. Joe Dawson is standing to the far right. The truck was specifically designed for the team before Marmon started producing them a few years later. (Photo courtesy of the Hoosier Auto Show and Swap Meet)*

It was almost 7:00 p.m. when the final event of the three-day program was complete. The sun was setting as the race teams began to clean up and the crowd started to file out of the Speedway in all directions. The buzz among the spectators as they left the grounds was how exciting the racing had been during the meet. There were over 30 new records set during three days of safe, competitive racing. Clearly, the Buick team was the class of the field with their new Marquette-Buick. The team won nine of the 26 races while being responsible for the majority of the records. But it wasn't only the Buicks that were successful. There were ten car manufacturers new to the Speedway, and five of them accounted for six victories. Additionally, there were two former Vanderbilt Cup winners included among the participating drivers – Harry Grant and George Robertson. Their presence at the Speedway was a testament as to how important the Indianapolis Motor Speedway had become in the sport of auto racing.

Despite the tremendous success of the three-day program, the Speedway management decided to cancel the 24-hour auto race, as well as the coinciding balloon races originally scheduled for August 12–13. Additionally, the auto races originally scheduled for September 2, 3, and 5 were rescheduled for Saturday and Monday only, September 3 and 5. A couple of reasons were rumored to be the cause of the changes. Some speculated that it was due to the disappointing crowds at the recently completed program, but others reasoned that there were not enough entries.

Sadly, just two days after the conclusion of the races, Tom Kincaid, the popular Indianapolis driver for the National team, was killed in an accident while testing at the Speedway. He was only 23-years-old. A five-year employee of the National Motor Car Company, he drove race cars for them the past two years. He had 12 victories to his credit, including the 100-mile Prest-O-Lite race at the Speedway in May 1910.

Apparently, since the National cars did not run well during the recent races, Kincaid had gone to the Speedway with his riding mechanic William Clifton, Johnny Aitken, W. G. Wahl, designer for the National Motor Car Company, and Charlie Merz, a driver for National. They wanted to try the cars out in an effort to improve them. Kincaid and Aitken started on a 50-mile test run when Aitken stopped for repairs after about 30 miles. Kincaid continued while Wahl, Clifton, and Merz were in the judges' stand timing. Since Clifton had stayed in the judges' stand, this was the first time that Kincaid had driven a car without a riding mechanic. He rounded the south turn and continued north on the backstretch. The men turned to await his coming at the north end of the frontstretch but he never came into sight. Scanning the course they noticed a hole in the fence along the backstretch that had not been there previously. Together with Aitken, they jumped into a car and hurried to the scene. Kincaid was found lying to the left of his car, partially against the fence and partially under the car, dead from multiple injuries. The big blue National was a twisted and dismantled mess, pinned in the fence and half buried under the soil. The car had taken out two fence posts that had been set in concrete, demolishing the fence for a distance of 25 feet.

A handkerchief was found on Kincaid's chest, giving rise to the theory that he reached for his handkerchief, which the National drivers wore fastened to their caps, as he sped along. Drivers frequently had to wipe an accumulation of dust and oil from their goggles while they were driving on the track. It was thought that something must have gone wrong with his car at that instant. Kincaid had set the brakes, and the skid marks on the brick course showed that the car turned sideways, sliding about 100 yards before crashing through the fence. Although all of the wheel mounts were intact, the car was so demolished that it was impossible to tell if something had broken just before the accident; however, that was the suspicion.

Charlie Merz said a couple of days later, "A fellow never knows when it is going to happen. All he can do is sit there and wait and see what is coming to him"[3]. Merz knew this better than anyone; it was his car that wrecked on the last day of the August 1909 races, killing three men. Meanwhile, Johnny Aitken was completely devastated. The two drivers boarded together on East 21st Street and were the best of friends. The other racing teams called them the "indigo twins", referencing the color of their National cars. Aitken decided not to participate in the races at Louisville and Cincinnati, scheduled to begin two days after the accident.

The loss of Tom Kincaid was an unexpected tragedy for everyone. Likewise, another big shock came later in July when the contest board of the AAA disqualified the Marquette-Buicks from competition in stock car classes for 1910. Not only did this prevent them from entering any further contests in 1910, but the board also ruled that all performances by the Marquette-Buick during the July races at the Indianapolis Motor Speedway were considered null and void. No record of the performances were permitted.

According to the contest board, the disqualification was made for three reasons. First and foremost, the Marquette-Buick was "not a stock car as defined under the 1910 contest rules of the AAA"[4]. Secondly, the Marquette-Buick was "not on sale or offered for sale to the public at the regular selling agencies of the Buick Motor Company or the Marquette Motor Company as required under the 1910 contest rules"[5]. Finally, according to the AAA, "the privilege of competing in the July races at Indianapolis under the name of Marquette-Buick was granted upon the condition that in the event of successful performances there were to be no advertisement of such performances under any other name than Marquette-Buick"[6]. That condition was violated by the advertisement in the *New York Herald* on July 10, 1910, referring to the performance of the Buick cars at Indianapolis on July 1, 2, and 4 with no mention being made of a Marquette-Buick.

Talk about a shake up in the results! The disqualification took six first-place finishes away from

uick (four for Burman and two for Louis Chevrolet) plus the elimination of 11 new records. The Marmon
nd National teams were the biggest benefactors of the ruling. Joe Dawson was awarded three wins and
ohnny Aitken two. Also, Billy Pearce was awarded first place in the 50-mile G & J trophy race, giving
AL an important victory. However, the one that had to hurt the most was Burman's victory in the Remy
irand Brassard and trophy race. He lost the weekly salary from the Brassard, the trophy, and three new
ecords set during the race. Joe Dawson was given the victory after having finished in second place, only
ve seconds behind Burman.

Additionally, the contest board also disqualified the Mercedes of Spencer Wishart. He had won the
ve-mile amateur race on July 4, but the board awarded the victory to Arthur Greiner, who finished second
o Wishart by 0.01 of a second. This gave Greiner his third victory for the three-day meet.

The rulings caused quite a stir throughout the sport of auto racing. Some thought that the Marquette-
uick would be reinstated in time for the September races at Indianapolis, but others contended that they were
o dominant in the races that it was obvious they were not stock cars as defined by the rules of the contest board.
he following weeks were full of speculation as to what might happen at the September meet.

*Chapter 9*

# The Last Auto Races Before the 500

After the July events at the Speedway, many of the drivers participated in races at Churchhill Downs in Louisville, Kentucky (home of the Kentucky Derby), and Elgin, Illinois. The Marmon team of Harroun and Dawson dominated the contests at Louisville. They finished first and second respectively in three races, Dawson picked up a victory in a five-mile event. Meanwhile, Al Livingstone, driving a National car as a private owner, made his mark on the sport of auto racing by winning a 192-mile contest on a road course at Elgin.

Shortly after the Elgin races, it was announced that Livingstone would drive for the National team in the September meet at Indianapolis. Many local fans were thrilled by the news that Livingstone would be joined by local favorite Johnny Aitken, who – along with the National team – had not raced since the death of Tom Kincaid. Also, two other local favorites, Charlie Merz and Howard Wilcox, were entered to drive for the National team. The famous Fiat driver from New York, Ralph DePalma, had confirmed that he was entered as did Chicago's Eddie Hearne, who would be defending the Speedway Helmet in his Benz.

One crowd favorite who was not entered in the program was Barney Oldfield. He stated in an interview with the *Indianapolis Star* just before the races that he would be racing on the East Coast. "I will not be at Indianapolis to take part in the special meet, nor will I be present in person to see the racing. I am booked to take part in the Brighton Beach races at New York on Saturday and Monday where I will meet George Robertson and other eastern drivers."[1]

Everyone's attention turned away from racing during late August when the western part of the country was plagued by some of the worst fires in history. Over 1,500 individual fires burned across Idaho, Montana, and into Canada. The "big blowup" – as many referred to it – came on August 20, 1910, burning over three million acres of forest and claiming at least 85 lives before early winter snows completely extinguished the flames. The effects of the fires were clearly seen in Indianapolis because the skies were so dark from ash that it caused the street lights to turn on during the day.

As the Labor Day weekend approached, it became more evident that the Buick team would not be at Indianapolis due to the disqualification of the Marquette-Buick; however, the 25 drivers entered represented 20 different car manufacturers. Seven of the car manufacturers would be making their Indianapolis debut. Two of them were the Parry and McFarlan. David Parry of Indianapolis started the Parry Auto Company in 1909. He had formerly been in business with his brothers at the Parry Manufacturing Company, one of the world's largest carriage factories before the turn of the century. Hughie Hughes was entered as the driver for Parry. The McFarlan Motor Car Company of Connersville, Indiana, entered two 1911 McFarlan Six models. W.J. Barndollar and Fred Clemens were the drivers.

The three days leading up to the program saw a beehive of activity at the Speedway. Some of the teams had come to Indianapolis straight from the Elgin races and practiced steadily during that time. The Marmon team provided a surprise when they rolled out two new Marmon cars that would be making their racing debut during the September races at the Speedway. Built by Howard Marmon and Ray Harroun, they were fitted with the same chassis as the six-cylinder Marmon Wasp, but they carried four-cylinder engines with 410 CID. The cars were to be driven by Harroun and Dawson during the free-for-all events. The cars were impressive in practice, completing fast laps at 87 mph.

*Scene in the garages during the early days at the Indianapolis Motor Speedway. (Photo courtesy of the Indianapolis Motor Speedway)*

As practice came to a close on Friday, September 2, everything was ready for the weekend's races. Although there were only two days of racing scheduled, they would be a full two days with 19 races and a one-mile time trial scheduled. Highlights of the program included a ten-mile free-for-all race for the Speedway Helmet, a 100-mile free-for-all, a 200-mile event open to stock chassis with engines of 600 CID or less, and the 100-mile contest for the Remy Grand Brassard and trophy. The Marmon team was eager for the opportunity to win the Remy again. By virtue of Harroun's Remy win in May and Dawson's win in July, the Marmon team could capture permanent possession of the Remy trophy by winning the September race. The complete program schedule was as follows.

### Saturday, September 3

- Event 1 – Trials for the one-mile record
- Event 2 - Five-mile race open to stock chassis with engines of 160 or less cubic inch piston displacement (CID)
- Event 3 – Five-mile race open to stock chassis with engines of 161 – 230 CID
- Event 4 – Five-mile race open to stock chassis with engines of 231 – 300 CID
- Event 5 – Five-mile race open to stock chassis with engines of 301 – 450 CID
- Event 6 – Five-mile race open to stock chassis with engines of 451 – 600 CID
- Event 7 – Ten-mile free-for-all race for the Speedway Helmet
- Event 8 – 100-mile free-for-all race
- Event 9 – Five-mile free-for-all handicap race
- Event 10 – Five-mile amateur race
- Event 11 – 100-mile race for the Remy Grand Brassard and trophy open to stock chassis with engines of less than 451 CID

### Monday, September 5

- Event 1 – Five-mile race open to stock chassis with engines of 160 or less CID
- Event 2 – Five-mile race open to stock chassis with engines of 161 – 230 CID
- Event 3 – Five-mile race open to stock chassis with engines of 231 – 300 CID
- Event 4 – Five-mile race open to stock chassis with engines of 300 – 450 CID
- Event 5 – Five-mile race open to stock chassis with engines of 451 – 600 CID
- Event 6 – Five-mile free-for-all handicap race
- Event 7 – Ten-mile free-for-all race
- Event 8 – 50-mile free-for-all race
- Event 9 – 200-mile race open to stock chassis with engines of 600 CID or less

Saturday started out cloudy with the threat of rain, but it turned into a beautiful day with the temperature at a comfortable 80 degrees. The spectators began swarming around the Speedway at noon with several thousand filling the grandstands by the start of the first race at 1:00 p.m. The Speedway was in pristine condition with flowerbeds at various spots around the grounds, complementing the lush green lawn of the infield. Military guards were stationed all around the grounds for security purposes. Seated in the main grandstand, the Maxwell-Briscoe band from New Castle, Indiana, provided music for the spectators. The cars also entertained the early crowd as the drivers practiced right up until the start of the first event.

Ralph DePalma started the day's events by bringing his big red 200-horsepower Fiat onto the track for a one-mile time trial. The Speedway offered a $100 prize if anyone could beat Barney Oldfield's track

*The crowd looking from the infield during the 1910 automobile races at the Indianapolis Motor Speedway. (Photo courtesy of the Detroit Public Library, National Automotive History Collection)*

record of 35.63 seconds set in May 1910 in his Benz. The trials started in the northwest turn so that the car would go by the main grandstand. DePalma fell a full three seconds short of the record after completing mile in 38.64 seconds. He made a second trial in his 90-horsepower Fiat Cyclone but could do no bette than 40.20 seconds. No other drivers made attempts at the record.

The five-mile race for stock chassis with engines of 160 CID or less was postponed until later in th day because the participants needed more time to prepare. This gave way to the first contest of the after noon, a five-mile event open to stock chassis with engines of 161 – 230 CID. It was an interesting lineup for the spectators that included two entrants in the Indianapolis-made Cole, a Firestone-Columbus, which had not been seen at the Speedway since the May races, and two car manufacturers new to the Speedway – Hudson and Staver-Chicago. The Hudson Motor Car Company began production at its Detroit, Michi gan, plant in June of 1909 and had just recently achieved the biggest first year sales in automobile histor by selling over 4,000 autos in the first year. The Staver Carriage Company of Chicago had been producing 2-cylinder cars since 1907, but only recently began producing 4-cylinder cars.

Louis Edmunds beat the field to the first turn in his Cole but was closely pursued by Keifer in the Staver-Chicago and Bill Endicott in the other Cole. Edmunds steadily built on the advantage throughou the first lap, leading Keifer by about nine seconds with Endicott another 11 seconds back. The Firestone Columbus of Lee Frayer experienced problems early in the race and dropped out before the end of the firs lap. Walter Olin, in the Indianapolis debut of the Hudson, did not fare much better as he was well off th pace during the first lap before eventually dropping out of the race. Meanwhile, Keifer and Endicott seemed to form an alliance as the two drivers chose to work together rather than race each other. This paid off for both of them, closing to within two seconds of Edmunds as the three streaked down the front straightaway for the final time. Edmunds managed to hang on to win in 5:05.50 to give Cole its first victory at the Indianapolis Motor Speedway. Keifer was given the nod over Endicott for second place in a time of 5:07.20 to Endicott's 5:07.79. The complete race summary follows.

| Place | Car # | Driver | Car | Laps | Led |
|-------|-------|--------|-----|------|-----|
| 1 | 6 | Louis Edmunds | Cole | 2 | 2 |
| 2 | 17 | Keifer | Staver-Chicago | 2 | 0 |
| 3 | 33 | Bill Endicott | Cole | 2 | 0 |
| 4 | 35 | Walter Olin | Hudson | 1 | 0 |
| 5 | 30 | Lee Frayer | Firestone-Columbus | 0 | 0 |

The next event was a five-mile race for stock chassis with engines of 231 – 300 CID. Besides the two Marmons, the contest featured two FAL cars and a Great Western. This race was also the Speedway debut for the McFarlan and the Cino. The Haberer & Company of Cincinnati, Ohio, had just begun producing the Cino in 1910.

*Frank Gelnaw and his riding mechanic sitting in a FAL car in Elgin, Illinois, one week before the September 1910 auto races at the Indianapolis Motor Speedway. (Chicago Daily News negatives collection, SDN-056234. Courtesy of the Chicago Historical Society)*

This race was just as closely contested as the previous one. Frank Gelnaw battled for the lead early, giving the FAL car a five-second advantage over the Marmon of Ray Harroun and Billy Pearce in another FAL car by the end of the first lap. The remainder of the field bunched up five seconds back with the two McFarlans another six seconds behind. Harroun and Pearce hooked up together, passing Gelnaw late in the second lap and quickly opening up a six-second gap as they drove side-by-side for the finish. In front of the frenzied crowd, Harroun barely nipped Pearce at the line to win in 4:35.66 to Pearce's 4:35.95. Gelnaw narrowly hung on to third place beating Dawson by only 0.36 of a second. Harry Endicott in a Great Western and William Fritsch in a Cino were a distant fifth and sixth, respectively. The McFarlans finished well off the pace in the last two positions. The final race summary follows.

| Place | Car # | Driver | Car | Laps | Led |
|-------|-------|--------|-----|------|-----|
| 1 | 26 | Ray Harroun | Marmon | 2 | 1 |
| 2 | 15 | Billy Pearce | FAL | 2 | 0 |
| 3 | 16 | Frank Gelnaw | FAL | 2 | 1 |
| 4 | 22 | Joe Dawson | Marmon | 2 | 0 |
| 5 | 37 | Harry Endicott | Great Western | 2 | 0 |
| 6 | 34 | William Fritsch | Cino | 2 | 0 |
| 7 | 24 | Fred Clemens | McFarlan | 2 | 0 |
| 8 | 23 | W.J. Barndollar | McFarlan | 2 | 0 |

At the start of the next event, the fans greeted Johnny Aitken with a thunderous applause as he drove onto the track to participate in a race for the first time since July. Adding to the interest of the contest, another car manufacturer was making its Indianapolis debut, the Speedwell Motor Car Company in Dayton, Ohio, builders of the Speedwell. The company's founder, Pierce Schenck, had selected Indianapolis driver Jap Clemens to drive the car during the September races at the Speedway. It would face stiff competition going up against eight other entrants, including the National, Marmon, and FAL teams in a five-mile race for stock chassis with engines of 301 – 450 CID.

To no one's surprise, Johnny Aitken and Joe Dawson quickly moved their National and Marmon entries to the front. The two rivals were literally inches apart as they completed the first lap racing wheel-to-wheel. About four seconds back were the Nationals of Charlie Merz and Arthur Greiner, closely followed by Clemens in the Speedwell and Pierce in the FAL car. Gelnaw in a FAL, Ireland in a Midland, and Frayer in a Firestone-Columbus were well off of the pace. Aitken and Dawson continued to put distance between them and the rest of the field while racing each other closely throughout the second lap. Aitken used a final surge of speed to pull away down the frontstretch, beating Dawson to the line by a little under two seconds with a time of 4:05.97. The local fans were standing on their feet cheering wildly as Aitken claimed the victory in his first race back. Some hated to see Dawson lose the race but everyone agreed that it was nice to see Johnny Aitken back where he belonged, winning races at Indianapolis. Arthur Greiner, who was another seven seconds back from Dawson, beat Charlie Merz to the line for third place by 0.40 of a second. The Speedwell had a good showing in its first race, finishing in fifth place just a little less than two seconds behind the fourth place Charlie Merz. The final race summary follows.

| Place | Car # | Driver | Car | Laps | Led |
|-------|-------|--------|-----|------|-----|
| 1 | 9 | Johnny Aitken | National | 2 | 2 |
| 2 | 10 | Joe Dawson | Marmon | 2 | 0 |
| 3 | 18 | Arthur Greiner | National | 2 | 0 |
| 4 | 11 | Charlie Merz | National | 2 | 0 |
| 5 | 5 | Jap Clemens | Speedwell | 2 | 0 |
| 6 | 15 | Billy Pearce | FAL | 2 | 0 |
| 7 | 16 | Frank Gelnaw | FAL | 2 | 0 |
| 8 | 29 | Ralph Ireland | Midland | 2 | 0 |
| 9 | 31 | Lee Frayer | Firestone-Columbus | 2 | 0 |

The five-mile event for stock chassis with engines of 451 – 600 CID that followed was primarily a National affair. Howard Wilcox, Arthur Greiner, and Charlie Merz, all driving Nationals, were entered against the Matheson driven by Charles Basle. The Matheson Motor Car Company run by Frank and Charles Matheson had moved from Grand Rapids, Michigan, to Holyoke, Massachusetts, before finding a permanent home in Wilkes-Barre, Pennsylvania, in 1906. The brothers had chosen French native and current Cincinnati resident Charles Basle to pilot their car for the Indianapolis races.

*Charles Basle and riding mechanic Neil Whalen sitting in a Matheson at Elgin, Illinois, in August 1910, just prior to the September 1910 auto races at the Indianapolis Motor Speedway. (Chicago Daily News negatives collection, SDN-056231. Courtesy of the Chicago Historical Society)*

The first lap of the race was hotly contested as Howard Wilcox led Arthur Greiner by less than a second. Merz and Basle were only about four seconds back from them. Wilcox and Greiner carried out a dazzling display of dicing throughout the second lap. Just when it appeared as if Wilcox had the advantage, Greiner would come storming back to lead by a wheel's length. Not to be denied, Wilcox would respond with another burst of speed as the two traded leads all the way to the finish. It became a two-car race when Merz and Basle began to fade back. At the finish, Wilcox edged out Greiner to claim the victory in 4:06.75, just 0.76 of a second ahead of Greiner. Merz had fallen about 12 seconds back from the two with Basle about a second and a half behind Merz. The race summary follows.

| Place | Car # | Driver | Car | Laps | Led |
|-------|-------|--------|-----|------|-----|
| 1 | 9 | Howard Wilcox | National | 2 | 2 |
| 2 | 18 | Arthur Greiner | National | 2 | 0 |
| 3 | 11 | Charlie Merz | National | 2 | 0 |
| 4 | 14 | Charles Basle | Matheson | 2 | 0 |

The excitement in the air began to build as the cars were brought to the track for the next contest, a ten-mile free-for-all for the Speedway Helmet. Not only were the spectators anxious to see who would win, but the notoriety of the entrants promised an intriguing race. Defending champion of the Speedway Helmet, Eddie Hearne, would be driving his Benz against the Nationals of Johnny Aitken and Charlie

Merz as well as the Fiat of Ralph DePalma. Many in attendance were pulling for DePalma. The handsome, even-tempered Italian was admired by all for his good sportsmanship. Charles Basle, entered in the Matheson, was the fifth entrant. Following the custom, defending champion Hearne wore the Speedway Helmet during the race.

The start of the race was a disaster for DePalma. He stalled his engine at the line, giving the rest of the field a considerable lead before he could get going again. With the Fiat at a handicap, Hearne's Benz was the class of the field in the early going. He completed the first five miles in 3:36.74, easily leading the second place Aitken by almost 21 seconds. DePalma, behind everyone else in the field, trailed the leader by almost a full minute! Hearne continued to accelerate his pace as he completed his second five miles in 3:26.67 to defend the Speedway Helmet in 7:03.41 for the ten miles. Merz finished about 45 seconds back in second place while DePalma recovered to complete the last five-miles in 3:33.45, but it was only good enough for third. Aitken fell off the pace during the last five miles to fade back to fourth place while the overmatched Matheson finished last. The race summary follows.

| Place | Car # | Driver | Car | Laps | Led |
|-------|-------|--------|-----|------|-----|
| 1 | 3 | Eddie Hearne | Benz | 4 | 4 |
| 2 | 7 | Charlie Merz | National | 4 | 0 |
| 3 | 2 | Ralph DePalma | Fiat | 4 | 0 |
| 4 | 8 | Johnny Aitken | National | 4 | 0 |
| 5 | 14 | Charles Basle | Matheson | 4 | 0 |

*Eddie Hearne wearing the Speedway Helmet. Hearne won the helmet race in July 1910 and successfully defended it in September 1910. (Photo courtesy of the Indianapolis Motor Speedway)*

Event number two, a five-mile race for stock chassis with engines of 160 or less CID, which had been postponed from earlier in the day, was the next contest to be held. The three starters were all driving the red, white, and blue Herreshoff cars. Walter Emmons and W.J. Smith had a back and forth affair going throughout the entire two laps. Emmons maintained a two-and-a-half second lead at the end of the first lap; however, Smith came back, just losing at the line by only 0.71 of a second. McCormick finished almost two minutes behind and was never a factor in the race. The race summary follows.

| Place | Car # | Driver | Car | Laps | Led |
|-------|-------|--------|-----|------|-----|
| 1 | 19 | Walter Emmons | Herreshoff | 2 | 2 |
| 2 | 21 | W.J. Smith | Herreshoff | 2 | 0 |
| 3 | 20 | E.R. McCormick | Herreshoff | 2 | 0 |

While the cars were getting ready for the 100-mile free-for-all race, the Michelin twins of the Michelin Tire Company were entertaining the crowd. The twins were made of automobile tires and operated by compressed air. Created in Nice, France, in 1908, their fame had spread throughout Europe and America.

Start of the 100-mile free-for-all race on September 3, 1910. Eventual winner Eddie Hearne (#3) in a Benz is in the first position. (Photo courtesy of the Indianapolis Motor Speedway)

The 100-mile free-for-all included 11 starters going after a $1,000 first prize. The race featured some very popular entrants: the Benz of Eddie Hearne, the Marmons of Harroun and Dawson, the Nationals of Johnny Aitken and Al Livingstone, plus the competitive FAL cars. This was Livingstone's first race at the Speedway and many were excited to see this young driver, who was noticed after his success at the Elgin, Illinois, races a few weeks earlier. The race also featured the return of the Westcott. Made in Richmond, Indiana, the Westcott had not been seen at the Speedway since the Wheeler-Schebler race in May. Young Harry Knight of Indianapolis was the driver for Westcott. Knight had just received his AAA driver's license on Friday! Another interesting twist to the race was the entry of an Indianapolis-made American to be driven by Indianapolis driver John Jenkins. Noted driver Louis Disbrow had purchased the car to drive in the Vanderbilt Cup race later in the year. Since it was still in Indianapolis, Disbrow decided to let Jenkins give it a shakedown at the Indianapolis races. This was the only race that the American was entered in during the two-day program.

The big Benz of Eddie Hearne lined up in the first position with John Jenkins in the American right next to him. Harry Knight and Joe Dawson followed in the next two positions. The Marmon of Ray Harroun and the National of Johnny Aitken lined up in the last two positions of the 11 starters. Many spectators wondered if Harroun and Aitken would take it easy at the beginning of the long race or immediately charge hard to the front. Likewise, it was no surprise to anyone that the Benz of Eddie Hearne rushed into the early lead. By the end of the first lap, with Hearne still in the lead, Livingstone passed the American of Jenkins for second. No one ever had a chance to see what Aitken's strategy would be because he dropped out of the race with engine trouble on the third lap. Joe Dawson, who had been running well, was forced to retire for the same reason on the next lap. At the end of the fourth lap, Hearne had about a nine-second lead over A Livingstone. John Jenkins was in third place about 30 seconds behind Livingstone and Harroun had made an aggressive charge to put himself in fourth place just one second behind Jenkins. Harry Knight was driving a good race and moved the Westcott into fifth place less than a half a second behind Harroun. The rest of the field trailed Knight by over 30 seconds.

*Johnny Aitken in the National #8. (Photo courtesy of the Indianapolis Motor Speedway)*

Over the next eight laps, or 20 miles, Hearne continued to pace the field. His lead over Livingstone stayed at a consistent nine seconds. Meanwhile, Harroun was locked in a fierce battle for third with Jenkins and Knight. The rest of the field had faded to at least two minutes behind these three cars.

Things changed dramatically over the next 12 laps. Livingstone was forced to surrender his second place position when his right rear tire blew on lap 13. The stop cost him one-and-a-half minutes, which allowed Harroun and Knight to each move up a position. During these laps, Jenkins began having trouble with the American, causing him to fall back to seventh place. He eventually dropped out of the race a few laps from the end. It appeared that Harroun's aggressive start had caught up to him, because he was forced to stop for tires on lap 18, or 45 miles; however, he worked his way back up to third at the end of 60 miles

By the 70-mile mark, Hearne was running away from the field. He had built up a lead in excess of two minutes over the rest of the cars. The best race was for the next three positions. Harroun led Knight and Livingstone, who had been plagued by a second stop for tires, by less than a minute. The rest of the field was a good five minutes back from this group.

Feeling comfortable with his lead, Hearne made a 24-second stop for oil just six laps from the end of the race. Harroun lost second position when he had to pit again for new tires. He was running an uncharacteristically aggressive race in pursuit of the Benz, but the pace proved to be too much for his tires. Harry Knight, who had not made a stop the entire race, took advantage of Harroun's misfortune by inheriting second place but was pressured by Livingstone just a few feet behind.

Hearne completed his impressive performance by capturing the victory in 1:19:58.09, an average of 75.030 mph. Harry Knight's performance was no less of an accomplishment as he drove the Westcott to a second place finish just one day after receiving his AAA driver's license! Al Livingstone faded somewhat at the end but still hung on to finish in third place – almost two minutes behind Knight but 37 seconds ahead of the fourth place Harroun. The FAL car of Billy Pearce finished in fifth position, the last car on the lead lap. The final race summary follows.

| Place | Car # | Driver | Car | Laps | Led |
|---|---|---|---|---|---|
| 1 | 3 | Eddie Hearne | Benz | 40 | 40 |
| 2 | 27 | Harry Knight | Westcott | 40 | 0 |
| 3 | 7 | Al Livingstone | National | 40 | 0 |
| 4 | 32 | Ray Harroun | Marmon | 40 | 0 |
| 5 | 15 | Billy Pearce | FAL | 40 | 0 |
| 6 | 16 | Frank Gelnaw | FAL | 39 | 0 |
| 7 | 14 | Charles Basle | Matheson | 38 | 0 |
| 8 | 36 | John Jenkins | American | 38 | 0 |
| 9 | 31 | Lee Frayer | Firestone-Columbus | 4 | 0 |
| 10 | 10 | Joe Dawson | Marmon | 3 | 0 |
| 11 | 8 | Johnny Aitken | National | 2 | 0 |

The next event was another wild and confusing handicap race. A total of 15 starters entered the contest. It was also the Indianapolis debut for Hughie Hughes and the Indianapolis-made Parry. W.J. Smith and Walter Emmons started first in their little Herreshoff cars. Four drivers began 16 seconds later; Louis Edmunds and Bill Endicott in the Cole cars, and W.J. Barndollar and Fred Clemens in the McFarlans. Another 18 seconds later, three more cars entered the race; the Midland of Ralph Ireland, the Cino of William Fritsch, and the Parry driven by Hughes. The Great Western of Harry Endicott and the Black Crow of Ed Stinson were added to the mix after another 10 seconds. Two more cars roared away from the start line 20 seconds later, Charles Basle in a Matheson and young Harry Knight in the Westcott. Finally, one minute and twenty-four seconds after the race had begun, the Nationals of Charlie Merz and Arthur Greiner were allowed to begin.

Louis Edmunds easily made up his 16-second handicap on the Herreshoffs to claim the lead before the end of the first lap. This race did not feature as many fluctuations in position as some handicap contests held previously. Basle and Knight made up their handicaps quickly, Greiner moved up several spots, and the Herreshoffs went straight to the back, but the rest of the placing did not change a great deal. Once Edmunds made it to the front, he never relinquished the lead, winning in a time of 5:01.66. Charles Basle was 15 seconds back in a Matheson and the rest of the finishers were spread out in two to four-second intervals. The race summary follows.

| Place | Car # | Driver | Car | Laps | Led |
|-------|-------|--------|-----|------|-----|
| 1 | 6 | Louis Edmunds | Cole | 2 | 2 |
| 2 | 14 | Charles Basle | Matheson | 2 | 0 |
| 3 | 24 | Fred Clemens | McFarlan | 2 | 0 |
| 4 | 27 | Harry Knight | Westcott | 2 | 0 |
| 5 | 29 | Ralph Ireland | Midland | 2 | 0 |
| 6 | 25 | Hughie Hughes | Parry | 2 | 0 |
| 7 | 34 | William Fritsch | Cino | 2 | 0 |
| 8 | 18 | Arthur Greiner | National | 2 | 0 |
| 9 | 37 | Harry Endicott | Great Western | 2 | 0 |
| 10 | 33 | Bill Endicott | Cole | 2 | 0 |
| 11 | 28 | Ed Stinson | Black Crow | 2 | 0 |
| 12 | 11 | Charlie Merz | National | 2 | 0 |
| 13 | 19 | Walter Emmons | Herreshoff | 2 | 0 |
| 14 | 21 | W.J. Smith | Herreshoff | 2 | 0 |
| 15 | 23 | W.J. Barndollar | McFarlan | 2 | 0 |

*Ralph Ireland and riding mechanic F. Sabin in a Midland at Elgin, Illinois, in August 1910. (Chicago Daily News negatives collection, SDN-056224. Courtesy of the Chicago Historical Society)*

A five-mile amateur race, the next scheduled event was cancelled due to the lack of entrants. The crowd didn't seem to mind since most of them were anxious for the final event of the day, the 100-mile Remy Grand Brassard and trophy race.

The 11 starters included three drivers who had just recently competed in the 100-mile free-for-all race: Joe Dawson, Billy Pearce, and Lee Frayer. Dawson and Frayer had only completed a few laps, but Pearce had gone the full 100-mile distance. Another hour and a half of racing would surely take its toll on the driver.

As the cars lined up, it looked like the favorites to win the race were in the first three starting positions, the Nationals of Charlie Merz and Howard Wilcox, plus the Marmon of Joe Dawson. No one really expected the other eight entrants to keep pace with them.

The first part of the race was a classic battle between Joe Dawson and Howard Wilcox. Dawson led the first lap by the smallest of margins over Wilcox and Jap Clemens. The Speedwell of Clemens took his

*Auto and pedestrian bridges at the Indianapolis Motor Speedway. (Photo courtesy of the Indianapolis Motor Speedway)*

turn at the front for the next two laps before giving way to Wilcox and Dawson on the fourth lap. Wilcox led Dawson by 0.44 of a second as they completed the fourth lap. Meanwhile, Clemens had fallen back about seven seconds with Merz another five seconds behind in fourth place. There was another gap of 50 seconds back to the Midland of Ralph Ireland in fifth with a tight race developing between the McFarlan of Fred Clemens and the Black Crow of Ed Stinson for sixth place.

Howard Wilcox continued to lead Dawson by just a fraction of a second through the 30-mile mark (12 laps) before Dawson took control on lap 13. By this time, Merz had put himself right on the tail of Dawson's Marmon, following him past Wilcox as the two quickly opened up a nine-second lead over him. Jap Clemens stayed within six seconds of Wilcox for fourth place as the race had become a four-car affair. The fifth place car of Ralph Ireland had fallen about two minutes behind Clemens with the rest of the field even further back.

By lap 16, Wilcox had fought his way around Merz, cutting into Dawson's lead by seven seconds. Over the next two laps, Wilcox guided his National around the Marmon of Dawson and the two began a furious dual for the lead over the next seven laps. Wilcox never lost the lead, but he never built a lead greater than one second. In the meantime, Merz stayed within 40 seconds of the two top cars and began to build a lead of over a minute on the Speedwell of Jap Clemens. Suddenly, misfortune struck the Marmon team. Joe Dawson retired from the race on lap 25 with engine trouble. With Dawson out of the race, it looked like Wilcox might have an easy ride to victory over the remaining 40 miles.

Charlie Merz apparently saw things differently. He was 28 seconds behind Wilcox at the 70-mile mark (28 laps), but in just four more laps he had cut Wilcox's lead down to two and a half seconds! The red Speedwell of Jap Clemens was still two minutes back in third place while the rest of the field trailed Clemens by at least five minutes. Merz continued his pursuit of Wilcox over the last 20 miles of the race but could never manage to get closer than two and a half seconds. Wilcox pulled away slightly at the end before winning in 1:23:03.56 for an average of 72.237 mph, nine seconds ahead of teammate Charlie Merz. Jap Clemens gave the Speedwell a good run, finishing in third place, two minutes behind Merz. These top three cars managed to go the entire distance without a pit stop. The rest of the field finished over six minutes behind Clemens. Billy Pearce was completely exhausted after manhandling his car in two 100-mile races nearly back-to-back. The race summary follows.

| Place | Car # | Driver | Car | Laps | Led |
|-------|-------|--------|-----|------|-----|
| 1 | 9 | Howard Wilcox | National | 40 | 32 |
| 2 | 11 | Charlie Merz | National | 40 | 0 |
| 3 | 5 | Jap Clemens | Speedwell | 40 | 2 |
| 4 | 29 | Ralph Ireland | Midland | 40 | 0 |
| 5 | 24 | Fred Clemens | McFarlan | 40 | 0 |
| 6 | 28 | Ed Stinson | Black Crow | 40 | 0 |
| 7 | 23 | W.J. Barndollar | McFarlan | 38 | 0 |
| 8 | 34 | William Fritsch | Cino | 37 | 0 |
| 9 | 15 | Billy Pearce | FAL | 31 | 0 |
| 10 | 10 | Joe Dawson | Marmon | 25 | 6 |
| 11 | 31 | Lee Frayer | Firestone-Columbus | 10 | 0 |

*Howard Wilcox receiving the Remy Grand Brassard and trophy after winning the 100-mile Remy race on September 3, 1910. (Photo courtesy of the Indianapolis Motor Speedway)*

Although no records were broken on the first day of competition, everyone viewed the program as a phenomenal day of racing. Seven car manufacturers had made their debut at Indianapolis and the racing was very competitive. Eddie Hearne had a good day by successfully defending the Speedway Helmet that he had won in July and winning the 100-mile free-for-all race. The National team had three wins to its credit to go along with three second-place finishes. Howard Wilcox, who had two of the victories for the National team, was beginning to make his mark as a talented race car driver.

Saturday evening after the races, Ray Harroun joined FAL car driver Frank Gelnaw for a ride in Carl Fisher's new balloon. George Bumbaugh, who built the balloon, piloted it to Millersville for an evening test flight. The 80,000-cubic-foot balloon was scheduled to participate in the Speedway balloon races later in the month.

Sunday afternoon provided an opportunity for the race teams to rest after several long days of hard work at the Speedway. Meanwhile, the Sunday *Indianapolis Star* published several interesting articles targeted at the many automobile enthusiasts in town for the races. One article praised the merits of the automobile. It was true that many "proclaimed the widespread purchase of automobiles to be an economic waste, which if not kept in check, would lead to the ruin of this country and other kinds of calamities."[2] However, the writer opened his case for the automobile by stating that the country was indebted to the automobile industry for the unprecedented prosperity during the last five years. He made a good point. As he asserted, one thing that was essential to prosperity was the free and rapid circulation of money. Money kept in circulation had a far greater impact on the economy than money locked up in safe deposit boxes or hidden in mattresses or under carpets. He also pointed out that the automobile industry provided labor for perhaps a million people. That was probably true when you consider not only those that produced the cars but also the workers that produced parts for them, those that built the machinery used in the plants, and the distributors that sold the cars. Many people wished to focus on what they perceived as negatives to the increasing popularity of the automobile without considering where this country might have been without it.

Another article told the story of how people were trying to improve the automobile. Most manufacturers were quick to claim that the automobile had arrived at practically a state of perfection with only minor refinements and improvements possible. The article reported that "out of the thousands of alleged improvements patented each year, less than five percent had any practical value and many of those were either cost prohibitive or had some minor defect."[3] One man who definitely would have disagreed with this assessment was Howard Marmon. While he was very pleased with the autos produced by Marmon, he was firm in his belief that they could be improved upon through new techniques and methods of engineering.

Labor Day 1910 in Indianapolis was a very busy day. The streets of Indianapolis were quickly filling up for a double celebration. The annual Labor Day parade was scheduled to begin at 9:00 a.m. followed by a circus parade. The police had close to 200 officers on duty and estimated the massive crowd at between 60,000 and 70,000 people. Washington Street from Pennsylvania Street west to Missouri Street was so crowded before the parade that people were forced to walk down the middle of the street. The last half-hour before the circus parade it was almost impossible to get through even by walking down the middle of the street. The sidewalks on either side of the street were lined with people all the way to White River with an additional scattering of spectators beyond the river to the circus grounds on West Washington Street. Many of these people had stood on the streets for nearly three hours to see the two parades. Fortunately, there were no problems with heat exhaustion as it was very humid with only a slight breeze for relief. Scores watched the parades from the tops of buildings. A break from the heat came around noon by way of a rain shower that sent thousands running for refuge. Every restaurant, lunch room, and store was full of men, women and children seeking shelter from the rain. Labor Park also hosted a throng of people throughout the day for various activities, including a seven-act vaudeville performance and a concert by the City Band.

The noon rain shower that sent the downtown parade crowd running for cover also dampened the Speedway. Despite the rain, spectators began arriving at the track around noon and filled portions of the main grandstand and the south bleachers within a half an hour. Although the sun darted in and out of the clouds, fans continued to file in until approximately 18,000 filled the stands by the time the first event was scheduled to start. Not a huge attendance by previous standards, but, considering the threatening weather and all of the other attractions of the day, it was respectable. The schedule of events for the day contained mostly five-mile races within the various classes plus free-for-all contests of 10, 50, and 200 miles.

Surprisingly, the majority of the big brick track was dry by 1:00 p.m. The Maxwell-Briscoe and Overland bands stopped playing around 1:15 p.m. when starter "Pop" Wagner began preparations for the events. Then, at 1:20 p.m., the field for the first contest of the day – a five-mile race open to stock chassis with engines of 160 CID or less – roared away from the starting line. This was a rematch of Saturday's event consisting of three Herreshoff cars.

Walter Emmons and W.J. Smith ran neck-and-neck for the full five miles. Emmons was given credit for leading the first circuit, but Smith gained the advantage as the cars headed into turn one. E.R. McCormick was far behind and dropped out after the first lap. Smith and Emmons continued to trade for the lead as they came out of turn four and headed for the judges' stand. Holding down the hood of his car with his hand, Emmons edged out Smith at the finish line by 0.42 of a second. The race summary follows.

| Place | Car # | Driver | Car | Laps | Led |
|-------|-------|--------|-----|------|-----|
| 1 | 19 | Walter Emmons | Herreshoff | 2 | 2 |
| 2 | 21 | W.J. Smith | Herreshoff | 2 | 0 |
| 3 | 20 | E.R. McCormick | Herreshoff | 1 | 0 |

Originally scheduled as event number seven, a ten-mile free-for-all race was moved up in the program to be run next. The lineup was the same as Saturday's dash for the Speedway Helmet with the addition of Ray Harroun. The red Fiat of Ralph DePalma who was closely pursued by Eddie Hearne in the big gray Benz led the six starters into the first turn. These two powered ahead of the rest of the field and the race quickly developed into a two-car contest. The Fiat and Benz battled fiercely. DePalma's Fiat held a one-and-a-half second lead at the end of five miles. Harroun was 35 seconds back in third place. Much to the disappointment of the crowd, the National of Johnny Aitken had dropped out after the first lap.

DePalma and Hearne remained in a fight for the lead, driving side-by-side most of the way. At the end of three laps, DePalma was barely in front of Hearne as the two started the final circuit of the contest. The close racing continued when Hearne put on a burst of speed down the frontstretch in an effort to pass DePalma but the Fiat answered the challenge as the two cars crossed the line in a dead heat. After a few minutes of deliberation, the victory was given to the Fiat of DePalma, his first at Indianapolis. The time of 6:48.30 was only 0.03 of a second faster than Hearne! Ray Harroun finished over a minute back in disappointing third place, edging out the National of Charlie Merz by 0.63 of a second. Charles Basle finished 25 seconds behind Merz in fifth place. The final race summary follows.

| Place | Car # | Driver | Car | Laps | Led |
|-------|-------|--------|-----|------|-----|
| 1 | 1 | Ralph DePalma | Fiat | 4 | 4 |
| 2 | 3 | Eddie Hearne | Benz | 4 | 0 |
| 3 | 32 | Ray Harroun | Marmon | 4 | 0 |
| 4 | 7 | Charlie Merz | National | 4 | 0 |
| 5 | 14 | Charles Basle | Matheson | 4 | 0 |
| 6 | 8 | Johnny Aitken | National | 1 | 0 |

*Ralph DePalma, driver of the Fiat. Later in his career DePalma would win the 1915 Indianapolis 500. (Photo courtesy of the Indianapolis Motor Speedway)*

*Cole driver Willard "Bill" Endicott. (Photo courtesy of the Indianapolis Motor Speedway)*

After two close races opened the program, the spectators remained enthusiastic as the cars lined up for the five-mile contest open to stock chassis with engines of 161 – 230 CID. Bill Endicott, driving an Indianapolis-made Cole, was greeted with cheers from the crowd as he lined up against Lee Frayer in a Firestone-Columbus and the Staver-Chicago of Kiefer.

Endicott and Frayer waged a spectacular dual throughout the first two and a half miles. Endicott had grabbed the lead late in the first turn, but Frayer came back to pass him as the cars entered turn three. Kiefer trailed the pair by six seconds. By the time the leaders were in front of the grandstand, Frayer held a one second advantage over Endicott. As the hometown crowd cheered him on, Endicott tried to overtake Frayer but could never get close enough to make a move for the lead. Frayer went on to claim his first victory at Indianapolis in 4:48.87, two-and-a-half seconds in front of Endicott. Kiefer had continued to fade and finished 17 seconds back in third place. The final race summary follows.

| Place | Car # | Driver | Car | Laps | Led |
|-------|-------|--------|-----|------|-----|
| 1 | 30 | Lee Frayer | Firestone-Columbus | 2 | 2 |
| 2 | 33 | Bill Endicott | Cole | 2 | 0 |
| 3 | 17 | Kiefer | Staver-Chicago | 2 | 0 |

Ray Harroun and Joe Dawson had the hopes of the Marmon team up for a one-two finish in the five-mile race for stock chassis with engines of 231 – 300 CID. Their biggest threat among the other seven starters was considered to be the FAL cars of Billy Pearce and Frank Gelnaw.

The Marmon of Harroun got off to a good start, but Pearce stayed with him and finally passed the Marmon as he built a lead of six seconds at the end of the first lap. The other FAL car of Gelnaw was in third, only one second behind Harroun. Dawson followed the fourth place McFarlan of W.J. Barndollar. It was clear from the start that Dawson's car was not running well, so it did not shock anyone when he was forced to drop out of the race with engine trouble on the second lap.

Harroun caught up with Pearce as the two drivers put on a thrilling show during the second lap. It was side-by-side racing from the backstretch to the finish. Harroun moved to the outside of Gelnaw and inched ahead as the two cars exited turn four. The Marmon held a slim margin as the cars roared down the frontstretch to give Harroun the win in 4:38.27. This would be Harroun's last victory at the Speedway until the 1911 Indianapolis 500. Pearce finished an agonizing one and a half second behind the winner. Gelnaw and Barndollar, six seconds back, had a similar battle for third place with Gelnaw claiming the position by 0.03 of a second. Fred Clemens ran another nine seconds behind the pair to give McFarlan two cars in the top five. The race summary follows.

| Place | Car # | Driver | Car | Laps | Led |
|---|---|---|---|---|---|
| 1 | 26 | Ray Harroun | Marmon | 2 | 1 |
| 2 | 15 | Billy Pearce | FAL | 2 | 1 |
| 3 | 16 | Frank Gelnaw | FAL | 2 | 0 |
| 4 | 23 | W.J. Barndollar | McFarlan | 2 | 0 |
| 5 | 24 | Fred Clemens | McFarlan | 2 | 0 |
| 6 | 37 | Harry Endicott | Great Western | 2 | 0 |
| 7 | 34 | William Fritsch | Cino | 2 | 0 |
| 8 | 25 | Hughie Hughes | Parry | 2 | 0 |
| 9 | 22 | Joe Dawson | Marmon | 1 | 0 |

*Billy Pearce and riding mechanic Bob Kutz sitting in a FAL car in front of the bleachers in Crown Point, Indiana, at the 1909 Cobe Cup race. (Chicago Daily News negatives collection, SDN-055226. Courtesy of the Chicago Historical Society)*

The next event featured the greatest finish ever witnessed at the Indianapolis Motor Speedway. The spectators anticipated a close contest between the National and Marmon cars in the five-mile race for stock chassis with engines of 301 – 450 CID and they were not disappointed. Harroun and Dawson were entered against the National trio of Aitken, Greiner, and Merz. Gelnaw and Pearce were also included in the FAL cars along with Jap Clemens in a Speedwell, Lee Frayer in a Firestone-Columbus, and Ralph Ireland in a Midland.

The race quickly developed into a four-car contest. Less than one second separated Aitken, Harroun, Dawson, and Greiner during the first lap as they passed the judges' stand in that order. Clemens had the Speedwell in fifth place; however, he was almost five seconds behind the lead pack. The race had played out like everyone anticipated – with the exception of Charlie Merz, who was well off the pace.

*Frank Gelnaw (#16), Joe Dawson (#22), Hughie Hughes (#25), and Fred Clemens (#24) at the start of a 5-mile race on September 5, 1910. Eventual race winner Ray Harroun (#26) can be seen behind and to the left of the #16 of Gelnaw while the McFarlan of Barndollar (#23) is to the immediate right of the #22 of Dawson, partially obscured by smoke. (Photo courtesy of the Indianapolis Motor Speedway)*

The second lap was one of the most competitive of all time. The four lead cars waged a stunning battle that never let up throughout the final two-and-a-half miles. Each took a turn at the lead, shuffling to obtain the most advantageous position for the finish. This continued until the cars came thundering out of the fourth turn four wide! It was a drag race all the way down the frontstretch as two Marmons and two Nationals sprinted across the line in a virtual dead heat! The thrilling finish electrified the fans who wildly cheered with excitement long after the race had ended. After several minutes of consultation among the officials and timers, it was announced to the anxious crowd that the National of Johnny Aitken had won the race. Aitken's time of 4:10.22 beat out Dawson's 4:10.56, Greiner's 4:10.90, and Harroun's 4:11.15. Less than one second had separated the first four finishers! Jap Clemens maintained his position behind th leaders to finish fifth in the Speedwell while the rest of the field finished far behind. The complete rac summary follows.

| Place | Car # | Driver | Car | Laps | Led |
|---|---|---|---|---|---|
| 1 | 9 | Johnny Aitken | National | 2 | 2 |
| 2 | 10 | Joe Dawson | Marmon | 2 | 0 |
| 3 | 18 | Arthur Greiner | National | 2 | 0 |
| 4 | 4 | Ray Harroun | Marmon | 2 | 0 |
| 5 | 5 | Jap Clemens | Speedwell | 2 | 0 |
| 6 | 16 | Frank Gelnaw | FAL | 2 | 0 |
| 7 | 31 | Lee Frayer | Firestone-Columbus | 2 | 0 |
| 8 | 15 | Billy Pearce | FAL | 2 | 0 |
| 9 | 11 | Charlie Merz | National | 1 | 0 |
| 10 | 29 | Ralph Ireland | Midland | 1 | 0 |

Charles Basle in a Matheson faced a tri of National drivers in the five-mile event fc stock chassis with engines of 451 – 600 CII Basle had his work cut out for him as he was u against Greiner, Merz, and Wilcox. Greiner ha finished third in the exciting race just con pleted; however, he was well rested, since it ha taken a while to sort out the order of the tc four finishers.

Wilcox grabbed the early lead whil Basle and Merz were wheel-to-wheel abou three seconds back from Wilcox. Greiner traile the field by another two seconds but had begu to make up ground on the second lap. Mear while, Wilcox lengthened his lead throughou the second lap, finishing the five miles i 4:09.89 to claim his third victory in two day of competition. A little over six seconds bacl Basle and Merz were having quite a contes Basle pulled off an upset when the Mathesor edged out Merz's National for second place b just 0.46 of a second. It was not a race win, bu still a huge accomplishment for Mathesor Greiner had closed the gap somewhat but sti finished about a second behind Merz in fourt place. The race summary follows.

*A spectator's view from the grandstands during the early days at the Indianapolis Motor Speedway. (Photo from a private collection)*

| Place | Car # | Driver | Car | Laps | Led |
|---|---|---|---|---|---|
| 1 | 9 | Howard Wilcox | National | 2 | 2 |
| 2 | 14 | Charles Basle | Matheson | 2 | 0 |
| 3 | 11 | Charlie Merz | National | 2 | 0 |
| 4 | 18 | Arthur Greiner | National | 2 | 0 |

A total of 17 cars faced starter "Pop" Wagner to begin the five-mile free-for-all handicap event. Although just about all of the teams had entered at least one car, Marmon had decided to sit out this contest to prepare for the 50 and 200-mile races that followed.

The small Herreshoffs driven by Walter Emmons and W.J. Smith were first off the line followed by the McFarlan of W.J. Barndollar 20 seconds later. Ten seconds after Barndollar, Bill Endicott in a Cole, Hughie Hughes in a Parry, and Lee Frayer in a Firestone-Columbus joined the race. Another five seconds later, four more cars were thrown into the mix; Louis Edmunds in a Cole, Ed Stinson in a Black Crow, William Fritsch in a Cino, and Ralph Ireland in a Midland. Billy Pearce in a FAL and Kiefer in a Staver-Chicago were added ten seconds after the previous four cars. Fred Clemens started in another McFarlan five seconds later. Ten seconds after the McFarlan, the Matheson of Charles Basle and the Speedwell of Jap Clemens started for turn one. Finally, 70 seconds after the first cars started, the big Nationals of Arthur Greiner and Charlie Merz were allowed to leave the starting line.

Barndollar and Frayer quickly made their way past the Herreshoff entries and raced each other closely throughout the entire five-mile distance. These two maintained a five second lead over the rest of the field and were never seriously challenged throughout the race. Barndollar drove a great race, beating Frayer at the finish line by 1.33 seconds for a time of 5:08.32. The win gave Barndollar and the Connersville-made McFarlan its first and only victory at Indianapolis. Fred Clemens in the other McFarlan was impressive as well. He picked his way through several cars to earn a third-place finish. The Nationals of Greiner and Merz, the last cars to start, could only make up time on half the field to finish ninth and tenth, respectively. The race summary follows.

| Place | Car # | Driver | Car | Laps | Led |
|---|---|---|---|---|---|
| 1 | 23 | W.J. Barndollar | McFarlan | 2 | 2 |
| 2 | 30 | Lee Frayer | Firestone-Columbus | 2 | 0 |
| 3 | 24 | Fred Clemens | McFarlan | 2 | 0 |
| 4 | 6 | Louis Edmunds | Cole | 2 | 0 |
| 5 | 25 | Hughie Hughes | Parry | 2 | 0 |
| 6 | 5 | Jap Clemens | Speedwell | 2 | 0 |
| 7 | 33 | Bill Endicott | Cole | 2 | 0 |
| 8 | 14 | Charles Basle | Matheson | 2 | 0 |
| 9 | 18 | Arthur Greiner | National | 2 | 0 |
| 10 | 11 | Charlie Merz | National | 2 | 0 |
| 11 | 19 | Walter Emmons | Herreshoff | 2 | 0 |
| 12 | 16 | Frank Gelnaw | FAL | 2 | 0 |
| 13 | 37 | Kiefer | Staver-Chicago | 2 | 0 |
| 14 | 28 | Ed Stinson | Black Crow | 2 | 0 |
| 15 | 34 | William Fritsch | Cino | 2 | 0 |
| 16 | 29 | Ralph Ireland | Midland | 2 | 0 |
| 17 | 21 | W.J. Smith | Herreshoff | 1 | 0 |

*William Fritsch and riding mechanic Charles Thorp in a Cino at Elgin, Illinois, in August 1910. (Chicago Daily News negatives collection, SDN-056219. Courtesy of the Chicago Historical Society)*

The spectators were on their feet as the eight cars in the 50-mile free-for-all race reported to the starting line. Five of the entrants in particular were seen as favorites for the $800 first prize. The red Fiat of Ralph DePalma and the gray Benz of Eddie Hearne were expected to give the Nationals of Aitken and Livingstone, along with the Marmon of Harroun, a good fight for the victory. The Firestone-Columbus of Frayer, the Westcott of Harry Knight, and the Matheson of Charles Basle were also entered but not expected to contend for the win.

Ralph DePalma put the hood of his big red Fiat out in front of the other starters as the cars sprang from the starting line on their way to the first turn. Hearne, Harroun, and Aitken fell in behind the leader, staying very close throughout the first two-and-a-half miles. DePalma held a slight lead over Hearne at the end of the first lap while Harroun, Aitken, and Livingstone followed closely behind. As DePalma's Fiat entered the first turn to begin the second lap, loud popping sounds could be heard coming from the back of the car. By the end of the second turn, Hearne's Benz had passed the Fiat, leaving DePalma and Harroun in a close battle for second place. Over the next five laps the two fought side-by-side for second place while Hearne built up a lead of two seconds. Aitken and Livingstone continued to race closely in fourth and fifth place, respectively. As expected, Basle, Knight, and Frayer occupied the final three positions several seconds back.

Harroun and DePalma began to catch Hearne when suddenly DePalma was forced to pit for a right rear tire on lap seven. Harroun found himself all alone in second position, less than one second behind Hearne. Incredibly, DePalma was forced to stop for tires again on lap 11, but this time Harroun had to stop as well. With no other serious challengers near him, Hearne had established a comfortable lead that seemed untouchable – provided he did not develop problems. Meanwhile, Harroun and DePalma were doing their best to come up through the field after their pit stops. DePalma had to stop for tires yet a third time on lap 16 and was never able to get any closer than fourth.

Hearne went on to win in a time of 38:02.85 for an average of 78.849 mph. Ray Harroun was one and-a-half minutes behind the Benz in second place. Livingstone was over a minute back from Harroun while DePalma had to settle for fourth. Aitken was well back in fifth place, the last car on the lead lap. The final race summary follows.

| Place | Car # | Driver | Car | Laps | Led |
|---|---|---|---|---|---|
| 1 | 3 | Eddie Hearne | Benz | 20 | 19 |
| 2 | 32 | Ray Harroun | Marmon | 20 | 0 |
| 3 | 7 | Al Livingstone | National | 20 | 0 |
| 4 | 1 | Ralph DePalma | Fiat | 20 | 1 |
| 5 | 9 | Johnny Aitken | National | 20 | 0 |
| 6 | 14 | Charles Basle | Matheson | 16 | 0 |
| 7 | 27 | Harry Knight | Westcott | 15 | 0 |
| 8 | 31 | Lee Frayer | Firestone-Columbus | 4 | 0 |

Despite a long day of racing, the crowd was still enthusiastic at 3:30 p.m. when the 12 starters lined up for the 200-mile event open to stock chassis with engines of 600 CID or less. The race started out on a positive note for the Marmon team as Harroun jumped out to the early lead. The first 20 miles (eight laps) provided a great race for the spectators because the top five cars were within 18 seconds of each other. After Harroun, the rest of the top five consisted of Aitken, Jap Clemens in the Speedwell, Livingstone, and Dawson. However, the remainder of the field had begun to fall back quickly.

*arting lineup for the 200-mile race on September 5, 1910. This was the last auto race at the Indianapolis Motor peedway before the 1911 Indianapolis 500. Eventual winner Johnny Aitken (#9) is the last car on the second row. Photo courtesy of the Detroit Public Library, National Automotive History Collection)*

Harroun continued to lead through the first 65 miles (26 laps) while building a lead of almost two inutes on Johnny Aitken and Al Livingtone. Aitken had been able to make up a lot of time after he spent full minute in the pits to replace a right front tire on lap 14. Dawson had moved into fourth place and rthur Greiner rounded out the top five.

On lap 27, Harroun came to the pits while leading the race. It was 2 minutes and 15 seconds before he could get back out on the track after stopping for gas, oil, and a new right rear tire. During that time, Aitken took over the lead but Harroun was able to get back out on the track in second place. Livingstone, Greiner, and Dawson completed the top five. The cars ran in that order for nearly 100 miles, during which time Harroun and Aitken waged a fierce battle while pulling away from the rest of the field. Many times during these laps, Harroun would electrify the crowd by shooting past the blue National of Aitken only to surrender the lead as the cars roared past the main grandstand. It was truly an exciting struggle between these two Indianapolis cars and their Indianapolis drivers.

*The view looking north along pit road during one of the races at the Indianapolis Motor Speedway. (Photo courtesy of the Detroit Public Library, National Automotive History Collection)*

Shortly thereafter, the promising performance of the Marmon cars came to a sudden halt. As Harroun was challenging Aitken for the lead on the backstretch late in the race, a coupling broke forcing him to drop out of the race. Fate struck another cruel blow almost immediately after that when Joe Dawson also left the race with engine problems. With the two Marmon cars out of the running, Johnny Aitken had a big lead over his National teammate, Al Livingstone. He went on to win easily in 2:47:54.74 for an average of 71.466 mph. Al Livingstone was five-and-a-half minutes back in second place with W.J. Barndollar another ten minutes behind him in third-place. Arthur Greiner had been a definite third-place finisher until he ran out of gas on the backstretch. By the time he could push his car around to the pits, he had fallen pelessly behind Barndollar. The McFarlan of W.J. Barndollar had an incredible race because he drove nstop for the entire 200 miles! Incidentally, toward the end of the race, a threatening cloudburst had put e track in such darkness that it made it very difficult for the starter and judges to determine which cars ssed by during the few remaining laps. The final race summary follows.

| Place | Car # | Driver | Car | Laps | Led |
|---|---|---|---|---|---|
| 1 | 9 | Johnny Aitken | National | 80 | 54 |
| 2 | 7 | Al Livingstone | National | 80 | 0 |
| 3 | 23 | W.J. Barndollar | McFarlan | 80 | 0 |
| 4 | 18 | Arthur Greiner | National | 80 | 0 |
| 5 | 24 | Fred Clemens | McFarlan | 79 | 0 |
| 6 | 28 | Ed Stinson | Black Crow | 78 | 0 |
| 7 | 10 | Joe Dawson | Marmon | 70 | 0 |
| 8 | 32 | Ray Harroun | Marmon | 68 | 26 |
| 9 | 5 | Jap Clemens | Speedwell | 48 | 0 |
| 10 | 16 | Frank Gelnaw | FAL | 40 | 0 |
| 11 | 14 | Charles Basle | Matheson | 40 | 0 |
| 12 | 29 | Ralph Ireland | Midland | 40 | 0 |

The Nationals were the big winners in the two-day program – victorious in six of the 18 races. oward Wilcox established himself as an up-and-coming driver with three victories, including the 100-ile Remy Grand Brassard and trophy race, while his teammate, Johnny Aitken, earned the other three ns for the National team. Eddie Hearne also won three races: the Speedway Helmet race, the 50-mile e-for-all, and a 100-mile free-for-all. Ray Harroun did have two victories for Marmon, but they were mewhat tempered by the fact that there could have been more victories had it not been for misfortunes in few of the other races.

Johnny Aitken's win in the 200-mile finale was a fitting end to the 1910 auto racing season at the eedway. He had the most wins at Indianapolis during the 1909 and 1910 seasons with 12 and was clearly e of the crowd favorites. Meanwhile, as the successful two-day program came to a close, everyone was ft to speculate what the 1911 season would bring to the great track. Rumors began to circulate that the eedway's partners were considering holding only one race at the Speedway; however, no schedule had en released to confirm that. As it turned out, no one had to speculate for long. The partners would soon ake a very big announcement that would shake up the world of automobile racing.

*Chapter 10*

# Balloons Return to the Brickyard

Earlier in the year the Aero Club of America had confirmed that St. Louis would host the 1910 James Gordon Bennett International Balloon Championship in October. At the same time, the Aero Club announced that the three entries reserved for American balloons would be decided by the results of the National Balloon Championship to be hosted by Indianapolis in September. The Speedway was the perfect place to host such an event as evidenced by the successful National Balloon Championship held in June 1909.

Since early July the local papers had carried stories about the September balloon championship, anticipating that it would be the greatest gathering of balloons ever seen. That prediction seemed more likely to come true when it was announced in August that the Speedway management decided to hold a free-for-all race for balloonists who were not eligible to enter the championship race. Entrants in the free-for-all were not required to be licensed pilots under the rules of the Aero Club of America. Carl Fisher even announced that the Speedway would be awarding a diamond-studded cup to the winner of the free-for-all event. With two races to be contested and participation in the International Balloon Championship at stake, it seemed likely that the world record of 12 balloons at one meet set in Berlin, Germany in 1908 would be surpassed.

The official entry list began to take shape a few days before the start of the races. Because the championship race would determine the American entries in the International race to be held in St. Louis, coupled with the fact that many of America's most experienced balloonists were from St. Louis, the city took a huge interest in the September races. Three balloons from the city were entered in the championship with another one entered in the free-for-all. The *Centennial*, a competitor in the championship, was the best known of the St. Louis balloons. It was formerly called the *St. Louis,* having won second place in the Centennial Week balloon race at St. Louis in October 1909. The balloon was owned by Harry Eugene Honeywell of the St. Louis Aero Club. Honeywell was the aide to Albert Bond Lambert in the *St. Louis 3* that captured third place in the National Championship at Indianapolis in June 1909. Honeywell would be the pilot in this race – aided by Wooster Lambert, Albert's younger brother.

The second St. Louis Aero Club entry was the *Million Population Club* piloted by Sylvester "Tony" Louis Von Phul with aide Joseph M. O'Reilly. The balloon's namesake was a club in St. Louis formed in an effort to boost the city's population to 1,000,000 people. The club had planned to send in excess of 100 people to Indianapolis to cheer on their balloon.

The third St. Louis Aero Club entry was the *Miss Sophia* piloted by William F. Assman. Named after Assman's daughter, the *Sophia* would have the benefit of experienced aide Paul McCullough who had been the aide to John Berry in the *University City* during the June 1909 National Championship race.

The *University City* with John Berry as the pilot was making a return to Indianapolis as the lone St. Louis representative in the free-for-all race. Many people were surprised that Berry did not enter the championship since he was one of the most experienced pilots in the country. Why did he make this decision? He said that he had a new balloon under construction but could not get it finished in time for the event. Since many of the contenders for the championship had new balloons, he did not wish to enter his old balloon.

"I may win in the free-for-all race," Berry said. "I'm sorry I could not get in the championship event with my new balloon; however, the old *University City* still takes me into the clouds notwithstanding it leaks like a sieve. I'll stay up as long as the old ship floats."[1]

*A fan's handwritten note to Sylvester "Tony" Von Phul and Joseph O'Reilly, pilot and aide in the Million Population Club balloon. The note was written just before the September 1910 balloon races from the Indianapolis Motor Speedway. (From the scrapbook of Joseph M. O'Reilly, courtesy of the Missouri Historical Society, St. Louis)*

Other noted entrants for the races were Clifford B. Harmon and Thomas Scott Baldwin, pilot and aide for the *New York*, and J.H. Wade, Jr., and A.H. Morgan, pilot and aide for the *Buckeye*, all of whom participated in the June 1909 races at Indianapolis. Alan Hawley and Augustus Post of New York, two of the most experienced American balloonists, were entered in the *America II* which was the very same balloon that Edgar W. Mix of the United States had piloted to victory in the 1909 James Gordon Bennett International Balloon Championship in Zurich, Switzerland. Alan Hawley was no stranger to Indianapolis having served as field manager of the June 1909 races at the Speedway. Indianapolis' hopes rested on Carl Fisher and George Bumbaugh, the only licensed pilots in Indianapolis, who were entered in the championship with Bumbaugh's new balloon the *Indiana II*.

Bumbaugh, one of the country's most experienced balloonists, was fortunate to be around for the balloon races. A few days after the July auto races, he ascended from the Speedway in the *Indiana* for an exhibition flight with two Ohio dentists, Dr. L.E. Custer of Dayton, who was entered in the upcoming free-for-all race, and Dr. C.W. Mills of Chillicothe. Carrying only eight bags of ballast, three of which were lost at the start, they ascended to 1,000 feet where they suddenly saw a storm that seemed to close in on all sides of them.

"We attained a height of 1,000 feet when we saw a storm approaching from the northwest," Bumbaugh explained. "I could tell that it was a heavy storm but I calculated that the same wind which was blowing the storm clouds would carry us before the storm. Before we realized it, the storm seemed to overtake and surround us. The balloon seemed to stand still in a lull. We were in utter darkness, everything was black and I knew that the other men were in the basket only by feeling for them."

"The rain blew against us in sheets. It blinded us. We shot up at least 2,000 feet. We had no sooner reached this height than we fell into a veritable hole in the air and the balloon dropped 800 feet. The wind whirled us, the rain beat on us, and I thought the gale would tear the bag to pieces. Several times we were carried by 'whooper ups' which took us to dizzy heights and no sooner did we reach them than we fell in a whirling vortex of air."

"We couldn't get above the clouds because of a lack of ballast. We were traveling at a rate of about 60 mph. The bag began to descend and after we were out of the clouds I could see that we were over Indianapolis. The balloon was straining and I was afraid the net would break. We skimmed housetops and the drag rope caught on trees and chimneys. When we struck high tension wires over Fall Creek there was a flash and I thought that static electricity had been generated in the bag and that it would explode. The drag rope wrapped around the wires and the balloon stood out straight before us. We lay flat on the side of the basket and the jolt almost knocked us out. After we had hit the wire I saw that we were dropping and so I jerked the rip cord and we landed safely in the trees. I dropped a rope and we came down unhurt."[2]

The ironic part of the story was that the balloon ended up landing only a few doors down from Dr. Mills' sister whom he was in Indianapolis to visit! All three men stated that they had never been through anything like that before and hoped they never would again. Unfortunately for George Bumbaugh, fate would have a similar adventure in store for him during the upcoming championship race.

Upon final confirmation of the entries, it was determined that there would be nine entrants in the National Championship and four entrants in the free-for-all. The total number of 13 balloons was short of what the Speedway management had anticipated but still enough to set a world record for the number of balloons in one meet. The pilots and aides for the two balloon races were as follows.

### National Championship Balloon Race Entrants

- Alan R. Hawley and Augustus Post of New York in the *America II*
- William F. Assman and Paul McCullough of St. Louis in the *Miss Sophia*
- Carl Fisher and George Bumbaugh of Indianapolis in the *Indiana II*
- Sylvester "Tony" Louis Von Phul and Joseph M. O'Reilly of St. Louis in the *Million Population Club*
- Arthur T. Atherholt and Conyers B. Graham of Philadelphia in the *Pennsylvania*
- Harry Eugene Honeywell and J. D. Wooster Lambert of St. Louis in the *Centennial*
- Charles Walsh of Kingston, New York and Samuel Reber, a U. S. Government official, in the *Hoosier II*
- J. H. Wade, Jr. and A. H. Morgan of Cleveland in the *Buckeye*
- Clifford B. Harmon and Thomas Scott Baldwin of New York in the *New York*

**Free-For-All Balloon Race Entrants**

- Albert Holtz and George R. Howard of Cincinnati in the *Drifter*
- Dr. L. E. Custer of Dayton, Ohio, (flew with no aide) in the *Luzerne*
- John Berry of St. Louis (flew with no aide) in the *University City*
- E. S. Cole and H. W. Jacobs of Topeka, Kansas, in the *Topeka*

Albert Bond Lambert, president of the St. Louis Aero Club, was selected to serve as Director of Contests in charge of presiding over the races. An accomplished balloonist in his own right, Mr. Lambert had considered entering the event in addition to his official duties but eventually decided against it.

*Photograph of a page included in a souvenir booklet prepared by the Million Population Club for the September 1910 balloon races held at the Indianapolis Motor Speedway. This page features some of the balloon pilots from St. Louis. (From the scrapbook of the St. Louis Aero Club, courtesy of the Missouri Historical Society, St. Louis)*

Trains carrying the pilots, aides, and their balloons began arriving in Indianapolis Wednesday afternoon. The balloons were then transported to the Speedway grounds where they were stored in the garages until Friday when the inflation process was scheduled to begin. Later in the week, spectators from around Indiana and the surrounding Midwest states began arriving in the city. Almost 100 members of St. Louis' Million Population Club arrived at Union Station Friday afternoon. The delegation, uniformed in white trousers, white hats, blue coats, and red belts came to Indianapolis in a special train of three Pullmans and a day coach. After being greeted at Union Station by the Indianapolis Trade Association, they formed ranks and marched around the business district accompanied by three Overland automobiles and the Indianapolis Military Band. They were then escorted to the Denison Hotel where they had an entire floor reserved.

Meanwhile, the pace at the Speedway quickened on Friday afternoon as preparations began for the races on Saturday. Several 40-foot squares of protective canvas were placed on the ground upon which the big gas bags were unfolded. The nets, which supported the baskets of the occupants, were then placed on top of the bags. After this was completed, several men began making the ballast for the balloons. Over 30 wagon loads of sand had been heaped up in mounds, and then carefully sifted, before being shoveled into canvas bags. Each bag of ballast contained about two gallons of sand and the men prepared 40-45 bags for each balloon.

The Aero Club of America had set up its headquarters in the Claypool Hotel just as it had for the 1909 races. However, it was the Denison Hotel that became the big center of activity and merriment the night before the races. There were smoking parties, story-telling groups and lots of music and dancing on nearly every floor. Many of the pilots who were busy making final preparations at the Speedway earlier in the day were staying at the Denison and could be seen throughout the crowds sharing stories with all who would listen.

John Berry of the *University City* amused a small group with a story about his decision to fly without an aide. He had told some people a few days earlier that he intended to go alone unless he could find a newspaper woman who would go with him. He reportedly had made arrangements with a St. Louis newspaper woman to accompany him in Saturday's race; however, it fell through when the woman's employer refused to permit her to make the journey. Apparently his wishes were made known in Indianapolis; Berry soon became overwhelmed with requests from Indianapolis women to accompany him into the skies. The bewildered pilot said that he had been sought out at his hotel as well as the Speedway and had even received numerous letters pleading for an opportunity to take a balloon ride. When asked whether he had made a decision, he announced with a grin that he would be flying solo on Saturday.

Joseph O'Reilly, aide for the *Million Population Club* balloon, was asked what he was taking in his balloon, upon which he instantly produced a handwritten list from his pocket. There were well over 30 items included which he quickly pointed out did not include any food items. The pilot, William Assman, was in charge of that. O'Reilly had included such essentials as a compass, gloves, rain coat, and toilet paper; however, he had also provided for a pipe and tobacco as well.

Likewise, H.E. Honeywell, pilot of the *Centennial* balloon, held the attention of the crowd as he answered questions about how hard it was to fly a balloon. "The pilot must watch his instruments constantly," Honeywell answered, "for there are conditions encountered which, if not counteracted at the proper moment, will cause a descent even when expansion is on from dawn until midnight. For instance, passing over water or a dense forest will all contract the gas, or a cloud passing over the sun, and mean the loss of several pounds of ballast. If the pilot should neglect his duty at this moment, it may, after he has started to descend, cost him the loss of several sacks of ballast to check the downward momentum."[3]

Cloudless skies and a gentle breeze from the south made Saturday an ideal day for a balloon race. There was absolutely no hint of the conditions that awaited the daring pilots in what would be one of the most treacherous evenings of ballooning ever encountered. By the scheduled start time of 3:00 p.m. sev-

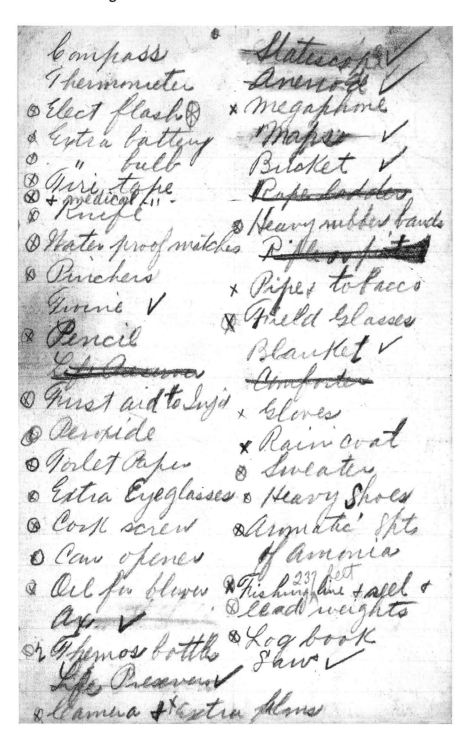

*A handwritten list of non-food items that Joseph O'Reilly, aide in the Million Population Club balloon, planned to carry with him during a balloon race. (From the scrapbook of Joseph M. O'Reilly, courtesy of the Missouri Historical Society, St. Louis)*

eral of the big balloons were nearly filled with gas as they sat tugging at their sandbag anchors ready t start the race. Unlike the 1909 races, where the balloons were inflated in front of the south bleachers, th Speedway management had the gas mains extended to a new filling station in front of the main grandstan by the start-finish line of the track. This allowed for closer viewing by a larger number of spectators.

There was some controversy over the starting time. Many of the contenders requested that the free for-all race begin at 3:00 p.m. with the championship race to start an hour later. They argued that th arrangement would be more desirable since the wind would be lighter by 4:00 p.m., allowing them to pas the night drifting slowly. Apparently, a decision was made to please all of the pilots and the first balloon set sail, free-for-all entrant the *Drifter*, did not ascend until shortly before 4:00 p.m. The new schedu called for the championship entrants to ascend after the free-for-all balloons at approximately 4:30 p.m.

There were over 6,000 eager spectators at the Speedway by the time the first balloon set sail. They came from all over the state plus many midwestern cities such as St. Louis, Chicago, Louisville, and Cincinnati. Many visitors in town for the Indiana State Fair also flocked to the Speedway to view the start of the races.

At 3:53 p.m. the *Drifter* – with 64,000-cubic-foot of capacity under the guidance of pilot Albert Holtz and aide George Howard of Cincinnati – slowly rose from the grounds heading to the northeast. The balloon carried 31 bags of ballast. The other entrants in the free-for-all race were supposed to follow the *Drifter* in five minute increments; however, none of the other balloons were ready to ascend because they had been working toward a 5:00 p.m. start time.

Finally at 4:56 p.m., an hour after the first balloon had set sail; the other entrants began to ascend from the Speedway in an order determined by a draw conducted at the Claypool Hotel on Friday night. Alan Hawley and Augustus Post sailed from the Speedway in the 80,000-cubic-foot *America II* with 33 bags of ballast. The big balloon, the largest in the competition, gently and gracefully rose into the air. Although not really noticed at the time, the *America II* was the only balloon to drift almost directly due east, a fact that would play a significant role in the outcome of the race.

Promptly at 5:00 p.m., William Assman and Paul McCullough set sail in the *Miss Sophia*. The 78,000-cubic-foot balloon, with 39 bags of ballast, skimmed the ground keeping the pair busy throwing out ballast all the way to the fence on the east side of the grounds. Assman tried to save as much ballast as possible, frantically casting out small portions of the ballast bags with a shovel.

As if right on cue, Carl Fisher and George Bumbaugh had the *Indiana II* with its 38 bags of ballast in the air promptly at 5:05 p.m. The Indianapolis Military Band struck up a lively tune, whistles screamed, hats were thrown, and spectators yelled their loudest as the hometown pilots floated above them. George Bumbaugh's daughter, Kathleen, could be seen waving to her father until he was well out of sight to the northeast.

The *Luzerne*, a free-for-all contestant and the smallest balloon in the races at 40,000 cubic foot, rose at 5:08 p.m. Dr. L.E. Custer, president of the Dayton Aero Club, flew the Club's entry without the services of an aide. He had told the Friday night crowd at the Denison that he could not compete with the bigger balloons so he would only be taking a short pleasure trip.

After a few minutes delay, a loud cheer erupted from the grandstand as "Tony" Von Phul and Joseph O'Reilly ascended at 5:17 p.m. in the *Million Population Club*. The St. Louis club members cheered wildly for their 78,000-cubic-foot balloon. After the initial ascent, the balloon began to come back down, causing Von Phul and O'Reilly to dump some of the 38 bags of ballast before clearing the fence surrounding the grounds. The balloon took a more northern route than the others had taken.

At 5:27 p.m., some ten minutes after the launch of the *Million Population Club,* John Berry ascended in the *University City*. Another free-for-all contestant, the balloon had a 78,000-cubic-foot capacity and carried 25 bags of ballast. Berry, as he had suggested on Friday night, flew without the services of an aide.

At 5:36 p.m. the 78,000-cubic-foot *Pennsylvania* gracefully took to the air carrying 26 bags of ballast. Pilot Arthur Atherholt and aide Conyers Graham of Philadelphia made the smoothest ascension as the balloon made a steady gradual climb to the northeast.

Right on the heels of the *Pennsylvania*, the 78,000-cubic-foot *Centennial* of H. E. Honeywell and Wooster Lambert was released and began to drift slowly to the northeast. The 21-year-old Lambert, a student at Princeton, had recently flown in an aeroplane with English aviator Claude Grahame-White on September 12 at the Harvard-Boston air meet.

By now the winds began to calm and the previous four balloons were still in sight when the small 40,000-cubic-foot *Topeka* started its journey from the Speedway at 5:46 p.m. The free-for-all entrant carried pilot E. S. Cole and aide H. W. Jacobs of Topeka, Kansas. The little balloon, sponsored by the Western Aero Association of Topeka, carried 22 bags of ballast as it drifted off to the northeast.

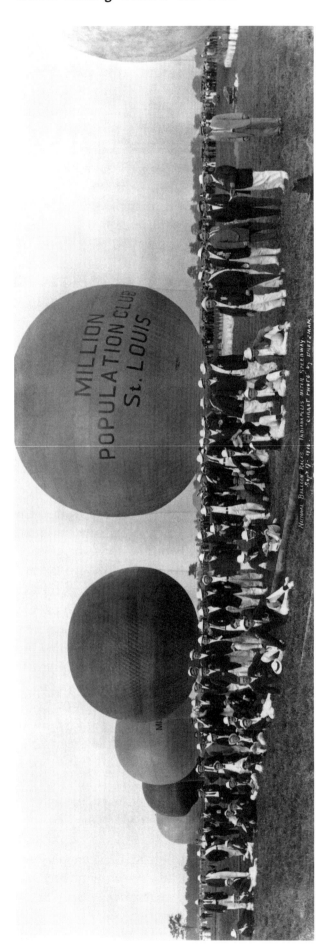

Members of the Million Population Club of St. Louis awaiting the start of the National Balloon Championship at the Indianapolis Motor Speedway on September 17, 1910. A roster of the members who made the trip to Indianapolis was: J.W. Alcorn, W.F. Assman, Judge C. Allison, George Ande, John H. Bardenheier, C.F. Blanke, D.L. Bollman, J.O. Banks, E.D.R. Browne, J.D. Brizzi, R.H. Bloeser, E.S. Borgelt, Frank Becker, J.H. Butler, Gus Becker, A.J. Butler, Jeff Casper, John F. Casey, C.H. Dieselhorst, E.A. Dunscomb, Bruce Dougan, F.W. Evers, Oscar B. Fischer, Eugene Fried, E.B. Fauber, Sam Gross, Vincent Gorley, G. Gartner; Tom Hause, Oscar Herkert, Judge Charles W. Holtcamp, Joseph E. Hoelzer, M. Hartmann, R.A. Heist, Dewey A. Hickey, Martin Hacker, Paul J. Hennrichs, Len Holdenreid, Joseph Hartmann, J. Hagen, Frank A. Hill, Edward Jerrald, C.E. Jewet, Otto F. Karbe, George C. Kirn, Al Kunze, Charles Kohler, H.L. Kohler, A.B. Koenig, Ernst Kist, Dr. L.E. Lehnberg, William E. Leach, J.H. Melton, W.O. Melton, C.H. Meinhard, William Meinshausen, Joseph Nager, Charles A. Nager; Steve Pensa, John Roedel, E.H. Roessel, Henry I. Roettger; O.G. Rode, George P. Roth, Otto Richter; Louis J. Reinstedler; Oscar Sontag, Louis Schmidt, A.C. Stuever; Colin M. Selph, William T. Schneeweis, Jerome J. Schotten, C.F. Stephens, Hugo Schick, R.R. Schneider; R.R. Schneider; Charles E. Schoenle, Al. Theis, George Wippermann, Clem Weick, Frank B. Warner; Robert Wey, Charles F. Wenneker; H. M. Schweppe, James B. Marquis, George Rose, E.L. Rose, H.L. Schunre. (Photo courtesy of the Missouri Historical Society, St. Louis)

The *Hoosier II* carried pilot Charles Walsh of Kingston, New York, and aide Colonel Samuel Reber of the United States Signal Corps who was in attendance to represent the government. The 79,000-cubic-foot balloon, built by George Bumbaugh and entered by the Aero Club of Indiana, ascended at 5:49 p.m. with 35 bags of ballast.

The Aero Club of Ohio entered the 78,000-cubic-foot *Buckeye* which methodically rose and drifted to the northeast with 39 bags of ballast. The pilot, 27-year-old J.H. Wade, Jr., was the son of one of Cleveland's wealthiest residents. His aide, A.H. Morgan also of Cleveland, was the president of the American Lithograph Company and the nephew of financier J.P. Morgan.

The *New York*, the last balloon to start, left the Speedway at 5:56 p.m. The big 78,000-cubic-foot balloon carried 36 bags of ballast as it rose in a northeasterly direction. The balloon was entered by the Aero Club of New York with pilot Clifford Harmon and aide Thomas Baldwin, both of New York. Harmon was a former head of the Aero Club of America.

As the last balloon drifted out of view, many of the spectators began to file out of the Speedway. Several got into their cars in an attempt to follow the balloons as far as the setting sun would allow. The 100 or so members of the Million Population Club even planned to stay in Indianapolis until late Sunday night to wait for word on the status of the St. Louis balloons.

Both the *Indianapolis Star* and *Indianapolis News* printed updates on the balloons over the next several days. Some who had been in the Noblesville area on Saturday saw the *Luzerne* descend back to earth just a few hours after the balloons had left the Speedway. The paper reported the next morning that the free-for-all contestant landed near Noblesville at 7:15 p.m. after a flight of about 20 miles in two hours and seven minutes.

The first progress reports of the remaining balloons came in the Monday edition of the *Indianapolis Star*. Many sightings had been made from cities and towns in Ohio, West Virginia, and Pennsylvania. A local newspaper office in Pittsburgh, Pennsylvania, reported receiving a note dropped from one of the balloons. The note was from "Tony" Von Phul and Joseph O'Reilly in the *Million Population Club*. It read, "We are now at 2,500 foot level traveling northeast with 14 sandbags. Don't think we will be able to stay up all night."[4] The balloons sparked a great deal of interest in Western Pennsylvania, holding down attendance at churches having afternoon services. Additionally, dispatches from many areas had indicated that nearly all of the balloons had encountered heavy rainstorms Saturday night.

The *Drifter*, a contestant in the free-for-all race, was one of the earliest balloons to report. Pilot Albert Holtz and aide George Howard of Cincinnati came to rest on a mountain peak near Littleton, West Virginia, at 1:08 p.m. Sunday afternoon. The pair was credited with covering 325 miles in 21 hours and 15 minutes. Mr. Howard talked about encountering a rainstorm near Muncie, Indiana, not long after the start of the race.

"In the vicinity of Muncie, Indiana," the pilot reported, "we encountered a very heavy rainstorm. After that, we needed every overcoat we had and at that were very cold. We threw off a considerable amount of ballast and were thus enabled to pass about it."[5]

The *Topeka,* another free-for-all contestant, had also filed its official report after having descended at 2:34 p.m. Sunday afternoon about 30 miles from Pittsburgh in Washington, Pennsylvania. The balloon had gone 325 miles in 20 hours and 48 minutes.

"The flight was a success in every way," stated pilot E. S. Cole. "The *Topeka* was never over 5,560 feet above the ground and our mean height was 2,000 feet. When we left Indianapolis, it looked like we would be carried over the Great Lakes, as the wind set in that direction, but it soon changed and we got into Ohio. We passed Columbus, Ohio, Sunday morning at sunrise and there, while about 1,500 feet up, we struck an air eddy which gave us much trouble, causing us to rise to a great height to get out of it. This took up much of our gas and brought us to the earth sooner than we had hoped for this afternoon. Saturday night was surely one of great anxiety for us, as it rained almost all of the time and was very dark."[6]

The final free-for-all contestant, the *University City*, landed in McKeesport, Pennsylvania, at 1:57 p.m. Sunday afternoon after a flight of 350 miles in 20 hours and 30 minutes. The 62-year-old Berry, who was flying alone, had made a remarkable flight considering his age and the age of his balloon. The *University City*, winner of the 1909 National Championship race from Indianapolis, had been used for years and was so dilapidated that many of his friends feared for his safety. Berry just laughed whenever his friends expressed their concern replying that he could "take care of himself" in case of an accident. The condition of the balloon was made obvious to all on Saturday as he continued to pour gas into it right up until the start of the race because it was leaking rapidly.

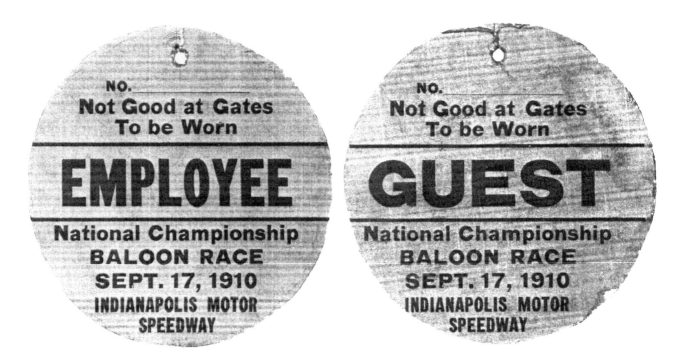

*Buttons worn by employees and guests at the September 1910 National Championship and handicap balloon races at the Indianapolis Motor Speedway. (From the scrapbook of Joseph M. O'Reilly, courtesy of the Missouri Historical Society, St. Louis)*

One of the first championship race contestants to report was the *Million Population Club*. The St Louis balloon made a descent near Trafford, Pennsylvania, at 2:33 p.m. Sunday afternoon after a 21 hou and 16 minute flight of 343 miles. Both Von Phul and O'Reilly were enthusiastic about the flight but were sorry that they were forced down.

"We left Indianapolis a little after dusk and a light northeastern wind started us in the genera direction of the lake. We had been in the air only a short time when it began to rain. Then we struck current that sent us along at a lively clip but the rain started to come down faster and we were getting soaked. The bag got heavy and sank a little. We threw out a little ballast and got back into the upper air. think we crossed the Ohio River at Warrington, Ohio. The night was the most remarkable that I had eve spent in my entire life. Up there among the clouds we seemed to be in a sea of dreams. Neither of us slep much. We didn't want to. Our highest altitude was 5,500 feet and the average was over 2,000 feet."

"When the sun came out our worst troubles began. We would run through clouds for awhile, an the sun would break through and strike our bag. The gas would shoot up for awhile, when the rain woul send us down. If we could have had fair weather, we would have broken records. At one time I saw si balloons. But when I was forced to come down whether I wanted to or not on account of the heavy bag, I could see only one man, and he may be the only one that passed me, and if that is true, I will be among the winners."[7]

Von Phul's prediction proved to be off slightly. Reporting before the other championship contenders, the balloon was eventually credited with a fourth place finish just missing the cutoff for the James Gordon Bennett International Balloon Championship in October.

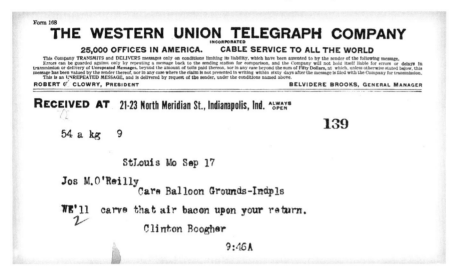

*A telegram to Joseph O'Reilly before the start of the September 1910 balloon races from the Indianapolis Motor Speedway. (From the scrapbook of Joseph M. O'Reilly, courtesy of the Missouri Historical Society, St. Louis)*

Carl Fisher had sent a dispatch to the *Indianapolis News* reporting that they had landed in the *Indiana II* at 5:10 p.m. Sunday evening ten miles west of Pittsburgh near Wilcox, Pennsylvania. Fisher stated they had also been caught in a storm. "The rain overtook us when we were about 20 miles east of Muncie. It came down in torrents but we were pleased that it was accompanied by a strong wind. It blew almost a gale and as we flew along in good running order we passed four or five of the other balloons in the darkness. We got by all of them except Hawley. The storm became fiercer (sic) and at 10:00 p.m. we were bowling along at great speed. It was during the night that we got into trouble and we had an experience I do not care to repeat."

"Near Degraff, Ohio, the rain and wind beat us down until our 600-foot drag rope was trailing. Suddenly, the end of the rope got caught in a tree and telegraph wires nearby. There we were, being whipped back and forth and up and down. The wind was so strong that the balloon would sweep almost to the ground and then when there would be a lull in the storm the bag would shoot upward 600 feet. Up and down we went, at times the balloon being beaten almost to the ground. We lost some of our equipment and ballast at the time. We shouted through a megaphone for some time when suddenly we saw a light approaching. A farmer came out with a lantern and after shouting at him for a time, we made him understand our predicament. We could not see anything except the light but we could hear the men below chopping at the tree. Finally we were cut loose and the balloon shot upward like a bullet. We stayed up all day Sunday and as we had only six bags of sand left we were compelled to descend, as the ballast was not sufficient for another night's trip."

"Our statiscope, which shows the ascent and descent, was broken and we were helpless to continue the flight. The rains poured down into our basket like a spout and we were almost drowned and frozen during Saturday night."[8]

The *Indiana II* was credited with an official distance of 320 miles after 24 hours and 5 minutes in flight. Fisher and Bumbaugh were awarded fifth place in the championship race. Monday's *Indianapolis News* carried the dispatch from Fisher as well as updates from some of the other balloons. Charles Walsh, pilot of the *Hoosier II*, had telegraphed the *Indianapolis News* on Monday morning that he and aide Samuel Haber of the United States government had landed in West Milton, Ohio, at 12:55 a.m. Sunday morning.

Exact details were not available at press time, but later the *Hoosier II* was credited with having gone 99 miles in seven hours and six minutes placing them ninth among the nine championship contenders.

Arthur Atherholt and Conyers Graham, pilot and aide for the *Pennsylvania*, had reported in a message to the *Indianapolis News* that they went down near Dexter, Ohio, at 12:28 p.m. Sunday afternoon. Atherholt had stated in his message that the heavy rains had forced them to the ground. The pair was later credited with an official distance of 218 miles to give them seventh place in the championship race.

The *Indianapolis News* also included a report that the *Centennial*, piloted by H.E. Honeywell with Wooster Lambert as his aide, had put their balloon down Sunday evening at 5:14 p.m. in Bush Valley, Pennsylvania. It was determined that the pair had made a flight of 379.5 miles in a 23 hour and 36 minute flight. It sounded as if they could have gone farther but decided against it due to their horrifying experience Saturday night.

"I landed Sunday evening because I did not want to experience another night like the one before. In the driving rain and cold and treacherous wind currents we spent such a night as I hope never to spend again. When we left Indianapolis we were caught by a northeastern breeze. Contrary to all expectations, we did not get near the lakes but were sent southward, crossing the Ohio River. Saturday night our troubles began. It had already begun to rain and grow cloudy and we soon lost sight of everything on terra firma. We had to go to 2,000 foot altitude to stay in the proper currents and the rain was fierce. It lashed the bag and soaked through. It beat into our faces and when we crouched down into the basket we became soaked and cold. All through the night we were at the mercy of the elements. When the weather is calm there is practically no sound up there but all night we were in an ocean of strange and hideous sounds."

"There was almost perfect darkness, the wind whistled and shrieked around the bag and the basket was swaying violently. We knew at times that our velocity was something terrible. But there was nothing to do but to trust Providence. The most welcome and beautiful sight I have ever seen in my life was the sunrise Sunday morning."[9]

*Armband worn by Joseph O'Reilly, aide in the Million Population Club balloon during the September 1910 National Championship balloon race at the Indianapolis Motor Speedway. (From the scrapbook of the St. Louis Aero Club, courtesy of the Missouri Historical Society, St. Louis)*

As of Monday night there were still four balloons that had not been heard from: *America II*, th Buckeye, the *New York,* and *Miss Sophia*. At the time it was assumed that these four balloons would b battling it out for the three coveted spots in the James Gordon Bennett International Balloon Champion ship in October. However, when the final results were announced days later, the *Centennial* was awarded a spot in the international race after determining that its distance of 379.5 miles was good enough for second place.

Finally, on Tuesday, September 20, the *Indianapolis News* provided word that all 13 balloons had been accounted for. As it turned out, the *New York* had been down since Sunday at noon. The balloon descended in Powellsville, Ohio, after traveling 198 miles in 18 hours and 4 minutes. This was only good enough for an eighth-place finish in the championship race. Apparently unmindful of the fact that the entire country had been concerned for the safety of his balloon, aide Thomas Baldwin appeared at the Aero Club of America rooms in New York late Monday to report the travels of the *New York*.

"I supposed, of course, that everyone knew about our having landed," Baldwin said in explaining his silence. "Although we were not in the air very long, we had a hard time of it and for 14 hours we had the hardest fight with adverse winds that I have ever experienced."[10]

William Assman and Paul McCullough, pilot and aide of *Miss Sophia*, had returned to earth in MacFarlan, West Virginia, at 5:08 p.m. on Sunday evening; however, it took them awhile to reach a telegraph office. Upon reaching Clarksburg, West Virginia, they wired the *St. Louis Globe-Democrat* to report their final destination.

"Landed last night in West Virginia. Got away in bad shape. Appendix never opened. Aide shook it all night and it opened little under expansion. Rained all night. Had to valve constantly to keep down. Passed over Middletown, Columbus, Athens, Wheeling. Threw out everything and landed with one and one-half sacks ballast."[11]

The *Miss Sophia* was credited with 269.5 miles in 24 hours and 8 minutes for a sixth-place finish in the championship race. This had to be a big disappointment for the St. Louis team, which wanted so badly to represent its city in the race for the international championship.

The final two balloons to descend back to earth, *America II* and the *Buckeye*, had made it all the way to Virginia. Pilot J.H. Wade, Jr. and his aide, A.H. Morgan, landed in Sowers, Virginia, at 7:29 a.m. Monday morning. The pair had stayed up for 37 hours and 38 minutes while floating along for 371 miles. The two men also talked about suffering through rain storms similar to what the other balloons had described. Wade sent a telegraph to the *Indianapolis News* from Christiansburg, Virginia, that read, "Balloon *Buckeye* landed on the mountains one mile southeast of Showalter, Floyd County, Virginia. Impossible to wire earlier."[12]

The efforts of the *Buckeye* crew earned them a third-place finish in the championship race, qualifying them for the James Gordon Bennett International Balloon Championships in October.

The *America II*, with Alan R. Hawley as pilot and Augustus Post as aide, did not land until 1:16 p.m. on Monday afternoon in Warrenton, Virginia. Their flight time of 44 hours and 20 minutes could have been exceeded according to Hawley; however, he was concerned about being carried out over Chesapeake Bay. The pair traveled 453 miles in that time to outdistance the rest of the championship contenders to claim first place.

A stroke of luck and some good strategy might have made all the difference in the race for the *America II*. All of the balloons were carried in a northeastern direction upon leaving the Speedway except the *America II*, which was carried due east. Additionally, Mr. Hawley reported that they maintained an incredible altitude of between 16,000 and 20,000 feet! This strategy seemed to pay off as Mr. Hawley reported in a wire to the *Indianapolis News* that they "met with little rain and no storms."[13] Theirs was the only balloon to avoid the heavy storms.

Despite avoiding the storms, Post and Hawley's flight was not without drama. They told the *Indianapolis News* how they met up with gunfire while drifting over eastern Ohio.

"The government should take steps at once to protect balloonists who are likely to be killed at any time by ignorant or vicious countrymen who persist in firing at them as they fly above farms", said Mr. Hawley. "While we were passing above Noble county Ohio Sunday evening I distinctly heard two bullets

*Alan Hawley and Augustus Post of the America II, winners of the 1910 National Championship balloon race hosted by the Indianapolis Motor Speedway. (Photo taken from a 1910 magazine)*

whistle past my ears and there were several reports. It was so serious that we actually decided that in the event of one of us was struck by a bullet the other should instantly descend."[14]

Although the Aero Club of America was disappointed that the storms kept the distances shorter than what had been hoped for, the championship race was viewed as a success. Based on the results of the National Championship race, the *America II, Centennial,* and *Buckeye* earned the right to represent the United States in the James Gordon Bennett International Balloon Championship at St. Louis in October. However, J.H. Wade, Jr., pilot of the *Buckeye,* withdrew shortly before the race to attend his grandmother's funeral. The Aero Club of America named "Tony" Von Phul and Joseph O'Reilly, pilot and aide of the *Million Population Club,* to replace the *Buckeye.*

Also in September, the four partners of the Indianapolis Motor Speedway turned the sporting world upside down when they publicized plans for the "greatest motor race in history". They announced that the Speedway would hold an International Sweepstakes race at the end of May 1911. The race, which was announced as being possibly 500 miles but at least 300 miles, would be open only to cars that could attain a 70 mph rate for a quarter of a mile (this was later increased to 75 mph). It would feature an incredible $30,000 in prize money! The Speedway itself was providing $20,000 – $25,000 with the tire, magneto, oil, carburetor, and other accessory companies expected to add to the total. Mr. Moross was scheduled to go to Europe to recruit entries for the race. The partners also announced that this race would likely be the only one run at Indianapolis during the 1911 season; however, the Speedway had applied for and been granted a September date by the AAA.

There had been rumors about such a race for several weeks leading up to the September events but none were confirmed until the *Indianapolis Star* came out with the story. The race teams were unanimous in their opinion that such a race would be a huge success. Starter Fred "Pop" Wagner spoke in the highest regard of the event.

"Such a race would be without parallel. This track would become famous in a day the world over. It would attract hundreds, yes, thousands, from Chicago, New York, Detroit, Denver and many from Europe. It would be a classic the likes of which was never known and months in advance the spotlight would play upon Indianapolis. Such a plan is overwhelming and would be nothing but a tremendous success and a credit to the men and the city where it was staged."[15]

## Seven Hours of Speed and Thrills

Spectators at the 500-Mile International Sweepstakes Race at the

## Indianapolis Motor Speedway

### DECORATION DAY, MAY 30, 1911

will see in action the cars and drivers whose names make the roster of Motordom's Hall of Fame complete. Such drivers as DePalma, Aitken, Burman, Chevrolet, Mulford, Dawson, Grant, Bruce Brown, Hemery, Wagner, Nazarro, Lytle, Strang and many others.

**RACE STARTS 1O A. M.**

---

**RACE STARTS 1O A. M.**

## $25,000,00 IN CASH PRIZES

## World's Most Daring Drivers

## Fastest Speed Cars Ever Built

Under the Management of the
### INDIANAPOLIS MOTOR SPEEDWAY CO.
#### Indianapolis, Indiana

C. G. FISHER, Pres.    J. A. ALLISON, Sec'y-Treas.

## Indianapolis Hotels Can Accommodate Any Size Crowd Conveniently

THE INDIANAPOLIS MOTOR SPEEDWAY CO. IS A MEMBER OF THE INDIANAPOLIS TRADE ASSOCIATION.

Greatest Race Course in the World

Greatest Inland City in the United States

---

## WARNER INSTRUMENT CO.

Call your attention to the
—— $25,000,00 ——
FIVE-HUNDRED MILE
### International Sweepstakes
AUTOMOBILE RACE
on the

## Indianapolis Motor Speedway

### DECORATION DAY, MAY 30, 1911

**RACE STARTS 1O A. M.**

---

**GREATEST RACE COURSE IN THE WORLD**

### Motordom's Supreme Speed Contest

Is to be staged at this famous 2½-mile brick course on DECORATION DAY, MAY 30, 1911. No race ever before planned has brought together such a galaxy of star drivers as will compete for the $25,000.00 gold purse, which is by far the largest ever offered for any one motor race.

### An All Day Battle of Cylinders

Will be fought by thirty of the master speed creators of Europe and America. Seven hours of racing in one continuous dash of 500 miles over the lightning-fast track assures the spectator of records broken in the longest contest ever held.

### Every Car Must Prove Worthy

Seventy-five miles an hour must be shown by every car that competes, which means that the greatest speed ever attained in any race will be necessary to win. Special racing cars, the masterpieces of the motor makers' art, will be seen earnest strife for a fortune in gold and glory.

### Purse Divided In Ten Prizes

The largest purse ever hung up for one great race—$25,000 in gold—is to be divided in ten prizes, as follows:

FIRST PRIZE ................ $10,000
Second Prize ................ $5,000
Third Prize ................ $3,000
Fourth Prize ................ $2,000
Fifth Prize ................ $1,500
Sixth Prize ................ $1,000
Seventh Prize ................ $800
Eighth Prize ................ $700
Ninth Prize ................ $600
Tenth Prize ................ $500

Many other special prizes are to be awarded to the winners.

### Location of Speedway

The Indianapolis Motor Speedway is located less than four miles from the heart of Indianapolis; twelve minutes by Big Four trains, twenty minutes by street car or interurban car service. The highways to the Speedway are excellent for automobile travel

The International Sweepstakes race will start promptly at 10 o'clock the morning of May 30, 1911. Postponed to Saturday, June 3, in case of rain.

### Indianapolis Motor Speedway Facts

The Indianapolis Motor Speedway has an area of 328 acres.
There are forty-one buildings, including garages, aerodromes, aviation sheds, etc.
The grandstands and boxes have a seating capacity of 60,000.
The entire grounds will accommodate upwards of 200,000.
There are parking facilities on the ground for 10,000 automobiles.
The turns are banked sixteen feet and have a radius of 1,500 feet.
Big Four railroad trains and interurban car service to the main gates of the grounds permit of the comfortable handling of 10,000 people every fifteen minutes.
The Speedway measures two and one-half miles to each lap, and has a surface of vitrified brick. 3,500,000 brick were required to pave the course.
A cement wall three feet in height by eleven inches in thickness extends around the outer edge of the turns.
Parking space for 9,800 automobiles is free.
Additional space for parking 200 automobiles has been set aside for reservations. This space may be reserved in advance and will be held for those purchasing same at 60.00 per automobile.
Box seats in the grandstands located in the main section of the grounds are $4.00 for each seat, this being in addition to price for admission into the grounds, which is $1.00. Each box contains six seats.
Main grandstand seats are reserved at $1.50 per seat, in addition to price of admission through the gate, which is $1.00. Reservations may be made by mail if remittance accompanies order.

---

*Front and back sides of a flyer promoting the first annual 500-Mile International Sweepstakes Race at the Indianapolis Motor Speedway. (Courtesy of a private collection)*

# Summary

The founders of the Indianapolis Motor Speedway would probably never have imagined that nearly 100 years after the building of the great track, it still remains as the premier racing facility in the world. Not only is the Indianapolis 500 the greatest race in the world, the Speedway has expanded to include three great classics each year, including NASCAR's Brickyard 400 and Formula One's United States Grand Prix. Through the years the Speedway crowds have witnessed great individual performances, heartbreaking defeats, tragedy, controversy, and plenty of drama. The events of 1909 and 1910 were no exception.

The Speedway opened with a great individual performance by 61-year-old John Berry. Competing against men half his age with a balloon much older than that of his competitors, he won the 1909 National Championship Balloon race from the Speedway. He even beat out the newer balloon that had been built to replace his *University City*!

Proving that the skies above the Speedway did not belong to John Berry alone, Walter Brookins thrilled the crowds at the 1910 aviation meet by soaring to new altitude records and completing maneuvers that amazed even the Wright brothers.

On the racetrack, Ray Harroun gave a dominating performance during the May 1910 Wheeler-Schebler race, leading 75 of the 80 laps. Cincinnati's Caleb Bragg followed that up by winning three races in one day while Chicago's Fred Huyck won three of the seven motorcycle races on August 14, 1909!

Who could forget the excruciating defeat suffered by motorcyclist Jake De Rosier at the hands of Ed Lingenfelder as De Rosier's body was perilously hurled along the tar and stone track or the agonizing defeat suffered by Bob Burman in the closing minutes of the May 1910 Cobe Trophy race after leading 75 of the 80 laps?

Tragedy struck during the first auto races held at the Speedway, claiming five lives and threatening the sanctioning of future auto races. Nearly a year later, tragedy struck again with the death of popular Indianapolis driver Tom Kincaid during a practice run.

The July 1910 auto races provided plenty of controversy when the Buick racing team came to town with their Marquette-Buicks. The powerful cars won practically everything they entered only to be disqualified weeks after the races.

What could be more dramatic than Johnny Aitken, the all-time leader in victories at the Indianapolis Motor Speedway, coming out of retirement after the death of his best friend and teammate to win the final race at the Speedway before the Indianapolis 500? Earlier in the day Aitken had warmed up by winning a thrilling race where the top four cars were separated by less than one second!

The events and decisions of these early years at the Indianapolis Motor Speedway shaped the future of the world's greatest race course. The whole thing could have easily ended after the tragic August races of 1909, but fortunately for us, the four founders were determined to make it work and their persistence paid off. Let us also not forget that the Speedway had plenty of competition in the early years. Besides competing with horse racing – clearly a more popular sport at the time – there were other race tracks such as Atlanta Speedway. A 20-year boom of the popular board tracks also began in 1910 starting with Playa-del-Ray in Venice, California. However, the Indianapolis Motor Speedway was blessed with good management that kept the track financially healthy and ran things smoothly for the participants and spectators alike. Perhaps this was something that was taken for granted at the time, but one only has to look at the fate of those other tracks (and there were a lot of them) to understand how fortunate Indianapolis has been.

After reading the story told here one can't help but have a greater appreciation of the rich tradition that sets the Indianapolis Motor Speedway apart from all of the other race tracks. When you set foot on the Speedway grounds, you walk where the four founders, along with Johnny Aitken, the Chevrolet brothers, Ray Harroun, the Wright brothers, and many others started it all back in 1909 and 1910.

Knowing this tradition, it's now easy to see why race teams put so much more effort into winning at Indy than any other place. I can understand their emotion as they express their desire to win a race at the Indianapolis Motor Speedway and their frustration when their efforts fall short. Perhaps one requirement of every rookie driver before competing at the Brickyard should be to read how it all started nearly 100 years ago.

# Whatever Happened To?

Whatever happened to these men after 1910? That has been a question that many people have asked since learning of the early history made at the Indianapolis Motor Speedway. Here is a brief summary of some of the participants and their activities after 1910, starting with the four founders of the Indianapolis Motor Speedway.

*The four founders of the Indianapolis Motor Speedway; Arthur Newby, Frank Wheeler, Carl Fisher, and James Allison. (Photo courtesy of the Indianapolis Motor Speedway)*

**Carl G. Fisher** – Carl Fisher sold the Prest-O-Lite Company to Union Carbide in 1917 for $9,000,000. He was also co-founder of the Empire Automobile Company and was instrumental in establishing the Lincoln Highway. Additionally, he is known as the primary developer of Miami Beach. He later sold his controlling interest of the Indianapolis Motor Speedway to Eddie Rickenbacker in August of 1927. Mr. Fisher died in Miami Beach on July 15, 1939, at the age of 65.

**James A. Allison** – James Allison sold his share of the Prest-O-Lite Company to Union Carbide at the same time as Carl Fisher, sharing part of the $9,000,000 proceeds. He was a co-founder of the Empire Automobile Company and, prior to WWI, he started the Allison Engineering Company in Indianapolis which later became a division of General Motors. Additionally, he served as a director of the American Fletcher Bank of Indianapolis. Mr. Allison died of pneumonia at his home in Indianapolis on August 4, 1928, at the age of 55.

**Arthur C. Newby** – Arthur Newby was co-founder of the National Motor Vehicle Company and the Empire Automobile Company. Prior to his involvement in the Speedway, he built the Newby Oval, a quarter-mile bicycle track. He made several financial gifts to various organizations including Earlham College and Butler University. He served on the Endowment and Building commissions at Butler University in addition to the Foundation board. Mr. Newby died in Indianapolis on September 11, 1933, at the age of 68.

**Frank H. Wheeler** – Frank Wheeler was co-founder and president of the Wheeler-Schebler Carburetor Company until his death. He was also involved with the Stutz Fire Engine Company of which he was vice president and the Wheeler-Langsenkamp Brass Company, both in Indianapolis. He took his own life at his home in Indianapolis on May 27, 1921, at the age of 57.

**Johnny D. Aitken** – Johnny Aitken is still the all-time leader of career wins at the Indianapolis Motor Speedway with 15. He started racing in 1905 and was a member of the National racing team that won the 24-hour race on the Indianapolis Fair Grounds track that year. He drove for the National racing team earning 12 wins at the Indianapolis Motor Speedway during 1909 and 1910 and won all three of the Harvest Day races at the Speedway in September of 1916, his last appearance as a driver at the Speedway. Aitken also participated in the 1911 and 1916 Indianapolis 500s. After retiring from racing at the start of WWI, he served as a vice president of the Allison Engineering Company. He died of bronchial pneumonia brought on by influenza, in Indianapolis on October 15, 1918, at the age of 33.

**Erwin G. Baker** – Erwin Baker, winner of the final motorcycle race held at the Speedway in August 1909, was born in Dearborn County, Indiana, and moved to Indianapolis at the age of 12. Baker had a talent for completing endurance runs in record time and went on to set several records. In 1914 he was given the nickname of "Cannonball" Baker after a newspaper writer compared him to the Cannonball Express train. He eventually shifted his talents to auto racing and finished 11th in the 1922 Indianapolis 500. He later was named the first commissioner of NASCAR. "Cannonball" Baker died in Indianapolis on May 10, 1960, at the age of 78.

**John Berry** – Captain Berry won the first National Championship Balloon race from the Speedway in 1909. He made his first balloon ascension in his hometown of Rochester, New York, at the age of 13 and piloted balloons up until his retirement at the age of 74. In 1915 he began flying airplanes as well. He spent most of his life in St. Louis where he founded an aerial and automobile school. He died in St. Louis on April 22, 1931, at the age of 83.

**Caleb S. Bragg** – Caleb Bragg was the son of a wealthy Cincinnati publisher and a graduate of Yale. He began his racing career in early 1910 and won three races at the Speedway in one day on May 30, 1910. He began flying airplanes in 1915, setting American altitude records in 1917. He later served as an Army test pilot during WWI. In the mid-1920s he was a successful motorboat racer. He was an executive in several engineering companies throughout his life and was also the first president of the Wings Club, founded in New York City after WWII to promote the advancement of aeronautics. He died in New York on October 24, 1943, at the age of 56.

**Walter R. Brookins** – Walter Brookins was the first student of the Wright brothers and later was named as their first instructor. He eventually left the Wright brothers' exhibition team and continued to set records for altitude and endurance. He was the founder of the "Early Birds," a club for individuals who flew an airplane or airship before December 17, 1916. He died on April 29, 1953, at the age of 63 and is buried at the Portal of Folded Wings Shrine to Aviation in North Hollywood, California.

**Bob Burman** – The famous Buick driver, Bob Burman, was born in Imlay City, Michigan, on April 23, 1885. He entered his first race in 1906 at Detroit, Michigan, and joined the Buick Motor Company as a driver in 1908. Burman had a very successful racing career at Buick and was credited with two wins at the Indianapolis Motor Speedway after four wins in July 1910 were taken away as a result of the disqualification of the Marquette-Buick. He won the first 250-mile Prest-O-Lite trophy race at the Speedway on August 19, 1909, and participated in the first five Indianapolis 500s. He died on April 8, 1916, from injuries suffered in a crash during the Corona Grand Prize Race at Corona, California. He was 30 years old.

**Louis Chevrolet** – Bob Burman's Buick teammate, Louis Chevrolet, was born on December 25, 1878, in Switzerland. He immigrated to the United States in 1900 and began racing for the Fiat Motor Company of New York in 1905. He later joined the Buick Motor Company where he had a successful racing career. Besides winning six races at the Indianapolis Motor Speedway during 1909 – 1910, he won the 400-mile Cobe trophy race of 1909 in Crown Point, Indiana, and participated in four Indianapolis 500s. He later joined the Buick Motor Company as a design and test engineer. He died on June 6, 1941, at the age of 62.

**Joe Dawson** – Joe Dawson is credited with six wins at the Indianapolis Motor Speedway including a victory in the Cobe trophy race on July 4, 1910, while driving for the Marmon team. He also won the 1912 Indianapolis 500 as a member of the National team. He participated in the Indianapolis 500 in 1911 and 1914, driving for Marmon, suffering severe injuries in the 1914 race. He ran an automobile service in Philadelphia for several years and served as the Philadelphia representative for the American Automobile Association. He died of a heart attack in Philadelphia on June 17, 1946, at the age of 57.

**Ralph DePalma** – Ralph DePalma is recognized as one of the all-time greats in auto racing. Known for his good sportsmanship, as well as his excellent driving skills, he was born in Italy and immigrated to the United States. His first appearance at Indianapolis was in August 1909, but his first win at Indianapolis came in September 1910, where he won a 10-mile free-for-all race driving a Fiat. He went on to drive in ten Indianapolis 500 races. He won only the 1915 race despite leading 612 laps during that time, a record that was not broken until the 1980s. During his 25-year career he won close to 2,000 races and was the 1912 and 1914 AAA National Champion. He died in 1956 at the age of 73.

**Jacob De Rosier** – "Jake" De Rosier recovered from his injuries sustained in an August 1909 motorcycle race at the Speedway and went on to win hundreds of races in the United States and Great Britain. He was known as one of the great motorcycle racers of all time. During his career, he rode for Indian and Excelsior before sustaining a career-ending leg injury in 1912 at the Los Angeles Motordrome. He died in Massachusetts almost one year later on February 25, 1913, at the age of 33 as a result of complications from surgery on the leg he had injured in Los Angeles in 1912.

**Ray Harroun** – Ray Harroun stands second in career wins at the Indianapolis Motor Speedway with eight. He won seven races during 1909 and 1910 and was the winner of the inaugural Indianapolis 500 in 1911, after which he announced his retirement from racing. Shortly after retirement he did engineering work for the Nordyke & Marmon Company and worked with the Maxwell racing team in 1914-15. He established the Harroun Motors Corporation in Wayne, Michigan, in 1917, producing Harroun autos until 1922. His company also produced munitions for the government during WWI. Harroun was employed in the auto industry until his retirement at the age of 79. He died in Anderson, Indiana, on January 19, 1968, at the age of 89.

**Alan R. Hawley** – Alan Hawley went on to win the James Gordon Bennett International Balloon race in October 1910 after winning the 1910 National Balloon Championship at the Speedway. In that race he and aide Augustus Post set a new American distance record of 1,172.9 miles. Mr. Hawley was a stock broker with his brother for several years before retiring in 1912. He was a founder of the Automobile Club of America and also served as the president of the Aero Club of America from 1913-19. He died in New York of heart problems on February 16, 1938, at the age of 69.

**Eddie Hearne** – Eddie Hearne has a total of six victories at the Indianapolis Motor Speedway, which puts him in a tie with Louis Chevrolet and Joe Dawson for third in all-time wins at Indianapolis. Hearne went on to race in nine Indianapolis 500s with a best finish of second in 1919. That was quite an accomplishment considering that he retired in 1912 only to come back after the war to continue his successful career until 1927. He also won the National Championship in 1923. Eddie Hearne died on September 2, 1955.

**Albert Bond Lambert** – Albert Lambert piloted the *St. Louis 3* to a third place finish in the 1909 National Balloon Championship at the Speedway and, as president of the St. Louis Aero Club, served as Director of Contests for the 1910 National Balloon Championship. Mr. Lambert was credited with making St. Louis one of the leading cities of flight in the early days of aviation and helped establish what is now called Lambert-St. Louis International airport. He was president of the Lambert Pharmacal Company for many years. The company was founded by his father, Jordan W. Lambert, and was known for making Listerine among other things. He was also one of the primary financial supporters of Charles Lindbergh's historic non-stop flight to Paris. Mr. Lambert died in St. Louis on November 12, 1946, at the age of 70.

**Charles Merz** – "Charlie" Merz was a popular Indianapolis driver for the National racing team during 1909 – 1910. He started his driving career at the young age of 17 in Indianapolis during November 1905. He participated in the first four Indianapolis 500s, with his best finishes being 4th in 1912 and 3rd in 1913. He was a veteran of both WWI and WWII, rising to a very high rank during WWII. He served as Chief Steward of the Indianapolis Motor Speedway from 1935 to 1940. Merz also formed the Merz Engineering Company in 1927, serving as president until his retirement in 1946. He died at his home in Indianapolis on July 8, 1952, at the age of 64.

**Berna Eli Oldfield** – "Barney" Oldfield was one of the most famous race car drivers of his time. He was born on June 3, 1878, in Wauseon, Ohio, and began his racing career in 1902. Although he did have four wins at the Indianapolis Motor Speedway during 1909 – 1910 and finished fifth in two Indianapolis 500 appearances, he was known more as the ultimate showman. He was most famous for holding speed records and participating in match races and exhibitions. He retired from active racing in 1918 but stayed close to the sport thereafter. He died on October 4, 1946, at the age of 68.

**Louis Schwitzer** – Winner of the very first auto race at the Indianapolis Motor Speedway, Schwitzer was born in Austria in 1880. He raced until 1912 when he joined the Speedway Technical Committee and served as chairman and honorary chairman until 1940. He also joined with Howard Marmon to design the engine for the Marmon Wasp that Ray Harroun drove to victory in the inaugural Indianapolis 500. After WWI, he started his own business in Indianapolis and manufactured automotive cooling fans. He later built water pumps and superchargers, among other things. He retired from the Schwitzer Corporation in 1964 and died in Indianapolis in 1967 at the age of 87. Each May since 1967, the Professional Society of Engineers has awarded the Louis Schwitzer Award for Engineering Excellence to a group or individual involved with the Indianapolis 500 who demonstrates innovative and engineering excellence.

**Lewis Strang** – Lewis Strang was a native of New York who began his racing career in 1905 at the age of 20. During his career, he earned victories in many big races including the 100-mile G & J trophy race at the Speedway in August 1909 as part of the Buick racing team. He finished 29th in the 1911 Indianapolis 500 as manager/driver for the Case team. Sadly, Strang was killed shortly thereafter on July 20, 1911, at the age of 26. He died as the result of injuries suffered in a freak accident while serving as a guide for an endurance run sponsored by the Wisconsin Automobile Club.

**Howard Wilcox** – Born in Crawfordsville, Indiana, "Howdy" Wilcox won five races at the Indianapolis Motor Speedway, including the 1919 Indianapolis 500. He started his racing career in 1906 at the age of 18 in Crawfordsville. Soon after, he worked as a mechanic for Johnny Aitken before becoming a driver for the National racing team. In 1911, he started what would later become known as the Yellow Cab Company with fellow driver Don Herr. Wilcox had an impressive string of starts in the Indianapolis 500, having started in every race from 1911 thru 1923. After being forced from the 1923 Indianapolis 500, he served as a relief driver for his teammate Tommy Milton who went on to win the race. He died on September 4, 1923, at the age of 35 from injuries suffered in an accident while driving a Duesenberg Special in the inaugural 200-mile race at Altoona Speedway in Altoona, Pennsylvania. At the time of his death he was the president of the Wilcox Sales Company.

# 1909 – 1910
# Racing Statistics
# Indianapolis Motor Speedway

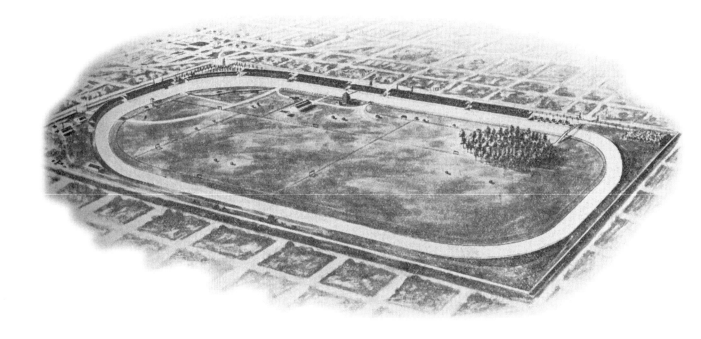

*Early aerial view of the Indianapolis Motor Speedway.*

# 1909 – 1910 Racing Statistics - Indianapolis Motor Speedway

## Number of Race Wins By Driver
## 1909 - 1910

| | | AUG 1909 | MAY 1910 | JUL 1910 | SEP 1910 | Total | |
|---|---|---|---|---|---|---|---|
| Johnny Aitken (1) | National | 2 | 4 | 3 | 3 | 12 | ( a ) |
| Ray Harroun | Marmon | 1 | 4 | | 2 | 7 | |
| Louis Chevrolet | Buick | 1 | 2 | 3 | | 6 | ( b ) |
| Eddie Hearne | Benz (2) | 1 | | 2 | 3 | 6 | |
| Joe Dawson | Marmon | 1 | 4 | | | 5 | ( c ) |
| Arthur Greiner | National | 2 | 3 | | | 5 | ( d ) |
| Barney Oldfield | Knox (3) | 1 | 3 | | | 4 | |
| Howard Wilcox | National | 1 | | 3 | | 4 | |
| Caleb Bragg | Fiat | 3 | | | | 3 | |
| Mortimer Roberts | Herreshoff | | | 3 | | 3 | |
| Tom Kincaid | National | 1 | 2 | | | 3 | |
| Bob Burman | Buick | 1 | 1 | | | 2 | ( e ) |
| Harry Grant | ALCO | | | 2 | | 2 | |
| Lewis Strang | Buick | 2 | | | | 2 | |
| Louis Edmunds | Cole | | | | 2 | 2 | |
| Walter Emmons | Herreshoff | | | | 2 | 2 | |
| Len Zengel | Chadwick | 1 | | | | 1 | |
| Louis Heineman | FAL | | | 1 | | 1 | |
| Ralph DePalma | Fiat | | | | 1 | 1 | |
| Lee Frayer | Firestone-Columbus | | | | 1 | 1 | |
| Leigh Lynch | Jackson | 1 | | | | 1 | |
| Wilfred Bourque | Knox | 1 | | | | 1 | |
| N. J. Sutcliffe | Maytag | | | 1 | | 1 | |
| W. J. Barndollar | McFarlan | | | | 1 | 1 | |
| Charlie Merz | National | 1 | | | | 1 | |
| George Robertson | Simplex | | | 1 | | 1 | |
| Louis Schwitzer | Stoddard-Dayton | 1 | | | | 1 | |
| Carl Wright | Stoddard-Dayton | 1 | | | | 1 | |
| Jack Reed | Stoddard-Dayton | | 1 | | | 1 | |
| Billy Pearce | FAL | | 1 | | | 1 | ( f ) |
| Totals | | 16 | 24 | 24 | 18 | 82 | |

(1) Johnny Aitken also won three races in one day at the Harvest Classic held on September 9, 1916, to give him a career total of 15 victories at the Speedway.
(2) The August 1909 win was in a Fiat.
(3) The August 1909 win was in a Benz.

( a ) Two July 1910 wins resulted from disqualification of the Marquette-Buick.
( b ) Forfeit of two wins in July 1910 due to the disqualification of the Marquette-Buick.
( c ) Three July 1910 wins resulted from disqualification of the Marquette-Buick.
( d ) One July 1910 win resulted from disqualification of the Mercedes.
( e ) Forfeit of four wins in July 1910 due to the disqualification of the Marquette-Buick.
( f ) One July 1910 win resulted from disqualification of the Marquette-Buick.

*Panoramic view of the infield at the Indianapolis Motor Speedway during the June 1910 aviation meet. (Photo courtesy of the Library of Congress)*

## Number of Race Wins By Car Manufacturer
## 1909 - 1910

| | AUG 1909 | MAY 1910 | JUL 1910 | SEP 1910 | Total | |
|---|---|---|---|---|---|---|
| National | 4 | 9 | 6 | 6 | 25 | ( a ), ( b ) |
| Marmon | 1 | 5 | 4 | 2 | 12 | ( c ) |
| Buick | 4 | 3 | 3 | | 10 | ( d ) |
| Benz | 1 | | 2 | 3 | 6 | |
| Fiat | 1 | 3 | | 1 | 5 | |
| Herreshoff | | | 3 | 2 | 5 | |
| Knox | 1 | 3 | | | 4 | |
| Stoddard-Dayton | 2 | 1 | | | 3 | |
| ALCO | | | 2 | | 2 | |
| Cole | | | | 2 | 2 | |
| FAL | | | 2 | | 2 | ( e ) |
| Chadwick | 1 | | | | 1 | |
| Firestone-Columbus | | | | 1 | 1 | |
| Jackson | 1 | | | | 1 | |
| Maytag | | | 1 | | 1 | |
| McFarlan | | | | 1 | 1 | |
| Simplex | | | 1 | | 1 | |
| Totals | 16 | 24 | 24 | 18 | 82 | |

( a ) Two July 1910 wins resulted from disqualification of the Marquette-Buick.
( b ) One July 1910 win resulted from disqualification of the Mercedes.
( c ) Two July 1910 wins resulted from disqualification of the Marquette-Buick.
( d ) Forfeit of six wins in July 1910 due to the disqualification of the Marquette-Buick.
( e ) One July 1910 win resulted from disqualification of the Marquette-Buick.

*Crushed rock ready to be rolled on the original racing surface prior to paving with brick.*

## Lap Leaders
## 1909 - 1910

| | | | | | |
|---|---|---|---|---|---|
| Ray Harroun | 138 | | Jap Clemens | 3 | |
| Johnny Aitken | 110 | | Len Zengel | 3 | |
| Bob Burman | 88 | ( a ) | Lee Frayer | 2 | |
| Eddie Hearne | 76 | | Louis Heineman | 2 | |
| Leigh Lynch | 48 | | George Robertson | 2 | |
| Lewis Strang | 42 | | John Ryall | 2 | |
| Joe Dawson | 37 | | W. J. Barndollar | 1 | |
| Howard Wilcox | 37 | | Wilfred Bourque | 1 | |
| Louis Chevrolet | 32 | ( b ) | Tobin DeHymel | 1 | |
| Tom Kincaid | 31 | | Frank Gelnaw | 1 | |
| Barney Oldfield | 19 | | Ben Kirscher | 1 | |
| Carl Wright | 14 | | Emmett Meddock | 1 | |
| Harry Grant | 12 | | Arthur Miller | 1 | |
| Caleb Bragg | 10 | | Bert Miller | 1 | |
| Arthur Greiner | 10 | | Billy Pearce | 1 | |
| Fred Ellis | 7 | | Jack Reed | 1 | |
| Mortimer Roberts | 7 | | unaccounted for | 7 | |
| Louis Scwitzer | 7 | | | 798 | |
| Arthur Chevrolet | 5 | ( c ) | | | |
| Ralph DePalma | 5 | | disqualified laps | 136 | |
| Frank Fox | 5 | | | 934 | |
| Charlie Merz | 5 | | | | |
| Gil Anderson | 4 | | | | |
| George DeWitt | 4 | | | | |
| Louis Edmunds | 4 | | | | |
| Walter Emmons | 4 | | | | |
| N. J. Sutcliffe | 4 | | | | |

( a ) 99 laps from July 1910 forfeited due to disqualification of the Marquette-Buick.
( b ) 8 laps from July 1910 forfeited due to disqualification of the Marquette-Buick.
( c ) 27 laps from July 1910 forfeited due to disqualification of the Marquette-Buick.

*Belt conveyor in the process of laying bricks on the Speedway's racing surface during 1909.*

## Participation by Car Manufacturer
## 1909 - 1910

| Car Name | Manufactured In | AUG 1909 | MAY 1910 | JUL 1910 | SEP 1910 |
|---|---|---|---|---|---|
| ALCO | Providence, Rhode Island | | | Yes | |
| American | Indianapolis, Indiana | Yes | Yes | | Yes |
| Apperson | Kokomo, Indiana | Yes | | | |
| Benz | Germany | Yes | Yes | Yes | Yes |
| Black Crow | Elkhart, Indiana | | Yes | Yes | |
| Buick | Flint, Michigan | Yes | Yes | Yes | |
| Chadwick | Pottstown, Pennsylvania | Yes | | Yes | |
| Christie | New York City, New York | Yes | | | |
| Cino | Cincinnati, Ohio | | | Yes | |
| Cole | Indianapolis, Indiana | Yes | Yes | Yes | |
| Cutting | Jackson, Michigan | Yes | | | |
| Darracq | France | Yes | | | |
| Diamond T | Chicago, Illinois | | Yes | | |
| E-M-F | Detroit, Michigan | | Yes | | |
| Empire | Indianapolis, Indiana | Yes | Yes | | |
| FAL | Chicago, Illinois | | Yes | Yes | |
| Fiat | Italy | Yes | Yes | | Yes |
| Firestone-Columbus | Columbus, Ohio | Yes | | Yes | |
| Fuller | Jackson, Michigan | | Yes | | |
| Great Western | Peru, Indiana | Yes | Yes | Yes | |
| Herreshoff | Detroit, Michigan | Yes | Yes | Yes | |
| Hudson | Detroit, Michigan | | | Yes | |
| Hupmobile | Detroit, Michigan | Yes | | | |
| Jackson | Jackson, Michigan | Yes | Yes | | |
| Knox | Springfield, Massachusetts | Yes | Yes | | |
| Lozier | Plattsburgh, New York | Yes | | | |
| Marion | Indianapolis, Indiana | Yes | Yes | | |
| Marmon | Indianapolis, Indiana | Yes | Yes | Yes | Yes |
| Marquette-Buick | Saginaw, Michigan | | Yes | | |
| Matheson | Grand Rapids, Michigan | | | | Yes |
| Maytag | Waterloo, Iowa | | Yes | | |
| McFarlan | Connersville, Indiana | | | Yes | |
| Mercedes | Germany | | Yes | | |
| Midland | Moline, Illinois | | Yes | Yes | |
| National | Indianapolis, Indiana | Yes | Yes | Yes | Yes |
| Parry | Indianapolis, Indiana | | | Yes | |
| Pope-Hartford | Hartford, Connecticut | Yes | Yes | | |
| Simplex | New York City, New York | | Yes | | |
| Speedwell | Dayton, Ohio | | Yes | | |
| Staver | Chicago, Illinois | | Yes | | |
| Stearns | Cleveland, Ohio | Yes | | | |
| Stoddard-Dayton | Dayton, Ohio | Yes | Yes | Yes | |
| Thomas | Buffalo, New York | Yes | | | |
| Velie | Moline, Illinois | Yes | | | |
| Warren-Detroit | Detroit, Michigan | Yes | Yes | | |
| Westcott | Richmond, Indiana | Yes | | Yes | |

Note 1) A Packard was driven by Walter Donnelly at the December 1909 brick tests.

*15-ton roller on one of the Speedway's banked turns during the brick paving process in 1909.*

## American Track Records
### Records Set at the Indianapolis Motor Speedway
### 1909 - 1910

| Class | Driver | Car | Date | Time |
|---|---|---|---|---|
| **Time Trials** | | | | |
| 1 Kilometer | Barney Oldfield | Benz | 5/30/10 | 21.45 |
| 1 Mile | Barney Oldfield | Benz | 5/30/10 | 35.63 |
| | | | | |
| **160 CID & under** | | | | |
| 5-miles | Mortimer Roberts | Herreshoff | 7/04/10 | 5:22.87 |
| 10-miles | Mortimer Roberts | Herreshoff | 7/02/10 | 10:37.59 |
| | | | | |
| **161 - 230 CID** | | | | |
| 5-miles | Louis Chevrolet | Buick | 7/01/10 | 4:35.47 |
| 10-miles | Louis Chevrolet | Buick | 7/02/10 | 8:55.40 |
| | | | | |
| **231 - 300 CID** | | | | |
| 5-miles | Joe Dawson | Marmon | 7/02/10 | 4:16.00 |
| 10-miles | Ray Harroun | Marmon | 5/27/10 | 8:16.80 |
| 25-miles | Ray Harroun | Marmon | 5/30/10 | 21:48.92 |
| 50-miles | Ray Harroun | Marmon | 5/30/10 | 42:31.33 |
| | | | | |
| **301 - 450 CID** | | | | |
| 5-miles | Tom Kincaid | National | 5/27/10 | 4:05.76 |
| 10-miles | Johnny Aitken | National | 7/02/10 | 7:55.12 |
| 15-miles | Johnny Aitken | National | 7/01/10 | 11:48.78 |
| 20-miles | Joe Dawson | Marmon | 5/27/10 | 15:57.63 |
| 75-miles | Joe Dawson | Marmon | 5/27/10 | 1:00:16.34 |
| 100-miles | Tom Kincaid | National | 5/27/10 | 1:23:43.11 |
| 250-miles | Bob Burman | Buick | 8/19/09 | 4:38:57.40 |
| | | | | |
| **451 - 600 CID** | | | | |
| 5-miles | Barney Oldfield | Knox | 5/30/10 | 4:01.36 |
| | | | | |
| **0 - 600 CID** | | | | |
| 200-miles | Joe Dawson | Marmon | 7/04/10 | 2:43:20.14 |
| | | | | |
| **Free-For-All** | | | | |
| 15 miles | Eddie Hearne | Benz | 7/04/10 | 10:25.17 |
| 20-miles | Eddie Hearne | Benz | 7/04/10 | 14:06.72 |

*Workers cleaning up the new brick racing surface during the paving process in 1909.*

## Winners of Special Races
## 1909 - 1910

|  | Date | Driver | Car |
|---|---|---|---|
| **Prest-O-Lite Trophy Race** | | | |
| 250-mile Prest-O-Lite trophy race (301 - 450 CID) | 8/19/09 | Bob Burman | Buick |
| 100-mile Prest-O-Lite trophy race (301 - 450 CID) | 5/27/10 | Tom Kincaid | National |
| **Wheeler-Schebler Trophy Race** | | | |
| 300-mile race (less than 600 CID) | 8/21/09 | Leigh Lynch | Jackson |
| 200-mile race (less than 600 CID) | 5/28/10 | Ray Harroun | Marmon |
| **Remy Grand Brassard & Trophy Race** | | | |
| 25-mile free-for-all open | 8/21/09 | Barney Oldfield | Benz |
| 50-mile race (231 - 300 CID) | 5/30/10 | Ray Harroun | Marmon |
| 100-mile race (301 - 450 CID) | 7/02/10 | Joe Dawson | Marmon ( a ) |
| 100-mile race (less than 450 CID) | 9/03/10 | Howard Wilcox | National |
| **G & J Trophy Race** | | | |
| 100-mile race (231 - 300 CID) | 8/20/09 | Lewis Strang | Buick |
| 50-mile race (231 - 300 CID) | 7/01/10 | Billy Pearce | FAL ( b ) |
| **Cobe Trophy Race** | | | |
| 200-mile race (less than 600 CID) | 7/04/10 | Joe Dawson | Marmon |
| **Speedway Helmet Race** | | | |
| 5-mile free-for-all race | 5/27/10 | Bob Burman | Buick |
| 10-mile free-for-all race | 7/01/10 | Eddie Hearne | Benz |
| 10-mile free-for-all race (Class D) | 9/03/10 | Eddie Hearne | Benz |
| **Ford Trophy Race** | | | |
| 10-mile free-for-all race | 8/20/09 | Len Zengel | Chadwick |
| **Miscellaneous races of 100 miles or more** | | | |
| 100-mile free-for-all race (Class D) | 9/03/10 | Eddie Hearne | Benz |
| 200-mile race (less than 600 CID) | 9/05/10 | Johnny Aitken | National |

( a ) Awarded 1st place after the Marquette-Buicks of Bob Burman and Louis Chevrolet were disqualified.

( b ) Awarded 1st place after the Marquette-Buick of Bob Burman was disqualified.

*Johnny Aitken driving a National on the Speedway's new brick racing surface during the December 1909 brick tests.*

## Winning Car Numbers
## 1909 - 1910

| Car # | AUG 1909 | MAY 1910 | JUL 1910 | SEP 1910 | Total |
|---|---|---|---|---|---|
| 9 | | 4 | | 6 | 10 |
| 19 | 1 | 3 | | 2 | 6 |
| 33 | 2 | 3 | 1 | | 6 |
| 3 | 1 | | | 3 | 4 |
| 35 | 1 | | 3 | | 4 |
| 6 | 1 | | | 2 | 3 |
| 7 | 1 | | 2 | | 3 |
| 8 | 2 | | 1 | | 3 |
| 14 | | 3 | | | 3 |
| 27 | 1 | | 2 | | 3 |
| 34 | 1 | 1 | 1 | | 3 |
| 46 | | 3 | | | 3 |
| 48 | | 2 | 1 | | 3 |
| 10 | | 2 | | | 2 |
| 12 | | | 2 | | 2 |
| 22 | | | 2 | | 2 |
| 26 | | | | 2 | 2 |
| 31 | | | 2 | | 2 |
| 36 | | 2 | | | 2 |
| 45 | | 1 | 1 | | 2 |
| 1 | | | | 1 | 1 |
| 2 | | | 1 | | 1 |
| 11 | | 1 | | | 1 |
| 15 | 1 | | | | 1 |
| 18 | 1 | | | | 1 |
| 23 | | | | 1 | 1 |
| 24 | 1 | | | | 1 |
| 30 | | | | 1 | 1 |
| 32 | | 1 | | | 1 |
| 41 | | 1 | | | 1 |
| 44 | | | 1 | | 1 |
| 50 | 1 | | | | 1 |
| 52 | 1 | | | | 1 |
| 90 | | | 1 | | 1 |
| Totals | 16 | 24 | 24 | 18 | 82 |

*Louis Chevrolet stopping for fuel during the Cobe trophy race at the Speedway in July 1910.*

## 1909 - 1910 Drivers Who Participated in the Indianapolis 500

**Johnny Aitken (2)**
1911 - 27th
1916 - 15th

**Charles Basle (1)**
1911 - 34th

**Caleb Bragg (2)**
1911 - 37th
1913 - 15th

**Bob Burman (5)**
1911 - 19th
1912 - 12th
1913 - 11th *
1914 - 24th
1915 - 6th

**Arthur Chevrolet (2)**
1911 - 36th
1916 - 18th

**Louis Chevrolet (4)**
1915 - 20th
1916 - 12th *
1919 - 7th *
1920 - 18th *

**Joe Dawson (3)**
1911 - 5th *
1912 - 1st *
1914 - 25th

**Ralph DePalma (10)**
1911 - 6th
1912 - 11th
1913 - 23rd
1915 - 1st
1919 - 6th
1920 - 5th
1921 - 12th
1922 - 4th
1923 - 15th
1925 - 7th *

**Fred Ellis (1)**
1911 - 38th

**Harry Endicott (2)**
1911 - 16th
1913 - 21st

**Bill Endicott (3)**
1911 - 26th *
1912 - 5th *
1913 - 27th

**Frank Fox**
1911 - 22nd *

**Lee Frayer (1)**
1911 - 13th

**Harry Grant (4)**
1911 - 33rd
1913 - 24th
1914 - 7th
1915 - 12th

**Arthur Greiner (1)**
1911 - 40th

**Ray Harroun (1)**
1911 - 1st *

**Eddie Hearne (9)**
1911 - 21st *
1912 - 20th *
1919 - 2nd
1920 - 6th
1921 - 13th
1922 - 3rd
1923 - 4th
1924 - 19th
1927 - 7th

**Don Herr (1)**
1913 - 26th

**Hughie Hughes (2)**
1911 - 12th
1912 - 3rd

**Harry Knight (2)**
1911 - 30th
1912 - 23rd

**Herbert Lytle (1)**
1911 - 32nd

**Charlie Merz (4)**
1911 - 7th
1912 - 4th
1913 - 3rd
1916 - 19th

**Barney Oldfield (2)**
1914 - 5th *
1916 - 5th

**Lewis Strang (1)**
1911 - 29th *

**Howard Wilcox (11)**
1911 - 14th
1912 - 9th
1913 - 6th
1914 - 22nd
1915 - 7th
1916 - 7th *
1919 - 1st
1920 - 19th
1921 - 23rd
1922 - 27th
1923 - 17th

**Spencer Wishart (4)**
1911 - 4th *
1912 - 15th
1913 - 2nd *
1914 - 17th

**Len Zengel (1)**
1912 - 6th

* Driver had relief help.

*Racing action on the front straightaway at the Indianapolis Motor Speedway during May 1910.*

## 2 ½ MILE SPEED TRACK

| MILES PER HOUR | 1 Lap 2½ M | | 2 Laps 5 M | | 3 Laps 7½ M | | 4 Laps 10 M | | 20 Laps 50 M | | 40 Laps 100 Miles | | | 80 Laps 200 Miles | | | MILES PER HOUR |
|---|---|---|---|---|---|---|---|---|---|---|---|---|---|---|---|---|---|
| | Minutes | Seconds | Minutes | Seconds | Minutes | Seconds | Minutes | Seconds | Minutes | Seconds | Hours | Minutes | Seconds | Hours | Minutes | Seconds | |
| 60 | 2 | 30.0 | 5 | 00.0 | 7 | 30.0 | 10 | 00.0 | 50 | 00 | 1 | 40 | 00 | 3 | 20 | 00 | 60 |
| ½ | 2 | 28.8 | 4 | 57.6 | 7 | 24.4 | 9 | 55.2 | 49 | 36 | 1 | 39 | 12 | 3 | 18 | 24 | ½ |
| 61 | 2 | 27.6 | 4 | 55.2 | 7 | 22.8 | 9 | 50.4 | 49 | 12 | 1 | 38 | 24 | 3 | 16 | 48 | 61 |
| ½ | 2 | 26.4 | 4 | 52.8 | 7 | 19.2 | 9 | 45.6 | 48 | 48 | 1 | 37 | 36 | 3 | 15 | 12 | ½ |
| 62 | 2 | 25.2 | 4 | 50.4 | 7 | 15.6 | 9 | 40.8 | 48 | 24 | 1 | 36 | 48 | 3 | 13 | 36 | 62 |
| ½ | 2 | 24.0 | 4 | 48.0 | 7 | 12.0 | 9 | 36.0 | 48 | 00 | 1 | 36 | 00 | 3 | 12 | 00 | ½ |
| 63 | 2 | 22.8 | 4 | 45.6 | 7 | 08.4 | 9 | 31.2 | 47 | 36 | 1 | 35 | 12 | 3 | 10 | 24 | 63 |
| ½ | 2 | 21.6 | 4 | 43.2 | 7 | 04.8 | 9 | 26.4 | 47 | 12 | 1 | 34 | 24 | 3 | 08 | 48 | ½ |
| 64 | 2 | 20.6 | 4 | 41.2 | 7 | 01.8 | 9 | 22.4 | 46 | 52 | 1 | 33 | 44 | 3 | 07 | 28 | 64 |
| ½ | 2 | 19.6 | 4 | 39.2 | 6 | 58.8 | 9 | 18.4 | 46 | 32 | 1 | 33 | 04 | 3 | 06 | 08 | ½ |
| 65 | 2 | 18.4 | 4 | 36.8 | 6 | 55.2 | 9 | 13.6 | 46 | 08 | 1 | 32 | 16 | 3 | 04 | 32 | 65 |
| ½ | 2 | 17.4 | 4 | 34.8 | 6 | 52.2 | 9 | 09.6 | 45 | 48 | 1 | 31 | 36 | 3 | 03 | 12 | ½ |
| 66 | 2 | 16.4 | 4 | 32.8 | 6 | 49.2 | 9 | 04.6 | 45 | 23 | 1 | 30 | 46 | 3 | 01 | 32 | 66 |
| ½ | 2 | 15.4 | 4 | 30.8 | 6 | 46.2 | 9 | 01.6 | 45 | 08 | 1 | 30 | 16 | 3 | 00 | 32 | ½ |
| 67 | 2 | 14.4 | 4 | 28.8 | 6 | 43.2 | 8 | 57.6 | 44 | 48 | 1 | 29 | 36 | 2 | 59 | 12 | 67 |
| ½ | 2 | 13.4 | 4 | 26.8 | 6 | 40.2 | 8 | 53.6 | 44 | 28 | 1 | 28 | 56 | 2 | 57 | 52 | ½ |
| 68 | 2 | 12.4 | 4 | 24.8 | 6 | 37.2 | 8 | 49.6 | 44 | 08 | 1 | 28 | 16 | 2 | 56 | 32 | 68 |
| ½ | 2 | 11.4 | 4 | 22.8 | 6 | 34.2 | 8 | 45.6 | 43 | 48 | 1 | 27 | 36 | 2 | 55 | 12 | ½ |
| 69 | 2 | 10.4 | 4 | 20.8 | 6 | 31.2 | 8 | 41.6 | 43 | 28 | 1 | 26 | 56 | 2 | 53 | 52 | 69 |
| ½ | 2 | 09.6 | 4 | 19.2 | 6 | 28.8 | 8 | 38.4 | 43 | 12 | 1 | 26 | 24 | 2 | 52 | 48 | ½ |
| 70 | 2 | 08.6 | 4 | 17.2 | 6 | 25.8 | 8 | 34.4 | 42 | 52 | 1 | 25 | 44 | 2 | 51 | 28 | 70 |
| ½ | 2 | 07.6 | 4 | 15.2 | 6 | 22.8 | 8 | 30.4 | 42 | 32 | 1 | 25 | 04 | 2 | 50 | 08 | ½ |
| 71 | 2 | 06.8 | 4 | 13.6 | 6 | 20.4 | 8 | 27.2 | 42 | 16 | 1 | 24 | 32 | 2 | 49 | 04 | 71 |
| ½ | 2 | 05.8 | 4 | 11.6 | 6 | 17.4 | 8 | 23.2 | 41 | 56 | 1 | 23 | 52 | 2 | 47 | 44 | ½ |
| 72 | 2 | 05.0 | 4 | 10.0 | 6 | 15.0 | 8 | 20.0 | 41 | 40 | 1 | 23 | 20 | 2 | 46 | 40 | 72 |
| ½ | 2 | 04.2 | 4 | 08.4 | 6 | 12.6 | 8 | 16.8 | 41 | 24 | 1 | 22 | 48 | 2 | 45 | 36 | ½ |
| 73 | 2 | 03.4 | 4 | 06.8 | 6 | 10.2 | 8 | 13.6 | 41 | 08 | 1 | 22 | 16 | 2 | 44 | 32 | 73 |
| ½ | 2 | 02.4 | 4 | 04.8 | 6 | 07.2 | 8 | 09.6 | 40 | 48 | 1 | 21 | 36 | 2 | 43 | 12 | ½ |
| 74 | 2 | 01.6 | 4 | 03.2 | 6 | 04.8 | 8 | 06.4 | 40 | 32 | 1 | 21 | 04 | 2 | 42 | 08 | 74 |
| ½ | 2 | 00.8 | 4 | 01.6 | 6 | 02.4 | 8 | 03.2 | 40 | 15 | 1 | 20 | 30 | 2 | 41 | 00 | ½ |
| 75 | 2 | 00.0 | 4 | 00.0 | 6 | 00.0 | 8 | 00.0 | 40 | 00 | 1 | 20 | 00 | 2 | 40 | 00 | 75 |
| ½ | 1 | 59.2 | 3 | 58.4 | 5 | 57.6 | 7 | 56.8 | 39 | 44 | 1 | 19 | 28 | 2 | 38 | 56 | ½ |
| 76 | 1 | 58.4 | 3 | 56.8 | 5 | 55.2 | 7 | 53.6 | 39 | 28 | 1 | 18 | 56 | 2 | 37 | 52 | 76 |
| ½ | 1 | 57.6 | 3 | 55.2 | 5 | 52.8 | 7 | 50.4 | 39 | 12 | 1 | 18 | 24 | 2 | 36 | 48 | ½ |
| 77 | 1 | 56.8 | 3 | 53.6 | 5 | 50.4 | 7 | 47.2 | 38 | 56 | 1 | 17 | 52 | 2 | 35 | 44 | 77 |
| ½ | 1 | 56.0 | 3 | 52.0 | 5 | 48.0 | 7 | 44.0 | 38 | 40 | 1 | 17 | 20 | 2 | 34 | 40 | ½ |
| 78 | 1 | 55.4 | 3 | 50.8 | 5 | 46.2 | 7 | 41.6 | 38 | 28 | 1 | 16 | 56 | 2 | 33 | 52 | 78 |
| ½ | 1 | 54.6 | 3 | 49.2 | 5 | 43.8 | 7 | 38.4 | 38 | 12 | 1 | 16 | 24 | 2 | 32 | 48 | ½ |
| 79 | 1 | 53.8 | 3 | 47.6 | 5 | 41.4 | 7 | 35.2 | 37 | 56 | 1 | 15 | 52 | 2 | 31 | 44 | 79 |
| ½ | 1 | 53.2 | 3 | 46.4 | 5 | 39.6 | 7 | 32.8 | 37 | 44 | 1 | 15 | 28 | 2 | 30 | 56 | ½ |
| 80 | 1 | 52.4 | 3 | 44.8 | 5 | 37.2 | 7 | 29.6 | 37 | 28 | 1 | 14 | 56 | 2 | 29 | 52 | 80 |
| ½ | 1 | 51.8 | 3 | 43.6 | 5 | 34.4 | 7 | 27.2 | 37 | 16 | 1 | 14 | 32 | 2 | 29 | 04 | ½ |
| 81 | 1 | 51.2 | 3 | 42.4 | 5 | 33.6 | 7 | 24.8 | 37 | 04 | 1 | 14 | 08 | 2 | 28 | 16 | 81 |
| ½ | 1 | 50.4 | 3 | 40.8 | 5 | 31.2 | 7 | 21.6 | 36 | 48 | 1 | 13 | 36 | 2 | 27 | 12 | ½ |
| 82 | 1 | 49.6 | 3 | 39.2 | 5 | 28.8 | 7 | 18.4 | 36 | 32 | 1 | 13 | 04 | 2 | 26 | 08 | 82 |
| ½ | 1 | 49.0 | 3 | 38.0 | 5 | 27.0 | 7 | 16.0 | 36 | 20 | 1 | 12 | 40 | 2 | 25 | 20 | ½ |
| 83 | 1 | 48.4 | 3 | 36.8 | 5 | 25.2 | 7 | 13.6 | 36 | 08 | 1 | 12 | 16 | 2 | 24 | 32 | 83 |
| ½ | 1 | 47.8 | 3 | 35.6 | 5 | 23.4 | 7 | 11.2 | 35 | 56 | 1 | 11 | 52 | 2 | 23 | 44 | ½ |
| 84 | 1 | 47.2 | 3 | 34.4 | 5 | 21.6 | 7 | 08.8 | 35 | 44 | 1 | 11 | 28 | 2 | 22 | 56 | 84 |
| ½ | 1 | 46.6 | 3 | 33.2 | 5 | 19.8 | 7 | 06.4 | 35 | 30 | 1 | 11 | 00 | 2 | 22 | 00 | ½ |
| 85 | 1 | 45.8 | 3 | 31.6 | 5 | 17.4 | 7 | 03.2 | 35 | 16 | 1 | 10 | 32 | 2 | 21 | 04 | 85 |
| ½ | 1 | 45.2 | 3 | 30.4 | 5 | 15.6 | 7 | 00.8 | 35 | 04 | 1 | 10 | 08 | 2 | 20 | 16 | ½ |
| 86 | 1 | 44.6 | 3 | 29.2 | 5 | 13.8 | 6 | 58.4 | 34 | 52 | 1 | 09 | 44 | 2 | 19 | 28 | 86 |
| ½ | 1 | 44.0 | 3 | 28.0 | 5 | 12.0 | 6 | 56.0 | 34 | 40 | 1 | 09 | 20 | 2 | 18 | 40 | ½ |
| 87 | 1 | 43.4 | 3 | 26.8 | 5 | 10.2 | 6 | 53.6 | 34 | 28 | 1 | 08 | 56 | 2 | 17 | 52 | 87 |
| ½ | 1 | 42.8 | 3 | 25.6 | 5 | 08.4 | 6 | 51.2 | 34 | 16 | 1 | 08 | 32 | 2 | 17 | 04 | ½ |
| 88 | 1 | 42.2 | 3 | 24.4 | 5 | 06.6 | 6 | 48.8 | 34 | 04 | 1 | 08 | 08 | 2 | 16 | 16 | 88 |
| ½ | 1 | 41.6 | 3 | 23.2 | 5 | 04.8 | 6 | 46.4 | 33 | 52 | 1 | 07 | 44 | 2 | 15 | 28 | ½ |
| 89 | 1 | 41.2 | 3 | 22.4 | 5 | 03.6 | 6 | 44.8 | 33 | 44 | 1 | 07 | 27 | 2 | 14 | 56 | 89 |
| ½ | 1 | 40.6 | 3 | 21.2 | 5 | 01.8 | 6 | 42.4 | 33 | 32 | 1 | 07 | 04 | 2 | 14 | 08 | ½ |
| 90 | 1 | 40.0 | 3 | 20.0 | 5 | 00.0 | 6 | 40.0 | 33 | 20 | 1 | 06 | 40 | 2 | 13 | 20 | 90 |
| ½ | 1 | 39.6 | 3 | 19.2 | 4 | 58.8 | 6 | 38.4 | 33 | 12 | 1 | 06 | 24 | 2 | 12 | 48 | ½ |
| 91 | 1 | 39.2 | 3 | 18.4 | 4 | 57.6 | 6 | 36.8 | 33 | 04 | 1 | 06 | 08 | 2 | 12 | 16 | 91 |
| ½ | 1 | 38.6 | 3 | 17.2 | 4 | 55.8 | 6 | 34.4 | 32 | 52 | 1 | 05 | 44 | 2 | 11 | 28 | ½ |
| 92 | 1 | 38.2 | 3 | 16.4 | 4 | 54.6 | 6 | 32.8 | 32 | 44 | 1 | 05 | 28 | 2 | 10 | 56 | 92 |
| ½ | 1 | 37.6 | 3 | 15.2 | 4 | 52.8 | 6 | 30.4 | 32 | 32 | 1 | 05 | 04 | 2 | 10 | 08 | ½ |
| 93 | 1 | 37.0 | 3 | 14.0 | 4 | 51.0 | 6 | 28.0 | 32 | 20 | 1 | 04 | 40 | 2 | 09 | 20 | 93 |
| ½ | 1 | 36.6 | 3 | 13.2 | 4 | 49.8 | 6 | 26.4 | 32 | 12 | 1 | 04 | 24 | 2 | 08 | 48 | ½ |
| 94 | 1 | 36.2 | 3 | 12.4 | 4 | 48.0 | 6 | 24.8 | 32 | 04 | 1 | 04 | 08 | 2 | 08 | 16 | 94 |
| ½ | 1 | 35.6 | 3 | 11.2 | 4 | 46.8 | 6 | 22.4 | 31 | 52 | 1 | 03 | 44. | 2 | 07 | 28 | ½ |
| 95 | 1 | 35.0 | 3 | 10.0 | 4 | 45.0 | 6 | 20.0 | 31 | 40 | 1 | 03 | 20 | 2 | 06 | 40 | 95 |
| ½ | 1 | 34.6 | 3 | 09.2 | 4 | 43.8 | 6 | 18.4 | 31 | 32 | 1 | 03 | 04 | 2 | 06 | 08 | ½ |
| 96 | 1 | 34.2 | 3 | 08.4 | 4 | 42.6 | 6 | 16.8 | 31 | 24 | 1 | 02 | 48 | 2 | 05 | 36 | 96 |
| ½ | 1 | 33.6 | 3 | 07.2 | 4 | 40.8 | 6 | 14.4 | 31 | 14 | 1 | 02 | 28 | 2 | 04 | 48 | ½ |
| 97 | 1 | 33.0 | 3 | 06.0 | 4 | 39.0 | 6 | 12.0 | 31 | 00 | 1 | 02 | 00 | 2 | 04 | 00 | 97 |
| ½ | 1 | 32.6 | 3 | 05.2 | 4 | 37.8 | 6 | 10.4 | 30 | 52 | 1 | 01 | 44 | 2 | 03 | 28 | ½ |
| 98 | 1 | 32.0 | 3 | 04.0 | 4 | 36.0 | 6 | 08.0 | 30 | 40 | 1 | 01 | 20 | 2 | 02 | 40 | 98 |
| ½ | 1 | 31.6 | 3 | 03.2 | 4 | 34.8 | 6 | 06.4 | 30 | 32 | 1 | 01 | 04 | 2 | 02 | 08 | ½ |
| 99 | 1 | 31.0 | 3 | 02.0 | 4 | 33.0 | 6 | 04.0 | 30 | 20 | 1 | 00 | 40 | 2 | 01 | 20 | 99 |
| ½ | 1 | 30.6 | 3 | 01.2 | 4 | 31.8 | 6 | 02.4 | 30 | 12 | 1 | 00 | 24 | 2 | 00 | 48 | ½ |
| 100 | 1 | 30.0 | 3 | 00.0 | 4 | 30.0 | 6 | 00.0 | 30 | 00 | 1 | 00 | 00 | 2 | 00 | 00 | 100 |

**INDIANAPOLIS MOTOR SPEEDWAY -- Greatest Race Course in the World**

*A timechart used for the races at the Indianapolis Motor Speedway during 1910. (Reproduced from a May 1910 Indianapolis Motor Speedway program provided by Dave Goss)*

*An Overland automobile going over a wooden incline during the hazard race at the Indianapolis Motor Speedway during May 1910.*

# August 1909 Stereoscopic Photographs

The first automobile races at the Indianapolis Motor Speedway were photographed by Lynn Skeels of the Stereo-Travel Company. During the three-day program Skeels made an outstanding series of 40 stereoscopic photographs. Today, they are among the rarest in existence. So rare in fact that, with the exception of a few published by *Car and Driver* magazine in a May 2003 article, this book includes 37 of them in print for the very first time. Presented in chapters 4 and 5 as single photos, they have been included on the following pages in the original double format as originated in 1909. These photographs were graciously provided to the author by Joe Freeman and Grant Meitzler.

Stereoscopic photographs work on the same principle as humans use to view images. The eyes of a human are roughly a couple of inches apart, causing each retina to see an image differently. When this information is transmitted to the brain, depth perception is created. Likewise, stereoscopic photos consist of a pair of pictures of one scene taken the same distance apart as the human eyes. Thus, using a stereo viewer such as the Holmes stereoscope shown below, viewing these photos produces a three dimensional effect. This was a very popular form of photography from 1860 to around 1920, making the stereo viewer a common item in households.

stereo viewer such as this Holmes stereoscope was used to view stereoscopic photographs, producing a three mensional effect. (Indiana Historical Society)

# August 1909 Stereoscopic Photograph Titles

1.   Start Event 2, Thursday, I.M.S. races, August 1909.
2.   Chevrolet after winning 10-mile race, Thursday, I.M.S., August 1909.
3.   Line-up for start Event 3, Thursday, I.M.S., August 1909.
4.   Ready for 250-mile race, Thursday, I.M.S., August 1909.
5.   Bourque and mechanic ready to start in 250-mile race, in which they lost their lives.
6.   Chevrolet in 250-mile race, Thursday.
7.   Start 50-mile, Friday, I.M.S., August 1909.
8.   Stoddard-Dayton, Switzer in 50-mile, Friday.
9.   missing
10.  Stopping for repairs, I.M.S., August 1909.
11.  missing
12.  Start 100-mile, Friday; Buick, Strang won. Time, 1hour 22min. 18 ½ sec.
13.  First lap 100-mile, Friday, I.M.S., August 1909.
14.  "In the Stretch," Marmon and two Buicks.
15.  Grand Stand, Judges Stand, etc., August 1909.
16.  Vast crowds lining fences, I.M.S.
17.  Guardian of the track.
18.  Marmon in 15-mile, Saturday.
19.  Cars in parking space, I.M.S.
20.  Getting ready—10-mile Amateur, Saturday.
21.  Starting 10-mile Amateur, Saturday.
22.  No. 29 in 10-mile Amateur, Saturday.
23.  Fiat, Hearne winning 10-mile Amateur, 9 min. 44 3/10 sec.
24.  Christie's world-beater. Record one mile in 28 7/10 sec.
25.  Waiting call to race.
26.  Oldfield winning 25-mile. Broke all records from kilometer to 25 miles. Time 21 min. 21 7/16 sec.
27.  National, Aitken winning 15-mile. 18 min. 27 5/10 sec.
28.  Watching them whiz by. I.M.S., August 1909.
29.  Start 200-mile race, Saturday, I.M.S., August 21, 1909.
30.  National, Aitken, lowering all records 25 to 100 miles. Time for 100 miles, 91 min. 41 9/10 sec.
31.  Brush between Buick and Apperson in 300-mile, Saturday.
32.  Stoddard-Daytons in the stretch.
33.  Rushing down at 80 miles an hour.
34.  missing
35.  37,600 people saw Saturday's races.
36.  "Don't go near the track."
37.  Crowds in the bleachers.
38.  At the half-mile. 300-mile, Saturday.
39.  Coming down the back stretch. 300-mile, Saturday.
40.  Jackson, two Buicks and Stoddard-Dayton at the mile. Middle 300-mile, Saturday.

1. Start Event 2, Thursday, I. M. S. Races, August, 1909.
Copyright, 1909, by Stereo-Travel Co.

2. Chevrolet after winning 10-mile race, Thursday. 8.55.4
I. M. S. August, 1909.
Copyright, 1909, by Stereo-Travel Co.

8. Line-up for start Event 3, Thursday, I. M. S. Aug, 1908.
Copyright, 1909, by Stereo-Travel Co.

4. Ready for 250-mile race, Thursday, I. M. S. August, 1909.
Copyright, 1909, by Stereo-Travel Co.

5. Borque and mechanic ready to start in 250-mile, in which they lost their lives.
Copyright, 1909, by Stereo-Travel Co.

6. Chevrolet in 250-mile race, Thursday.
Copyright, 1909, by Stereo-Travel Co.

7. Start 50-mile Friday. I. M. S. August, 1909.
Copyright, 1909, by Stereo-Travel Co.

8. Stoddard-Dayton, Switzer, in 50-mile, Friday.
Copyright, 1909, by Stereo-Travel Co.

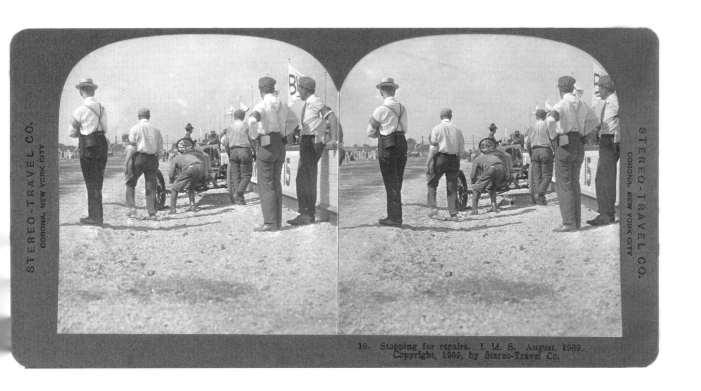

10. Stopping for repairs. I. M. S. August, 1909.
Copyright, 1909, by Stereo-Travel Co.

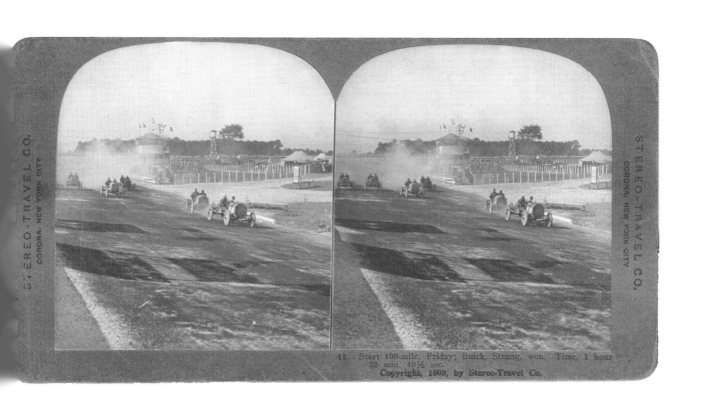

12. Start 100-mile, Friday; Buick, Strang, won. Time, 1 hour
32 min. 48½ sec.
Copyright, 1909, by Stereo-Travel Co.

13. First lap 100-mile, Friday. I. M. S. August, 1909.
Copyright, 1909, by Stereo-Travel Co.

14. "In the Stretch," Marmon and two Buicks.
Copyright, 1909, by Stereo-Travel Co.

STEREO-TRAVEL CO.
CORONA, NEW YORK CITY

STEREO-TRAVEL CO.
CORONA, NEW YORK CITY

15. Grand Stand, Judges, Stand, etc. I. M. S. August, 1909.
Copyright, 1909, by Stereo-Travel Co.

STEREO-TRAVEL CO.
CORONA, NEW YORK CITY

STEREO-TRAVEL CO.
CORONA, NEW YORK CITY

16. Vast crowds lining fences. I. M. S.
Copyright, 1909, by Stereo-Travel Co.

17. Guardian of the track.
Copyright, 1909, by Stereo-Travel Co.

18. Marmon in 15-mile, Saturday.
Copyright, 1909, by Stereo-Travel Co.

19. Cars in parking space. I. M. S.
Copyright, 1909, by Stereo-Travel Co.

20. Getting ready—10-mile Amateur, Saturday.
Copyright, 1909, by Stereo-Travel Co.

21. Starting 10-mile Amateur, Saturday.
Copyright, 1909, by Stereo-Travel Co.

22. No. 29 in 10-mile Amateur, Saturday.
Copyright, 1909, by Stereo-Travel Co.

23. Fiat, Hearne, winning 10-mile Amateur, 9 min. 44 3/10 sec.
Copyright, 1909, by Stereo-Travel Co.

24. Christie's world-beater. Record one mile in 28 7/10 sec.
Copyright, 1909, by Stereo-Travel Co.

25. Waiting call to race.
Copyright, 1909, by Stereo-Travel Co.

26. Oldfield winning 25-mile. Broke all records from kilometer
to 25 miles. Time, 21 min. 21 7/16 sec.
Copyright, 1909, by Stereo-Travel Co.

27. National, Aiken, winning 15-mile. 13 min. 27 5/10 sec.
Copyright, 1909, by Stereo-Travel Co.

28. Watching them whiz by. I. M. S. August, 1909.
Copyright, 1909, by Stereo-Travel Co.

29. Start 300-mile race, Saturday, I. M. S. August 21, 1909.
Copyright, 1909, by Stereo-Travel Co.

30. National, Aiken, lowering all records 25 to 100 miles. Time
for 100 miles, 91 min. 41 9/10 sec.
Copyright, 1909, by Stereo-Travel Co.

31. Brush between Buick and Apperson in 300-mile, Saturday.
Copyright, 1909, by Stereo-Travel Co.

32. Stoddard-Dayton in the stretch.
Copyright, 1909, by Stereo-Travel Co.

32. Rushing down at 80 miles an hour.
Copyright, 1909, by Stereo-Travel Co.

35. 37,000 people saw Saturday's races.
Copyright, 1909, by Stereo-Travel Co.

36. "Don't go near the track."
Copyright, 1909, by Stereo-Travel Co.

37. Crowds in the bleachers.
Copyright, 1909, by Stereo-Travel Co.

# References

Newspapers:
*Indianapolis Star*
*Indianapolis News*
*Indianapolis Sun*
*Detroit News*
*Detroit Times*
*Detroit Free Press*
*Flint Journal*
*New York Times*
*Chicago Tribune*
*St. Louis Globe-Democrat*
*St. Louis Post-Dispatch*
*St. Louis Republic*
*St. Louis Star-Times*

*The Marmon Heritage*
By George Philip Hanley and Stacy Pankiw Hanley

*INDIANA CARS: A History of the Automobile in Indiana*
By Dennis E. Horvath and Terri Horvath

*Indianapolis 500-Mile Race History*
By Floyd Clymer

*Saga of the Roaring Road*
By Fred J. Wagner
As told to John M. Mitchell

*500 Miles to Go*
By Al Bloemker

*An Investigation into the Rise and Fall of the Automobile
Industry in Indiana*
B.A. Thesis, Harvard University, Boston, MA
Carl J. Weinhardt

*The Encyclopedia of Indianapolis*
By David J. Bodenhamer and Robert G. Barrows

*The Papers of Wilbur and Orville Wright*
*Including the Chanute-Wright Letters*
*Volume Two 1906 – 1948*
Edited By Marvin W. McFarland

Brochure:
*The Brickyard: The Legendary Bricks of Indy*
By Tom Rollings and John E. Blazier

*The Pacesetter*
*The Untold Story of Carl G. Fisher*
By Jerry M. Fisher

*Castles in the Sand*
*The Life and Times of Carl Graham Fisher*
By Mark S. Foster

*BROOKLANDS*
*Ballantine's Illustrated History of the Car*
By P. J. Wallace

*The Illustrated Directory of Motorcycles*
By MBI Publishing Company
Edited by Mirco De Cet

*Antique Motorcycles*
Volume 5 Number 2 Summer 1966
"Annual Review of 1909 Motorcycles"

*Fabulous Hoosier*
By Jane Fisher

*Nordyke & Marmon Company*
*An Institution*
By Nordyke & Marmon Company

*Automobile Quarterly*
Volume 35 Number 2 May 1996
"Carl G. Fisher: Indiana's Best Kept Secret"
L. Spencer Riggs

*Automobile Quarterly*
Volume 19 Number 4 Fourth Quarter 1981
"Speed King In a Silk Shirt – The Career of Bob Burman"
By Russ Catlin

*Speed Age Magazine*
October 1951
"When Indianapolis Was Born"
By Russ Catlin

*The Automobile*
September 1, 1909
"Inauguration of Indianapolis Speedway 1909"

*The Automobile*
December 16, 1909
"Indianapolis Speedway is Ready"

*The Automobile*
June 2, 1910
"Records Fall at Indianapolis"

*The Automobile*
July 7, 1910
"Cobe Trophy Feature of "Fourth" at Indianapolis"

*The Automobile*
September 8, 1910
"Labor Day Events at Indianapolis"

# Notes

## Chapter 1

1. *Nordyke & Marmon Company: An Institution* by Nordyke & Marmon Company, June 1920.
2. *Indianapolis News*, Tuesday March 16, 1909.
3. Ibid.

## Chapter 2

1. *Indianapolis Star*, Friday June 4, 1909.
2. *Indianapolis News*, Saturday June 5, 1909.
3. *Indianapolis Star*, Sunday June 6, 1909.
4. *St. Louis Republic*, Wednesday June 9, 1909.
5. *Indianapolis Star*, Sunday June 6, 1909.
6. Ibid.
7. Ibid.
8. Ibid.
9. Ibid.
10. Ibid.
11. Ibid.
12. Ibid.
13. Ibid.
14. *Indianapolis News*, Monday June 7, 1909.
15. *St. Louis Globe-Democrat*, Wednesday June 9, 1909.
16. Ibid.

## Chapter 3

1. *Indianapolis Star*, Friday August 13, 1909.
2. *Indianapolis Star*, Sunday August 15, 1909.
3. Ibid.
4. Ibid.

## Chapter 4

1. *Indianapolis Star*, Wednesday August 18, 1909.
2. *Indianapolis Star*, Friday August 20, 1909.
3. *Indianapolis Star*, Sunday August 22, 1909.
4. *Detroit News*, Sunday August 22, 1909.

## Chapter 5

1. *The Brickyard: The Legendary Bricks of Indy*, by Tom Rollings and John E. Blazier
2. *Indianapolis Star*, Sunday December 19, 1909.
3. Ibid.
4. Ibid.

## Chapter 6

1. *Indianapolis Star*, Monday May 9, 1910.
2. Ibid.
3. Ibid.
4. *Indianapolis Star*, Saturday May 28, 1910.
5. *Indianapolis Star*, Sunday May 29, 1910.
6. Ibid.
7. *Indianapolis Star*, Tuesday May 31, 1910.
8. *Indianapolis Star*, Sunday May 29, 1910.

**Chapter 7**

1. *Indianapolis Star*, Monday June 13, 1910.
2. *Indianapolis Star*, Tuesday June 14, 1910.
3. Ibid.
4. Ibid.
5. Ibid.
6. Ibid.
7. Ibid.
8. *Indianapolis News*, Tuesday June 14, 1910.
9. *Indianapolis Star*, Wednesday June 15, 1910.
10. Ibid.
11. Ibid.
12. *Indianapolis Star*, Thursday June 16, 1910.
13. *Indianapolis News*, Wednesday June 15, 1910.
14. *Indianapolis Star*, Friday June 17, 1910.
15. Ibid.
16. *Indianapolis News*, Friday June 17, 1910.
17. *Indianapolis Star*, Saturday June 18, 1910.
18. Ibid.
19. *Indianapolis Star*, Sunday June 19, 1910.
20. Ibid.

**Chapter 8**

1. *Indianapolis Star*, Sunday July 3, 1910.
2. Ibid.
3. *Indianapolis Star*, Thursday July 7, 1910.
4. *Indianapolis News*, Thursday July 28, 1910.
5. Ibid.
6. Ibid.

**Chapter 9**

1. *Indianapolis Star*, Tuesday August 30, 1910.
2. *Indianapolis Star*, Sunday September 4, 1910.
3. Ibid.

**Chapter 10**

1. *Indianapolis News*, Friday September 16, 1910.
2. *Indianapolis Star*, Wednesday September 6, 1910.
3. "Piloting a Balloon", by H. E. Honeywell, Aircraft Magazine, September 1910.
4. *Indianapolis Star*, Monday September 19, 1910.

5. Ibid.
6. Ibid.
7. Ibid.
8. *Indianapolis News*, Tuesday September 20, 1910.
9. *St. Louis Globe-Democrat*, Tuesday September 20, 1910.
10. *Indianapolis News*, Tuesday September 20, 1910.
11. *St. Louis Globe-Democrat*, Tuesday September 20, 1910.
12. *Indianapolis News*, Tuesday September 20, 1910.
13. *Indianapolis News*, Tuesday September 20, 1910.
14. Ibid.
15. *Indianapolis Star*, Tuesday September 6, 1910.

# ORDER FORM

**3 Easy Ways to Order *INDY: Racing Before the 500***

**1) Visit our website at:** www.indianareflections.com

**2) Call toll free:** 1-877-501-1909 (between 8:00 am – 8:00 pm EST)

**3) For postal orders mail this form to:**
Indiana Reflections
1197 The Pines, Suite 500
Batesville, Indiana 47006

---

**Billing Information (please print clearly):**

Name:_____

Address:_____

City:_____ State:_____ Zip:_____

Telephone (optional):_____ Email (optional):_____

**Shipping Information (if different from billing information):**

Name:_____

Address:_____

City:_____ State:_____ Zip:_____

|  | Quantity | | Total |
|---|---|---|---|
| ***INDY: Racing Before the 500*** | _____ | x $59.95 = | _____ |

6% sales tax  (Indiana addresses only)……………………………….. _____
Standard Shipping (5-6 days) $4.00, each additional book $2.00………………………….. _____
Priority shipping (2-3 days) and AK, HI or Int'l orders add $5.00………………………….. _____

Total Cost _____

Payment method (check one): ___ Check     ___ Money Order     ___ VISA     ___ MasterCard
If paying by credit card:

Card Number: _____ Card ID (3 digit code on back of card):_____

Name on card: _____ Exp. Date _____

# ORDER FORM

**3 Easy Ways to Order *INDY: Racing Before the 500***

**1) Visit our website at:** www.indianareflections.com

**2) Call toll free:** 1-877-501-1909 (between 8:00 am – 8:00 pm EST)

**3) For postal orders mail this form to:**
Indiana Reflections
1197 The Pines, Suite 500
Batesville, Indiana 47006

**Billing Information (please print clearly):**

Name:_____

Address:_____

City:_____ State:_____ Zip:_____

Telephone (optional):_____ Email (optional):_____

**Shipping Information (if different from billing information):**

Name:_____

Address:_____

City:_____ State:_____ Zip:_____

|  | Quantity | Total |
|---|---|---|
| ***INDY: Racing Before the 500*** | _____ x $59.95 = | _____ |
| 6% sales tax (Indiana addresses only)................................. | | _____ |
| Standard Shipping (5-6 days) $4.00, each additional book $2.00................................. | | _____ |
| Priority shipping (2-3 days) and AK, HI or Int'l orders add $5.00................................. | | _____ |
| | Total Cost | _____ |

Payment method (check one): ___ Check ___ Money Order ___ VISA ___ MasterCard
If paying by credit card:

Card Number: _____ Card ID (3 digit code on back of card):_____

Name on card: _____ Exp. Date _____

IUPUI
UNIVERSITY LIBRARY
755 WEST MICHIGAN STREET
INDIANAPOLIS, IN 46202-5195

WITHDRAWN